CENSORSHIP OF THE MOVIES

THE SOCIAL AND POLITICAL CONTROL OF A MASS MEDIUM

Richard S. Randall

The University of Wisconsin Press
Madison, Milwaukee, and London

To my mother and the memory of my father

Published by the University of Wisconsin Press
Box 1379, Madison, Wisconsin 53701
The University of Wisconsin Press, Ltd.
27–29 Whitfield Street, London, W.1

Published 1968; Second printing 1970

Printed in the United States of America
SBN 299-04731-8 cloth, 299-04734-2 paper
LC 68-14035

Note to the Second Printing

In the two short years since the first edition of this book appeared, the crumbling inhibitions on cinematic content have fallen away at an ever quickening pace. For many who love the movies and are excited by their power to communicate, this expanding freedom is welcome, if not overdue. The readiness in films to explore political, social, and psychological themes and the infusion of much new, young, and independent creative talent are giant steps in the maturing of the medium as an art. Probably no less can be said for the correspondingly steady rise of a sophisticated and appreciative constituency for this new moviemaking, including not only a larger audience of experienced moviegoers but also an increasingly rich professional criticism and commentary.

A major consequence of this widening freedom is that each year, or as it sometimes seems, each month, the movies come to deal more fully, more explicitly, and more often with sex and with violence. Much of this pursuit is inseparable from art and from some of the best moviemaking we have. Some of it, offered in the name of art, is merely specious and profitable. And some of it, without pretension, is aimed solely at those morbid and demeaning recesses of the human spirit long familiar to the pornographer. These developments have called forth an outpouring of angry and often undiscriminating criticism that today is probably unprecedented in its volume and intensity. These attacks have more and more become concerned with the protection of youth, the movies being seen as destructive of moral values and emotional well-being. Unhappily, we are still not much closer to knowing how justified or unjustified these fears may be. As a matter of more certain knowledge, we must still await the comprehensive and definitive studies that may indicate whether a steady offering of sex and violence is actually damaging or whether it is merely offensive to conventional sensibilities.

Demands on policy-makers are not subject to the same scholarly patience, however. And it is not surprising to find that, with the exception of traditional boards of censors, the currents of censorship analyzed in this book have not slackened, but rather have actually quickened and cut deeper still. In the last two years we have seen an increasing number of punitive measures introduced in Congress, the state legislatures, and town and city councils, an increasing number of prosecutions of exhibitors, and an increasing amount of official and informal harassment of exhibitors.

It was largely in response to this agitation and to the threat of new governmental prior censorship posed by it that the movie industry, through the Motion Picture Association, began to classify films late in 1968. Movies are rated as to their suitability for youth *G* ("general audience"), *GP* (all ages admitted, parental guidance suggested), *R* ("restricted audience"—persons under 17 not admitted unless with parent or guardian), and *X* (persons under 17, or 18 in some areas, not admitted), and an attempt is made to enforce the *R* and *X* ratings at the theatre. This major innovation represents a reversal of the industry's long-standing opposition (largely for boxoffice reasons) to any kind of classification. Although great effort has gone into the rating system, its effectiveness in either easing censorship pressure or in protecting youth from supposedly harmful films remains in doubt. One question arising is whether the massive voluntary cooperation required of production, distribution, and exhibition interests in a highly decentralized industry can be maintained in the face of ever present temptations to profit commercially by paying only lip service to the system or by outright disregard of it. Another is whether the voluntary system can *ever* hope to reach many of the kinds of films now provoking censorial reaction. Finally, it is unclear whether the rating operation can win and hold public confidence. To do so it must avoid absurd rulings as well as those appearing to make the system merely the convenient tool of the major companies, two faults which drained the Motion Picture Code of much of its credibility.

Overshadowing the rating system and, for that matter, the entire film medium itself is the growing politization of the obscenity issue. Obscenity has broken out of its former judicial confines and has done so largely because the judiciary has almost eliminated it as a legal concept and has, at least at the appellate level, become increasingly unresponsive to the censorship interest. Because of this and the accompanying record traffic in erotica, obscenity is now an electoral issue as well. It has entered presidential campaigns for the first time and may be establishing itself as an inviting target for executive crusade, the sort which could also be used to divert attention from more serious political problems. In addition, obscenity has become a factor in a growing number of state and local legislative and judicial elections. Perhaps most striking of all, it played a part in the defeat of the nomination of former Associate Justice Abe Fortas to the Chief Justiceship of the Supreme Court, with members of the Senate actually viewing in their chambers a film made up of clips of movies found not obscene by the Supreme Court in cases in which Fortas voted with the majority.

It is clear that in the matter of sex and violence the media of communication are now caught up in a kind of cultural revolution. What is not so clear is that the end result will be a higher level of practicing tolerance and sophistication. In two years many of the social and political hazards for the movies chronicled in these pages have grown and become more general. The gap between the American free speech society and the American mass democratic society has widened, as have a number of other divisions in the country. And though this gap is by no means as serious as the division over foreign policy or race relations, it is of such a political, social, and ideological character that it is likely to reinforce those divisions. Management of the obscenity problem would very likely have an effect of easing these greater tensions, as failure to manage it would likely exacerbate them.

R. S. R.

New York City
January, 1970

Preface

Most studies of censorship and free speech have been written by authors drawn to their work by libertarian interests. This one is no exception. I hasten to make this point at the outset, the more to reassure a later doubting reader. Traditional studies of censorship and free speech have been studies in the law—analyses of doctrine and judicial workmanship, often with strong normative direction. As essential as these works have been and are, they often leave many questions unanswered and unasked, in some instances too many for the good of freedom of speech itself. Before public policy, including judicially made policy, can be fully evaluated and recommendations be soundly made, we need to know something about the factual setting out of which constitutional litigation, legislation, and public dispute arise. Abstractions of the First Amendment need to be related to the political, social, and economic factors which they affect. Before we know what to do about governmental prior censorship in law, for example, we must know what governmental prior censors do in fact. Before we know what the limits of free speech should be, we need to know what the condition of free speech is.

Until very recently, a partisan of free speech writing about movie censorship need not have worried about taking careful aim. The censorial woods were full of inviting targets, both menacing and absurd. So many battles needed winning that almost any attack at any point could be justified. With the advent of the 1960's, however, this "open season" closed. The censorial enemy was ousted from many long-held redoubts, and the content of movies radically transformed as a result. So rapid and dramatic have these changes been that they now challenge many traditional libertarian assumptions. Today, the movies are a mass medium set at liberty in a mass democratic society that is still marked by censorial impulse and resourcefulness. Under these circumstances, securing and enlarging the freedom of speech becomes a far more complex task than it was in the past. Today, an analysis that merely welcomes each new emancipating court decision, and calls for more of the same, may come close to a kind of mindless libertarianism that serves freedom of speech not well at all.

I hope this book will be at least a small step in the other direction. Its aim is to relate the legal doctrine of a mass medium to the operating controls of a mass society. In Chapters 2, 3, and 4, I have examined the law of movie censorship in its procedural and substantive aspects. Though I hope this has been done in more than a routine way, the reader who believes he has already read enough analyses of movie censorship and obscenity decisions may prefer to skip these chapters. The operations of governmental prior censorship itself are dealt with in Chapters 5 and 6. Their analysis is based on interviews with censors on major state and city licensing boards and in the United States Bureau of Customs, and with film proprietors and lawyers who deal with them. Chapters 7 and 8 explore the wider world of censorship in a mass society, which encompasses control through criminal prosecution, extra-legal action by officials, the pressures of private groups, and the film industry's efforts at self-regulation. An attempt to evaluate the state of free speech in motion pictures is made in Chapter 9.

If, here and there, I have been unkind to the movies or to their proprietors, it is not from ill will, but is, in fact, a lover's quarrel. My affection for the movies is unremitting, stretching back, I suppose, to a childhood of long and enchanted Saturday afternoons and the projected events and stories that filled not only a local silver screen, but a young imagination as well. And from such basic stuff, I suspect, springs at least one reason for this work itself.

Research for this book has put me in the debt of many persons, and acknowledgment of this good fortune is a welcome task. The following lawyers, critics, censors, clergymen, legislators, government counsel, producers, directors, writers, distributors, exhibitors, and other industry figures were kind enough to grant interviews and were generous with their knowledge: Miss Hildegarde Albrecht, Marvin Aspen, William P. Bagwell, Jr., Felix Bilgrey, Richard Brandt, Vincent Canby, Howard Clark, Bosley Crowther, Irving Fishman, Daniel Frankel, Elwood L. Gebhart, Mrs. Margaret K. Gregory, Robert J. Gurney, Jr., Mrs. Marie Hamilton, Nico Jacobellis, Elmer Jahncke, Edward Johnson, Elia Kazan, Mrs. Polly Kirk, Henry Kratz, Si Lax, Michael Linden, Monsignor Thomas F. Little, Ephraim London, Luigi Marano, Michael F. Mayer, Charles E. McCarthy, Radley H. Metzger, Sergeant Robert Murphy, Carl Peppercorn, Harry Perlewitz, Louis M. Pesce, Martin Quigley, Jr., Henry Rago, Vincent Redding, George Regan, Donald S. Rugoff, Patrolman Stanley Russell, Miss

Barbara Scott, Edward Solomon, Miss Eleanor Suske, Julius Tannenbaum, Gore Vidal, Valentine Wells, Mrs. Lollie C. Whitehead, and Irving Wormser.

For having made available various specific data, I also wish to thank the Reverend Patrick J. Sullivan, executive secretary, National Catholic Office for Motion Pictures; Geoffrey M. Shurlock, director, Production Code Administration of the Motion Picture Association of America; Kenneth W. Sain, assistant corporation counsel, City of Chicago; John F. Davis, clerk of the United States Supreme Court; Paul C. Spehr, Audio-Visual Section, Library of Congress; Earl Young, Scientific, Photographic, and Business Equipment Section, Department of Commerce; Lou Greenspan, editor, *The Journal of the Producers Guild of America;* Mrs. Marion Kelly, Cleveland Heights *Sun-Press;* the research staff of the American Civil Liberties Union, New York; and the film-library staff of the Museum of Modern Art, New York.

I am particularly indebted to David Fellman of the University of Wisconsin for advice and encouragement. My appreciation also goes to Robert J. Rosicky and to Evelyn Stein, two excellent assistants. Finally, I wish to thank the Graduate School of the University of Wisconsin, the Trustees of the William F. Vilas Estate, and the Research Council of the University of Nebraska, whose financial assistance at various points made the undertaking and conclusion of this work a far easier task.

RICHARD S. RANDALL

Lincoln, Nebraska
January, 1968

Contents

Part V   Conclusion

Tables

I

INTRODUCTION

1

A Medium of Controversy

Over the years, the movies have probably been the most attractive, popular —and worried about—of all media of communication. Their extraordinary power to capture reality and give it representation in the most simply understood terms has not only guaranteed them a large following, but convinced many persons that they have a special capacity for harm. In a mass society this power and popularity has aroused a strong censorship interest that has shadowed the movies since their beginning and taken a toll of free expression. No other medium has been subject to quite the intensity or variety of moral measurements and restraints as have the movies.

Following a somewhat stormy infancy, an effective combination of state and local boards of censors, organized religious pressure, and the film industry's own code of regulation succeeded in curbing much of the screen's potential for offensive and threatening depiction. As a result, an entire generation of Americans grew up with the "family" film—an artistically immature, morally safe, and highly profitable entertainment. But in the 1950's this reign of stability and affluence was interrupted by two events eventually leading to a radical change in the content of movies. One was the advent of television; the other, the inclusion of movies within the constitutional guarantees of free speech. The former had a devastating economic effect on the motion picture business. As the number of television sets in American homes increased four-fold during the fifties, movie theatre admissions fell by 50 per cent. Television succeeded in displacing the movies completely as the prime supplier of American "family" entertainment, leaving the older medium to search for a new social and cultural identity as well as a new solvency. At the same time, the movies were acquiring a new freedom in the law. In the now-famous *Miracle* case, the United States Supreme Court held that motion pictures, which had never before been considered anything more than a business enterprise in the law, were a medium of speech entitled to the protection of the First Amendment. This ruling and other decisions narrowing the range of proscribable obscenity became the basis for a series of cases limiting the authority of governmental censors.

As a result of these developments, the movies have never been freer in the law nor more provocative in content. The new liberties and economic imperatives have made possible films of quality and maturity that were all too uncommon before, but they have also produced unprecedented excesses in the detailing of erotica, nudity, and violence. Such elements have come to play an increasingly important role in "major" films, that is, movies produced for a general audience. They have also given rise to the aptly named "exploitation" film—the nudist camp, "girlie," and sado-masochistic feature—now an established and gainful sector in the film business.

In effect, the movies have succeeded in breaking down a traditional division of labor among the media of communication. Like their sister mass media—newspapers, radio, and television—they address an almost unlimited audience. But unlike those media, all of which are controlled to an extent by advertisers, movies now deal with a content that was previously limited almost entirely to the elite channels of the hardcover book and the theatre. In this breach the movies raise, in somewhat acute form, a larger question of how a free-speech society can coexist with a mass democratic society. Popular sovereignty and unfettered expression, seldom mixing easily at any time, are particularly apt to be in unstable combination when the speech in question involves sex and morality, which touch so often upon elemental hopes, fears, and frustrations.

This book deals with the multifarious methods by which conventional values have been defended against the challenge of motion picture freedom. By far the most debated of these has been prior censorship—the licensing of films by governmental censors before exhibition. Because it requires that speech be submitted to and approved by administrative boards before it can enter the "free marketplace of ideas," such censorship has usually been considered to be the classically illiberal method of limiting expression. The distinction between prior and subsequent restraint has had a long history in American law, and the possible, if not probable, dangers presented to free speech by the former method have been well catalogued. In fact, many libertarians have argued that prior restraints are totally incompatible with the principles of the First Amendment, and that the movies, which are still obliged to submit to the authority of a number of state and local boards of censors and to United States Customs inspection, are consequently a kind of second-class medium of speech.

Yet today the boards of censors, on the losing side in most legal contests, have been forced into so many changes that their effect on freedom of speech is not at all clear from the mere fact that their restraint is "prior." In particular, the difference between prior censorship and subsequent restraint through the criminal law, the method of control preferred by most libertarians, has become increasingly modest. Today prior censorship is in need of reexamination both in the law and in actual operation, not only with regard to its direct effect on free speech, but also in order to evaluate the role it plays in relation to other controls on the medium.

By the same measure, the traditional libertarian absorption with prior censorship and the preferred alternative of the criminal process presents an increasingly narrow analytic approach to the problem of free speech. Its emphasis on formal governmental controls tends to overlook the operation of other controls, particularly the demonstrated capacity of public officials for extralegal action against movies, as well as the role of private groups in the restriction of films. With the movies having greater freedom in the law than ever before, effective censorial restrictions are likely to be increasingly of an informal kind, often freely crossing governmental-nongovernmental lines. The libertarian controversy over the method of control and the censorial controversy over the content of films are thus interrelated. An analysis of movie censorship confined to the action of government within its constituted powers risks a seriously distorted picture not only of free speech and censorial pressures today, but of the role of public officials in a democratic system as well.

Though it is assumed here that the censorship interest in movies is a persistent fact of political and social life, the purposes for which freedom in motion pictures should be limited will not be considered. The censorship interest covers a multitude of fears, and this book is not a brief for any of them. Yet it is worth noting that not all censorial concerns involve morbid or irrational reactions or the defense of particularist values. The desire to protect the public—the viewers—from depiction of excessive erotica or violence is a concern held reasonably by many reasonable persons. Unfortunately, at the present time there is no conclusive evidence that the movies do or do not have harmful effects. On the other hand, there is widely held "common sense" opinion that, under particular circumstances, they can and do contain matter that may injure viewers, particularly youthful viewers. Unless and until proven groundless, the concern over possible harmful effects of erotica and violence is likely to be one that many reasonable men and women will consider worthy of representation in public policy.

However, in the pages that follow, the censorship interest is considered as political energy, pressure, or force rather than as value. In the American mass democracy, marked as it is by a considerable freedom of action and association and by a responsiveness of public officials to popular demands, the censorship interest tends to find some kind of accommodation. The actual limits to freedom of speech in the film medium depend, in large measure, on how this accommodation takes place.

II

THE MOVIES
AND THE LAW

2

From "Business" to "Speech"

The Coming of a Medium[1]

Novelty and Power

From their very beginning the movies were an object of public concern. In a heterogeneous society they were nothing if not intrusive. In fact, almost everything about them seemed calculated to place strain upon the accepted and established. They were the first medium of communication without roots in either elite or folk culture. Their appeal was made directly to an undifferentiated public in the mass without any evolution to such an audience through a process that would temper their content. Having neither history nor tradition, they were a kind of instant medium, possessing a franchise that could hardly be left unencumbered for long.

The movies were also a public medium. They could not be wrapped up, taken home, and savored in private. Even in the early days when their chief outlet was the peep-show machine, viewing was a public activity. When they graduated completely to the theatre, their social character became pronounced. There in a darkened balcony or orchestra, even the solitary moviegoer could enjoy a sense of vicarious companionship and the comfortable feeling of sharing in a social enterprise.

Economically, the movies depended almost entirely upon those who paid their way in to see them. With few exceptions, no advertisers influenced the content of the pictures out of a need to sell products of their own. The movies were essentially a consumer's medium; and, as the moviemakers soon learned in a maelstrom of competition, what the moviegoer-consumer could be tempted to see was not always what was good for him, or at least what others thought good for him.

Above all, the movies were popular. They captured the imagination as almost nothing else had, simply because they moved. Even in a technically

9

primitive stage they came closer to representing reality for most people than had any other form of communication. The early effect that could send patrons in front row seats running out of the theatre when a locomotive came roaring toward the camera might wear off, but not so the romance of movement and focus. The medium was a kind of psychic magnet, not only creating an illusion of reality but enormously simplifying the communication process itself. The camera (and the film editor) did all the work, directing the viewer's attention and anticipating his needs before even he, himself, was aware of them. Little or no effort was required to watch a movie. Education, intellect, and even literacy were dispensable.

If the unveiling of the movies can be fixed with any precision, it would probably be the night of April 14, 1894, when Thomas A. Edison's Kinetoscope made its commercial debut in a Broadway parlor in New York City. Within two years this machine, into which only one customer at a time could peek, was joined with the "magic lantern" device so that the "movies" could be projected onto a screen and entertain an entire audience.

At first, films were used to fill out vaudeville shows or offered as added attractions in traveling carnivals and amusement parks. But the enthusiasm they aroused soon made them features in their own right. After the turn of the century the doors of the nickelodeon—the five-cent theatre devoted entirely to motion pictures—opened in nearly every sizable city in the country.

The early films, simply depicting a motion rather than telling a story or conveying an idea, were not imaginative efforts. Yet even within these narrow limits they could be sensational. A kiss of May Irwin and John C. Rice which ran for fifty feet thrilled thousands at the same time it was decried as a "lyric of the stockyards." The scene also excited moviemakers by showing them the direction in which huge profits might be pursued. In 1903, *The Great Train Robbery,* the first connected narrative, led the way to hourlong films, which in turn opened the doors to a tide of lurid westerns and slapstick comedies.

Excesses were inevitable, and the sensationalism of a few productions brought moralistic attention to the entire medium. Also, with the screen now achieving a steady audience drawn largely from the working classes and immigrants in the cities, its potential for molding the thoughts and actions of the masses became disturbingly apparent to many persons (just as many Marxists were later aggrieved by the potential of the movies for distracting the masses from pursuit of a class interest). Nor did discord within the industry do anything to improve its image. Cut-throat practices frequently bordered on criminal behavior, with accusations of theft and copying not uncommon. In many quarters the movies were increasingly viewed as a disreputable and possibly subversive enterprise. With convention thus offended, if not outraged, it was certain that this injury would be followed not far behind by the law.

Prior Restraint—Archetypes

The first recorded protest against a movie, involving an entertainment called *Dolorita in the Passion Dance,* the rage of the peep-show parlor on the Boardwalk in Atlantic City, came just two weeks after Edison's machine was introduced. It was followed by others. A pantomime of a bride's wedding night preparations was closed by a court order in New York, the judge denouncing it as an "outrage upon public decency."[2] Later, the Children's Society of New York brought about the arraignment of a theatre manager because his establishment was allegedly packed with youngsters watching *The Great Thaw Trial.* In Rhode Island, members of the Murphy clan threatened to descend upon Providence and suppress *Murphy's Wake,* which featured an imbibing "corpse" in the title role. The following year the mayor of New York tried to close all nickelodeons as immoral places of amusement.

At first, official attempts to curb movies employed local business-licensing laws. In Delaware, owners of movie houses were subject to heavy license fees on the ground that their business constituted a "circus" within the meaning of existing statutes.[3] A similar result was obtained in New York, where movies were grouped with "public cartmen . . . hawkers . . . ticket speculators . . . and bowling alleys."[4] In Deer River, Minnesota, an annual merchant's license fee of $200 was deemed not excessive for a town of 1,000 because movie houses were "among those pursuits which are liable to degenerate and menace the good order and morals of the people."[5]

These early and sundry measures failed either to have much effect on the content of movies or to still protests against them. Continued pressures led inevitably to a search for more systematic and certain forms of control. In a two-year period beginning in 1907, pre-exhibition censorship of the movies was introduced in Chicago and New York. Its respective forms—governmental licensing and nongovernmental regulation supported by the film industry itself—were the forerunners of the major controls on the movies in later years.

Chicago passed an ordinance requiring police inspection and licensing of all films to be shown in the city. It gave authority to the chief of police, with right of appeal to the mayor, to withhold a permit if in his judgment a film was "immoral" or "obscene."[6] The city had more than one hundred nickelodeons at this time, many of them open all night.

Two years later in *Block* v. *Chicago,* the first movie censorship case, the ordinance was upheld by the Illinois Supreme Court. At issue was the refusal of permits for *The James Boys* and *Night Riders.* According to the court, the purpose of the ordinance was to secure decency and morality in the motion picture business, "and that purpose falls within the police power" unless constitutional rights were transgressed. In this case the court was satisfied that none were. The standards of "immoral" and "obscene" were adequate, since "the average person of healthy and wholesome mind" knew what the words meant. Furthermore, the court thought that films like the two in question could "represent nothing but malicious mischief, arson, and murder. They are both immoral, and their exhibition would necessarily be attended with evil effects upon youthful spectators."[7]

The same year the *Block* case was decided, a group of public-spirited citizens in New York City formed the National Board of Censorship (later to be called the National Board of Review) to preview and evaluate films before release to the public. Its creation was in direct response to threats of New York officials to close down movie houses in the city. With a liberal bent and an avowed aim of heading off governmental censorship, the board won the financial and moral support of the film industry, which agreed to abide by its decisions. Yet it was just this arrangement that was eventually the board's undoing. In the years following World War I, its rulings grew far too permissive for those who were concerned about the content of movies, and a number of the films it approved were considered objectionable even by some moviemakers themselves. Moreover, the board's financial dependence on the industry cast doubt upon its objectivity, and eventually it was attacked in the press as a tool of the moviemakers. The failure of the country's first experiment with voluntary nongovernmental prior censorship was complete when New York State passed a licensing law in 1921.*

Even while the National Board of Review functioned as a censorship agency in New York, governmental licensing had become the prevailing pattern of community response to agitation against movies. In 1911 Pennsylvania enacted the first state censorship law. A board of three was authorized to review all films to be shown in the state and issue permits for those that were "moral" and "proper," and to withhold them from those that were "sacrilegious, obscene, indecent, or such as tend, in the judgment of the board, to debase or corrupt morals."[8] The legislatures of Ohio and Kansas passed similar laws in 1913, and three years later, Maryland became the

---

* The National Board of Review has continued to function, though in a substantially less influential role. Today it serves chiefly as an agency for mobilizing social organizations which want to improve the content of films without resort to governmental censorship. It publishes the monthly *Films in Review.*

fourth state to adopt film censorship. At about the same time, the constitutionality of such laws was upheld by the United States Supreme Court in *Mutual Film Corp.* v. *Ohio.*

The Federal Factor

Though the Bureau of Customs has had authority to scrutinize imported films since passage of the Tariff Act of 1930, the United States is one of the few countries which has never had a national censorship of movies. The federal government's role in control of the medium has been largely indirect, though this has not been for any want of interest in outright federal censorship. The Hughes Bill of 1915, for example,[9] one of the first efforts in this direction, would have set up a five-member Federal Motion Picture Commission in the Department of the Interior to license all films before they could enter interstate commerce. It was defeated, only to be followed by frequent, in fact almost annual, attempts to establish official censorship at the national level.

Yet the failure of these measures was no index of their influence. Though the film industry eventually found it could live with state and local licensing, it invariably managed to pull itself together in all-out opposition to proposals for federal control. In these efforts, the moviemakers may have been stirred less by the fear of federal censorship per se, than by fear that such censorship would ultimately lead to federal regulation of business practices as well. This always-present threat of national action was one of several Damoclean swords that eventually persuaded the industry to regulate itself.

Three federal enactments were aimed at the content of movies during this early period, but none appears to have had much consequence for the medium. The Tariff Act of 1913[10] gave the Secretary of the Treasury power to censor imported films. However, the power was not spelled out, and it was not until passage of the Tariff Act of 1930,[11] authorizing the Bureau of Customs to examine imported films, that the federal government became really active in this area.

Another measure, passed just before American entry into World War I, forbade civilians to wear the uniform of any military service on the stage or screen unless it were done in ways that would not bring discredit or reproach upon the services. The law is still on the statute books, though no reported cases appear to have arisen under it.[12]

In 1912, Congress barred from interstate commerce "any film or other pictorial representation of any prize fight" intended for public exhibition.[13] The law was hastily passed after Jack Johnson, the Negro heavyweight champion, had decisively beaten the white former champion, Jim Jeffries. Since Jeffries had come out of retirement to reclaim the championship from the "dark menace" of the world of sport, it was believed circulation of the films might cause racial disturbances. Newsreels and short subjects were mainly affected by the statute, which was not infrequently violated. It was repealed in 1940.[14]

Threat and Counterthreat

The years immediately following World War I were well suited to a showdown over the content of movies. The nation had lived through one great struggle to find itself tested in another in which many old ways and values were challenged by new. Much of the country seemed bent on racing headlong into a Jazz Age at the same time that at least another part of it was determined to do no such thing. The movies, which unhesitatingly took new liberties at every turn, were caught up in this larger struggle. Increasing demands for their censorship were the small arms of a much larger reactive arsenal that included the Volstead Act and the Palmer Raids among its heavier weapons. Their mission was the defense of a way of life made insecure by change. "Back to normalcy" was naturally prejudicial to a medium that now claimed 40,000,000 admissions a week and seemed to have an ever-increasing influence on American habits.

Some excuses can be made for the industry. The postwar period was intensely competitive, with much shifting and consolidation of ownership cutting across production, distribution, and exhibition lines. Many of the films provoking the greatest protest were made by small, fly-by-night promoters. Even so, the industry as a whole showed little sense of public responsibility and did practically nothing to anticipate the growing reaction to its product. Anything that made money was permissible, and the surefire hits in the twenties were erotica and crime. As one film historian has noted,

Sophisticated sex had suddenly become big box office, whether in comedies or played straight. Drinking scenes abounded in pictures, despite the recent adoption of prohibition. Divorce, seduction, the use of drugs were presented in film after film as symbols of the fashionable life.[15]

Thus the portrayal of vice and immorality seemed well on its way to becoming a multimillion-dollar business. In the view of a leading trade publisher, who was later to become a co-author of the Motion Picture Production Code, much of the film medium portrayed "false sex standards, incitements to sexual emotion, glorification of crime and criminal, and debasing brutality."[16]

In reaction, the entire industry was indicted for the transgressions of a part. Civic groups, women's clubs, literary societies, educators, clergymen, and professional reformers attacked the moral tone of the movies. Editorials and articles inveighing against cinematic indecency and immorality appeared in leading magazines. A survey sponsored by the General Federation of Women's Clubs found that of 1,765 films examined, 21 per cent were "bad" and 59 per cent "not worthwhile."[17]

Protests were intensified because of what happened off the screen as well as on. The industry had recently moved to Hollywood, where life was supposedly glamorous and wicked, and moviemakers, unaware that certain restraint was a price exacted for dealing with the mass of the population, operated on the theory that bad publicity was better than no publicity at all. The industry's prime asset, the star system, became involved. Created out of popular demand and built entirely on a foundation of mass identification, it allowed large numbers of people to see something of themselves in the human archetypes who were paraded on the screen in film after film. When the medium was hit by a series of sex, murder, and drug scandals involving some of its leading personalities, this relationship was damaged and reaction against the movies reached a peak.

Yet the protesting forces were not consolidated and were far from being in accord on what should be done. Throughout the brief history of films, agitation against their content had always exceeded the desire for governmental censorship. As the first attempts at prior restraints in New York and Chicago a decade earlier indicated, critics generally fell into one of two camps. There were the moderate reformers, who believed cooperation with the industry was the most fruitful course and who usually had misgivings about official censorship. In contrast, there were those critics of a more punitive or pessimistic bent, who looked to the law. It was this group that succeeded in having nearly one hundred censorship bills introduced in thirty-seven states in 1921 alone. Meanwhile, the moderates brought heavy pressure to bear on the industry to clean up its own house.

Crest and Stability

In spite of the extreme claims of some of the agitators, it is doubtful that the movies can be called the cause of the supposed "moral indifferentism" of the post-war years. If they were even a kind of early accomplice of the Jazz Age, it was probably only through coincidence. The medium already had a well established reputation for excess, and in the postwar years it found a permissive climate in which this vice could flower. Whether the movies reinforced the new morality and how much so if they did remains an interesting, if unanswered, question. Many of their detractors were willing to believe they were a prime mover. Their defenders countered that movies merely reflected their times. Actually, any established guilt lay somewhere in between—movies reflected *and exaggerated* the new age. Yet for many of the jury, this alone was enough to convict for the greater crime of causation.

In late 1921 and early 1922 two events brought the struggle to a temporary resolution. In August, 1921, New York State established a licensing system for motion pictures. Though four other states had already set up similar boards of censors, New York's action was an especially hard blow to the industry. Not only did the state represent the country's major film market, but the censorship law, which was bitterly fought by the National Association of the Motion Picture Industry, a trade organization mainly of producers, marked the failure of what was once considered a noble experiment in voluntary censorship. The National Board of Review had already lost the confidence of protesting groups in the state, and the National Association, hoping to step into this void, had asked the legislature for a year's grace to allow the industry to reform itself. This proposal was turned down.

Now, almost out of desperation, the industry made a move to improve its image and to ease the pressures for official censorship. In doing so, it borrowed an invention from organized baseball. A year earlier, baseball owners, trying to weather a scandal of their own, had named a stern-faced jurist, Kenesaw M. Landis, "Czar" of the sport. In March, 1922, the movie industry reached into President Harding's Cabinet to hire the Postmaster General, Will H. Hays, and put him at the head of a new organization, the Motion Picture Producers and Distributors of America. His was a difficult, twofold task: to launch a public relations campaign, and to persuade individual moviemakers to tone down their more sensational and lurid films for the good of the entire industry. As a national figure and a Presbyterian elder, as well as a man of considerable persuasiveness, Hays was well suited for the job. It was not until 1930, however, that the "Hays Office," as the MPPDA came to be called, took up the task of formal self-regulation with the creation of the Motion Picture Production Code. And it was not until four years after that, that the code was fitted with effective enforcement powers. Still, Hays' appearance on the scene, and his partial success in improving the industry's public image and in more or less keeping the lid on its product, helped to ease moviemakers out of the difficulties in which they had found themselves in the early twenties.

In strict terms, it is probably inaccurate to speak of equilibrium at any time where control of the film medium is concerned. Yet after 1922, pressures for censorship did seem to abate for a time. Toward the end of the twenties and in the early thirties, protests were to increase again and result not only in the creation of the Motion Picture Production Code but in the formation of the Roman Catholic Legion of Decency as well. It was probably only after 1934 that the censorship situation in the country could be said to have achieved a kind of stability.

After enactment of the New York licensing law and the industry's first concerted attempt to reform itself, only one other state, Virginia, initiated film licensing and that was in 1922 in the swell of protest.[18] Later, in 1932,

Massachusetts achieved much the same effect as licensing, under a Lord's Day Observance statute.[19] The law, which included other entertainment besides movies, provided that only films "in keeping with the character of the day and not inconsistent with its due observance" could be shown on Sunday. It gave mayors the power to grant or withhold permits.

Two other states, Connecticut and Rhode Island, also enacted laws that directly or indirectly affected motion picture content. The Connecticut law, which was on the statute books only two years, required that all films shown in the state be registered with the state tax commissioner and that a tax be paid on each. The commissioner was authorized to revoke the registration of any film that he found "immoral or of a character to offend the racial or religious sensibilities of any element of society."[20] The Rhode Island law shifted the censorship problems to the community level by giving local police the power to require permits for films if they chose to do so. No standards or procedures were mentioned in the act.[21]

The number of cities and towns with prior censorship varied over the years. The exact number operating at any one time is not known, since the licensing boards in many smaller communities were inactivated from time to time.* In the larger cities with licensing systems—Chicago, Detroit, Memphis, Atlanta, Boston—the prior restraint authority or apparatus had already been established by 1922. Morris Ernst and Pare Lorentz found that in the five years following 1922, forty-five censorship bills were introduced in state legislatures, thirty-four of them in the 1923–1925 period. All forty-five were defeated.[22]

By 1922 censorship of motion pictures had fallen into a characteristic pattern—governmental control at the state and local level in many key areas and a degree of self-regulation at the production level. The former was the product of popular demand, the latter of fear of the former and of federal control. Neither institution completely satisfied the agitators, though self-regulation was probably the more effective in stilling protests, since it tended to have much wider support than did control through governmental censorship. Yet self-restraint was far from self-operating. It required organization and will. In the twenties, an increasingly centralized industry was beginning to develop organization. In fact, the years in which self-regulation was to work most effectively—the thirties and forties—were the very ones during which the industry was the most highly centralized. The will, on the other hand, proved to be a reluctant partner. In fact, wedding motion pictures to the moral concerns of the day has always required some sort of political or economic shotgun—at first, governmental censorship or the

* The highest estimate, to my knowledge, is ninety, made in 1950 by Lester Velie in "You Can't See That Movie," *Collier's,* May 6, 1950, p. 11. (See Table 2, page 79, for municipalities with prior censorship ordinances in the 1960's.)

threat of it, and later, the pressure of the Legion of Decency. This fact was sometimes forgotten by many of those beguiled by the workings of self-regulation. Furthermore, shotguns are dangerous weapons, and those who wielded them often did not see well enough to aim properly. It is not surprising that the marriages effected were not always brilliant matches.

Self-regulation notwithstanding, governmental censorship of movies was destined to move on to serve its own ends. Left to itself, it developed idiosyncrasies and self-justifying ways that no reasonable amount of industry self-restraint could head off or put to rest.

The *Mutual Film* Period

A Decision of 1915

Prior censorship of the movies first came before the Supreme Court at a time when that form of control was receiving increasing attention at all levels of government. The case, *Mutual Film Corp.* v. *Ohio,* had far-reaching consequences not only because of the issue the Court decided, but because it was to be the only movie censorship case it heard for thirty-seven years. For many latter-day students of civil liberties the decision was an unfortunate one, a step backward authorizing the unlimited censorship of movies and one insensitive to the medium's potential. Though some of this criticism appears to be well taken in retrospect, the decision was not an unreasonable one in its time.

The Mutual Film Corporation was a Detroit company which purchased films from producers and leased them to exhibitors in Ohio and other states. In the case before the Court, it had sought to enjoin enforcement of Ohio's prior-censorship law. The company claimed that the statute imposed an unlawful burden on interstate commerce, that it was an invalid delegation of legislative power to the board of censors because it failed to set up precise standards by which films were to be approved or rejected, and that it violated the free speech guarantees of the Ohio Constitution and the First Amendment.

A unanimous Court, speaking through Justice McKenna, ignored the federal free-speech claim and rejected the other contentions. McKenna disposed of the commerce argument by saying that when films were in the hands of the exchanges (of which Mutual Film was one), ready to be rented to exhibitors, they were mingled with other property in the state, at least as much as they could be considering their nature. At that point, accordingly, they were subject to regulation by the state.

On the delegation-of-power question, the provisions of the statute did not run the risk of leaving the censors' decisions to "whim" or "caprice," because "its terms, like other general terms, get precision from the sense and experience of men."[23]

On the question of whether movies fell within the free-speech guarantees of the state constitution—the issue that was to make *Mutual Film* a critical decision—McKenna declared:

The exhibition of motion pictures is a business pure and simple, originated and conducted for profit . . . not to be regarded, nor intended to be regarded by the Ohio Constitution, we think, as part of the press of the country or as organs of public opinion. They are mere representations of events, of ideas and sentiments published or known; vivid, useful, and entertaining, no doubt, but . . . capable of evil, having power for it, the greater because of their attractiveness and manner of exhibition.[24]

Once the Court found movies not to be speech, it was unnecessary to take up the claim of federal protection. Indeed, that question—eventually to become central to the prior censorship of motion pictures—was premature in 1915. The First Amendment was not then regarded as binding upon the states, nor was it even to begin to be so until *Gitlow* v. *New York,* a decade later.

Criticism of the *Mutual Film* decision is usually addressed to McKenna's characterization of the movies and to his attempts to distinguish the medium from the constitutionally protected speech and press of the country. Much of the criticism may reflect the understandable dissatisfaction with the censorship that developed in the years following the case. Yet several points can be made in the Court's defense.

Three lines of reasoning are apparent in the effort to distinguish motion pictures. First, the movies were primarily entertainment rather than vehicles for ideas. This was a risky kind of distinction to make, for, as the Court itself was to note many years later in referring to the printed media, "what is one man's amusement, teaches another's doctrine."[25] Yet, even if shortsighted, this distinction was not entirely unreasonable when measured against either the state of the film medium in 1915 or the scope of constitutionally protected speech. The movies were still largely in their nickelodeon stage, and it is doubtful that many among those who watched them or produced them thought that they dealt in ideas or were organs of public opinion. In terms of a role in the functioning of the political system—the major frame of reference for free speech questions at the time—the movies of 1915 could hardly be compared with the press of the country. In fact, not until *Hannegan* v. *Esquire* in 1946 did the Supreme Court actually hold that materials that were characteristically entertainment were protected speech.

Second, McKenna thought the movies were "a business, pure and simple, originated and conducted for profit." This was clearly a poor distinction. If taken literally it was irrelevant, since almost all newspapers and book-publishing houses have been run for profit. In its argument here, the Court may have been influenced by the undisguised cupidity of many of those in the movie industry at the time, and by their lack of any sense of public service. Nevertheless, McKenna's reasoning was unfortunate. Its impact was all the worse because, in its simple phrasing—probably the most facile in the opinion—it became the most widely cited of his attempted distinctions in the case.

Finally, the Court believed that the movies had a special capacity for evil. This was not proven in 1915 and, in fact, remains an open question today. Yet there was no doubt at all, then or now, that movies possessed an unusual power. Because of this, and particularly in the absence of proof to the contrary, it was not unreasonable for the Court to believe that they might be especially harmful and therefore would require special controls. In fact, the entire decision might have rested on this point alone, and would have been stronger if it had. The possibility of a special capacity for harm was to be noted by the Court in two of its later motion picture censorship decisions, *Burstyn* v. *Wilson* (the *Miracle* case) in 1952, and *Times Film* v. *Chicago* in 1961. And it is apparently this question that underlies the modern Court's continued willingness to sustain prior censorship.

In *Mutual Film* the Court was presented with the problem of freedom in a mass medium for the first time. Throughout his opinion, McKenna was concerned with the power and influence of the movies. He spoke of their public character, of their possible excitement of "prurient interest," and of the fact that they were shown to mixed audiences which included children —the very concerns at the center of the censorship controversy today. Asked to accord the nation's first mass medium all the rights of the press while it was still in its infancy, the Supreme Court proceeded with caution. McKenna may have overstated the distinctions separating the movies from speech, yet in 1915, at least, his error was pardonable.

Moreover, in upholding prior censorship, the Court clearly indicated that such censorship had limited purpose. Licensing was permissible, not because movies were without value, but because states had an interest in protecting "public morals and welfare" against the medium's capacity for evil. What this evil might be was not detailed, but McKenna's discussion leaves little doubt that it lay in the realm of sexual morality and not in that of political or social ideas. He spoke of audiences "not of women alone nor of men alone, but together," of "things which should not have pictorial representation in public places," and of the possibility that a "prurient interest might be excited and appealed to." And where the Mutual Film company had charged that imprecise standards in the licensing statute might allow a censor to exercise "unjust discrimination against some *propagandist* film" (emphasis added), McKenna answered by saying that the standards would "get precision from the sense and experience of men," and thus preclude "such *variant judgments*" (emphasis added). As it turned out, this was a bad guess, but again it did indicate that the Court had certain expectations. Finally, McKenna noted that "the Ohio statute gives a review by the courts . . . of the decision of the board of censors."[26]

Clearly the Supreme Court did not contemplate unlimited censorship of movies. Allegations to the contrary are unfair, though to an extent understandable, since unlimited censorship or something very close to it actually did come about in the years following the decision. It came about in large measure because the courts, including the Supreme Court, allowed it to come about. And in that, the Court may be judged at fault.

The Problem of Supervision

Social controls that may be acceptable in the abstract can often work unreasonable burdens in actual operation. As things turned out, response to popular demands for some kind of control of movies was one thing; limitation of a resulting censorship apparatus was quite another. In setting up prior censorship, state legislatures and city councils chose a device which, by its very nature, invited abuse. As executive agencies, prior-censorship boards were less likely to be restrained by any balance of forces that might have existed in the law-making branch. The boards were not designed to reflect diverse elements in the community, and in their task orientation they often came to represent the interests of a few active censorial groups. Under these circumstances, extreme decisions on emotionally charged questions of public morality were not surprising. They were, in fact, compounded by a willingness of some boards to give themselves over completely, from time to time, to the idiosyncrasies of their members.

To curb these tendencies broad review by the courts was vital. Except in a very few instances, however, it was not forthcoming. This was unfortunate when the censors, as it became clear, abused their discretion on the questions of what was "indecent" or "sexually immoral" on the screen; but it was far worse in the thirties, when they turned their attention increasingly to political and social ideas.

In the face of widening censorship, the *Mutual Film* decision, with its overstated distinctions and dated characterization of the movies, was inadequate if left to stand alone. It was, nevertheless, a decision upon which limitations on censorship might have been built. Since it had not held movies to be without value, the Supreme Court might even have worked through the property right in films without reaching the free speech issue at all, had it chosen to do so. However, the Court remained silent.

At the same time, lower courts seemed to ignore the sense of limitation contained in the *Mutual Film* opinion. Judges repeatedly refused to substitute their own judgment for that of the censors. Usually the only issue on review was whether the examining officials had acted arbitrarily or in bad faith. The courts were not to be "constantly called upon to permit motion picture reels to be reproduced before them, and sit as supercensors thereof."[27] Accordingly, it was impossible for a film proprietor to reach a court without an a priori judgment against him. If he exhibited without a license as a test case, he was guilty of a crime under the typical statute. On the other hand, appeal of the denial of a license was on the narrow issue of administrative discretion only, and then the film proprietor carried the burden of proof. Moreover, the courts became increasingly permissive about what was within the censors' discretion.

Not surprisingly, then, only a handful of cases were won by exhibitors or distributors in the years following the *Mutual Film* decision. Extreme circumstances were required for the film interests to have any chance of prevailing. For example, in 1928 the Supreme Court of Ohio found that refusal of a permit for a film of the Dempsey-Tunney fight of 1927, based on "general knowledge of its character" rather than on an actual examination required by statute, was the exercise of more discretion than it could allow.[28] In another case, action by the Detroit Police Censor Bureau banning the film *Youth of Maxim* on the grounds that it was "Soviet propaganda and is likely to instill class hatred and hatred of existing government and social order in the United States" was reversed, because discretion had been exceeded in applying the statutory standard of "immoral" to the film. The police, the court noted acidly, did not have the duty "of preserving the international relations between the United States of America and the Union of Soviet Socialist Republics."[29]

In the meantime, however, newsreels and current events films, the part of the medium most like the press and an obviously inviting field for political censorship, were held to be subject to licensing.[30] In New York, Pennsylvania, and Kansas, newsreels were finally rescued from prior censorship by the legislatures. Some states extended similar exemptions to films used by the learned professions if not shown in places of amusement.

The arrival of talking pictures in 1927 presented an unusual opportunity for reexamining the constitutional status of the medium, or, at the very least, for restating the original narrow purposes of censorship. Sound was the outstanding technical advance in movies since the projection technique itself had been perfected before the turn of the century. Yet no court was either willing or imaginative enough to come to grips with the development. In a test case in 1929, *In re Fox Film Corp.*, the Pennsylvania Supreme Court found that sound films were no different from those that were silent.

The same year Vitagraph Films, which owned a phonographic device to synchronize speech with the screen, was required to file its disks with the licensing board.[31]

Though a new legal theory for motion pictures was long overdue in the thirties, it was not until 1948 that any court was even willing to hint at it. The fact that the court involved was the United States Supreme Court was heartening, though the statement itself was merely a dictum. In *United States* v. *Paramount Pictures,* the great antitrust prosecution in the film industry, Justice Douglas observed that "we have no doubt that motion pictures, like newspapers and radio, are included in the press whose freedom is guaranteed by the First Amendment."[32] So fertile was the field upon which these few words of nourishment fell that a foliage of test cases and law review articles was quick to spring up.[33] Yet the dry spell was not quite over; that would await the *Miracle* case in 1952.

Censorship Extraordinary

"The sense and experience of men" which Justice McKenna hoped would prevent "whim and caprice" in censorship was not self-executing. It required judicial supervision, and when that supervision was not given, the movies, in the words of Zechariah Chafee, Jr., had to "run a gauntlet of a host of big and little despots."[34] Where these censors operated under ill-defined standards, as they did in most licensing jurisdictions, it was inevitable that many of them would go beyond their original mandate as guardians of the public's morality and attempt to be guardians of its social and political thought as well. Perhaps social change in the thirties and war in the forties encouraged these additional concerns, just as the Jazz Age had amplified the protest against sex and immorality on the screen. In any case, censorship of the political and social content of films accounted for many of the worst abuses of the *Mutual Film* period. At the same time, there is little doubt that such censorship also hastened the day when movies were brought under constitutional free-speech protection.

The cavalcade of censorial action during the period has been well chronicled.[35] Noted here are a few of the rulings which became the subject of litigation and which were actually upheld by appellate courts. The latitude given the censors on the question of sexual immorality, the bellwether of censorship, is revealed in an early Pennsylvania decision in which suppression of *The Brand* was upheld. The protagonist in the film had run away from her husband to live in adultery. The state supreme court thought that any film which failed to pay "the highest deference and respect to the sanctity and purity of the home and family relation between husband and wife" could be barred from exhibition in the state.[36]

On the question of violence, Chicago censors were upheld in 1925 in refusing to license *Deadwood Coach,* which featured a stagecoach holdup and a great deal of shooting. The Illinois court offered a definitive comment on depiction of violence, at the same time giving great reach to the statutory standard of "immoral":

Such pictures should not be shown unless plainly harmless. Where "gun-play," or the shooting of human beings is the essence of the play and does not pertain to the necessities of war, nor the preservation of law and order, is for personal spite or revenge, and involves the taking of law into one's own hands, and thus becomes a murder, the picture may be said to be immoral. . . .[37]

Outright censorship of political ideas was sustained in a number of cases in the thirties. A Pennsylvania court affirmed the state licensing board's right to cut several rather mild anti-Fascist statements from a pro-Loyalist film based on the Spanish Civil War.[38] In *Thayer Amusement Corp.* v. *Moulton,* allegations by the Providence, Rhode Island, police department that the Soviet film *Professor Mamlock* was "Communist propaganda" were enough to sustain a ban in the state.

Beginning in 1915 with *Birth of a Nation,* which portrayed supposed excesses of Reconstruction, courts sustained the right of communities to censor films touching upon race questions.[39] In fact, the last two cases appealed to the Supreme Court before the *Miracle* decision involved such films. In the *Curley* case,[40] Memphis' censor, Lloyd Binford, had explained in a letter to United Artists Corporation that

the Memphis Board of Censors . . . is unable to approve your *Curley* picture with the little Negroes, as the South does not permit Negroes in white schools nor recognize social equality between the races even in children.[41]

His action was sustained by the Tennessee Supreme Court, which held that the movie company had not complied with provisions of the state's foreign corporation laws and, therefore, lacked standing to challenge the censorship order.

Finally, Atlanta's ban on *Lost Boundaries*—the story of a Negro doctor and his family who "pass" for white—on the ground that the film was "likely to have an adverse effect on the peace, morals, and good order of the city," was upheld by the Fifth Circuit Court of Appeals in *RD-DR Corp.* v. *Smith.*

It was fitting then that when the Supreme Court held motion pictures to be protected by the First Amendment in the *Miracle* case, the immediate issue before the Court—whether "sacrilegious" could be used as a licensing standard—was one of the censorship of a social idea.

The *Mutual Film* period—the years between 1915 and 1952—was marked by unbridled censorship. This was hardly surprising under the circumstances, since administrative censorship of a mass medium tended toward excess, in the absence of close judicial supervision. This was all the more likely where such censorship was in the volatile and ill-defined realm of public morality and where it was administered by patronage appointees often lacking liberal education. For these reasons, the lesson to be drawn from the nation's unfortunate experience with censorship during the *Mutual Film* period can be qualified: the experience indicates that prior restraint is a difficult institution to manage, but not that excesses are ordained or immutable.

Yet in spite of this, the censorship of the *Mutual Film* period continues to serve as the major frame of reference for many libertarians in judging the licensing of motion pictures. This "lag" is unfortunate, since it tends to distort public dialogue on the question. For example, in twenty-five references made to specific rulings of licensing boards by Chief Justice Warren in his long and notable dissenting opinion attacking prior censorship in the *Times Film* case of 1961, twenty-four were from the *Mutual Film* period, and the single one taken from the nine years between the *Miracle* decision and his opinion had been reversed by a court![42]

The doors open to abuses of the sort that occurred during the *Mutual Film* period have been gradually closed, and as they have, the relevance of those censorial extremes to prior censorship today is fast diminishing.

The *Miracle* Decision

Irresistible Forces

By the time of the ruling in the *Miracle* case, *Burstyn* v. *Wilson*—that motion pictures were entitled to protection of the First Amendment—not only had censorial excesses become commonplace and in obvious need of correction, but two other developments made it hard to ignore motion pictures as a medium of speech. The first of these was the technical and artistic advance of the medium itself. The other was an expanding constitutional theory of free speech in which the absence of the movies was increasingly conspicuous.

The years between the *Mutual Film* and the *Miracle* cases were marked by a steady refinement in the mechanics of both production and projection. Developments of more sensitive film stocks and faster lenses increased the precision of the camera and led to experimentation in photographic techniques. These advances were complemented by the remarkable innovation of synchronizing sound and picture.

Such technical progress heightened the sense of realism offered by the screen, and augmented its story-telling and documentary powers. The men and women who made movies showed increasing sophistication and imagination in their work. Features were longer, more unified in theme, and more ambitious artistically. Many were adaptations of classics or of current literature. Many more went beyond the mere intent to entertain and dealt critically with social and political ideas and values.* These developments not only made comparisons with the medium of the nickelodeon era difficult, but went far to remove whatever doubt remained that the screen could play, and in fact was playing, a role in the formation of public opinion.

World War II saw motion pictures accorded some of the same privileges as the press and radio by the executive and legislative branches of government. In 1941 President Roosevelt declared that the medium should not be subject to war censorship by the government. In a price control bill, Congress included films with the press in granting exemption from licensing as a condition of sale or distribution.[43] At the Inter-American Conference in Mexico City, in 1944, the United States was one of the signatories to a resolution urging the speedy abandonment of wartime controls on the press, radio, and motion pictures when hostilities ended.

During the years in which the movies were being regulated by the states as a business, the Supreme Court had developed a formidable constitutional right of free speech against abridgment by state authority. So advanced had this doctrine become by the end of World War II that it seemed only a matter of time before a place would be found in it for motion pictures. Development of the theory went back to 1925, when the Court first announced, in *Gitlow* v. *New York,* that freedom of speech would be protected against unreasonable state action. In the next quarter century the Court struck down a variety of state and local laws abridging communication.

In one series of cases, several types of speech were held to be protected from government interference except under narrow and clearly drawn laws relating only to the time and place of communication, and administered only in the interest of maintaining order in public places.[44] In other cases, regulation of the content of speech was found to be unlawful except upon a

---

* Among such films in the years before the *Miracle* decision were *Pinky, Intruder in the Dust* (race relations), *Gentleman's Agreement* (anti-Semitism), *All the Kings Men, Citizen Kane* (demagoguery), *The Ox-Bow Incident* (mob emotion), *Lost Weekend* (alcoholism), *Knock on Any Door* (juvenile delinquency), *Whistle at Eaton Falls* (labor-management relations), *Dark Past* (psychoanalysis), *Burning Cross* (the Ku Klux Klan), *The Snake Pit* (conditions in mental hospitals), *Iron Curtain* (Communism), *Tomorrow the World* (Nazism), *Grapes of Wrath* (social migration, poverty), *Live Today for Tomorrow* (euthanasia). An extensive list of such films, including some of those mentioned above, appears in Brief for Appellant at 13, *Burstyn* v. *Wilson,* 343 U.S. 495 (1952).

showing by the government that publication would lead to a clear and present danger of incitement to violence, criminality, or breach of the peace; or except where the utterance fell into certain narrow categories—defamation, "fighting words," and obscenity.[45] These latter categories were considered to be entirely outside the scope of constitutional protection, because of their slight social value in comparison with the harm their publication might do. In still other cases, statutes affecting free speech were held to violate due process of law where, because of vague criteria, they failed to give warning of what communications might fall within their proscriptions, or failed generally to define a crime clearly enough for a reasonable man to know when he was committing it.[46]

The leading prior-censorship decision in this period was *Near* v. *Minnesota,* in 1931, in which the Court held that a state could not enjoin future issues of a newspaper solely on the basis of obscene or defamatory character of past issues. Such an action, according to Chief Justice Hughes, who spoke for the Court, was a prior restraint on speech and, as such, it violated the First Amendment's chief guarantees. The decision settled the general rule that publications, even by "miscreant purveyors of scandal," were not subject to prior restraints and that "subsequent punishment for such abuses as may exist is the appropriate remedy."[47]

However, the doctrine was complicated by a dictum in which the Chief Justice set out a number of exceptions.

No one would question but that a government might prevent actual obstruction to its recruiting service or the publication of the sailing dates of transports or the number and location of troops. On similar grounds, the primary requirements of decency may be enforced against obscene publications. The security of the community life may be protected against incitements to acts of violence and the overthrow by force of orderly government.[48]

The Chief Justice gave no indication how prior restraint in the exceptional cases could be imposed. For example, it was not clear whether prior restraint was to be limited merely to those utterances already shown to present an exceptional case, or whether it could include an administrative apparatus set up to discover exceptional cases.

When the Supreme Court did at last include motion pictures in the theory of free speech, in the *Miracle* case in 1952, the decision was hailed as a courageous one. In one sense it was, for it was made in the face of powerful pressures at the state and national level. But in a larger sense the Court had moved with great care. By 1952, First Amendment rights were fairly well established against interference by the states, the movies had demonstrated a capacity for dealing with social and political controversy, and the state and local censorship that controlled the medium had consistently gone beyond its original purpose and exceeded reasonable bounds.

"A Medium for the Communication of Ideas"

The unusual series of events that preceded the litigation in the *Miracle* case can only be summarized here.[49] The film, *The Miracle,* forty minutes long, was made in Italy by Roberto Rossellini. It had been joined with two short French films, which were never part of the controversy, to form the trilogy feature *Ways of Love.* The story concerned a simple-minded peasant girl, played by Anna Magnani, who is seduced by a bearded stranger she imagines to be St. Joseph. Later she gives birth to a son who she believes is the Christ child. Though *The Miracle* itself received mixed reviews, *Ways of Love* was eventually selected by the New York Film Critics as the best foreign-language film of 1950.

The trilogy had originally received a license from the New York State Motion Picture Division and opened at the Paris Theatre in New York City, December 12, 1950. The first overt protest came twelve days later when the city commissioner of licenses threatened to suspend the theatre's business license because he found *The Miracle* "officially and personally blasphemous." At this point the film's distributor, Joseph Burstyn, entered the controversy and succeeded in having the license commissioner enjoined from further interfering with exhibition.[50] Shortly after this, Cardinal Spellman, head of the Roman Catholic Archdiocese of New York, publicly denounced the film and called upon Catholics throughout the country to avoid the film and any theatre showing it.

In the weeks that followed, members of the Catholic War Veterans, sometimes numbering more than 1,000, picketed the Paris Theatre. They were, in turn, counterpicketed by token representation from Protestant and interdenominational groups. The theatre itself received several bomb threats. Each time it was emptied by police, but no bomb was found. The management was given a series of fire summons for allowing standees in the rear of the theatre. Ephraim London, counsel for Burstyn, suspected that his telephone line to the distributor had been tapped. And pressure from the Catholic hierarchy in the city forced the New York Film Critics to abandon plans to use the large and prestigious Radio City Music Hall for presentation of their annual awards, one of which was the recognition of *Ways of Love.*

Finally, after claiming to have received hundreds of protests, the state Board of Regents, parent body to the Motion Picture Division, agreed to review the division's approval of the film. On February 16, 1951, after hearings, the Regents revoked the license on the ground that the film was sacrilegious, and therefore censorable under New York's licensing law. Burstyn then brought his action to review the Regents' finding. He was unsuccessful in New York courts, with the Court of Appeals voting 5 to 2 to uphold "sacrilegious" as a valid censorship standard.[51]

In February, 1952, the United States Supreme Court agreed to hear the case—its first on film censorship in thirty-seven years. In its decision three months later, the Court considered only whether motion pictures were a medium of speech protected by the Constitution, and whether the censorship standard "sacrilegious" in the New York law was a permissible one.

Justice Clark, speaking for the Court, declared that "it cannot be doubted that motion pictures are a significant medium for the communication of ideas." And, as such, they were within the free speech and free press guarantees of the First and Fourteenth Amendments.[52]

This recognition, Clark said, could not be diminished either on the ground that they were exhibited for private profit, or that they were designed to entertain as well as inform, or that they might possess a greater capacity for evil than other forms of expression. The last "hypothesis," he said, might be "relevant in determining the permissible scope of community control, but it does not authorize substantially unbridled censorship. . . ." Thus Clark answered each of Justice McKenna's attempts, thirty-seven years earlier, to set the movies apart. To the extent that this reevaluation of the medium was inconsistent with the one in *Mutual Film,* Clark said the earlier decision was overruled.

On the question of whether motion pictures, as a medium of speech, could still be subject to prior censorship, Clark pointed out that freedom of expression was the general rule, even though the Constitution does not require absolute freedom to exhibit every motion picture of every kind at all times and all places. Referring to the *Near* rule against prior restraints on free speech, he said that such limitations would be recognized only in "exceptional cases," and that even then the state would have the heavy burden of demonstrating that the particular restraint in question presented such a case.

The state had not so demonstrated here. The standard of "sacrilegious" was

far from the kind of narrow exception to freedom of expression which a state may carve out to satisfy the adverse demands of other interests of society. . . . the state has no legitimate interest in protecting any or all religions from views distasteful to them which is sufficient to justify prior restraint upon the expression of those views. It is not the business of government in our nation to suppress real or imagined attacks upon a particular religious doctrine, whether they appear in publications, speeches, or motion pictures.[53]

And here Clark noted the serious consequences that could result from the use of a "broad and all-inclusive" standard of "sacrilegious." Under it the censor would be

set adrift upon a boundless sea amid a myriad of conflicting currents of religious views, with no charts but those provided by the most vocal and powerful orthodoxies. . . . Under such a standard the most tolerant censor would find it virtually impossible to avoid favoring one religion over another, and he would be subject to an inevitable tendency to ban the expression of unpopular sentiments sacred to a religious minority.[54]

Finally, having observed that each method of communication tended to present its own peculiar problems of control, Clark emphasized that it was not necessary for the Court to decide "whether a state may censor motion pictures under a clearly drawn statute designed and applied to prevent the showing of obscene films."[55]

Though the Court was unanimous, there were two concurring opinions. In a brief one, Justice Reed noted that since the Court had not foreclosed the states from licensing motion pictures, "our duty requires us to examine the fact of the refusal of a license in each case to determine whether the principles of the First Amendment have been honored."[56]

In a very long opinion in which he was joined by Justices Burton and Jackson, Justice Frankfurter undertook a scholarly survey of the meaning of the term "sacrilegious." As a result, he found the definition of the term by the New York Court of Appeals to be so vague as to violate due process of law when used as a standard for denying a license. He would have decided the case on this ground, finding it unnecessary to determine whether or not there had been a violation of free speech.

The New Directions

In deciding to hear the *Miracle* case, the Supreme Court had moved cautiously. From the very beginning, New York's standard of "sacrilegious" was highly vulnerable, open to challenge not only on grounds of free speech, but also on those of freedom of religion. Whatever merit the standard may have had as public policy had been clearly impaired by events which preceded the litigation. The row over the film in New York City indicated an absence of any unity of public opinion. Christians were divided, with a number of Protestant leaders actively supporting the film, and several Catholics in arts and letters in disagreement with their spiritual leaders on the issue.

The case thus presented a very different situation from *RD-DR Corp.* v. *Smith,* in which the Supreme Court had denied certiorari two years earlier. In that case the Atlanta censor had refused to license *Lost Boundaries,* in which a Negro "passes" for white. The reason given was the necessity of protecting the "peace, morals, and good order" of the city. There, the aim embodied in the standard, if not the particular application of the standard, *was* a legitimate interest of government. Moreover, the effective public opinion in the community at the time—which is to say, the white opinion —was undoubtedly largely united on the question. In contrast, New York's position was a poor one. The "public" outrage over the film was almost exclusively that manifested by a single, well defined group objecting to something that was offensive for the most part only to itself. Under these circumstances, the legal controversy over a "sacrilege" in *The Miracle* was an ideal vehicle for taking the larger step of bringing the entire medium under the First Amendment.

On the prior-censorship question the Supreme Court chose a middle ground. On the one side, near-unrestricted censorship was the prevailing situation. On the other, Ephraim London, counsel for Burstyn, had argued for freedom to exhibit a film under any circumstances. London won the case and a great change in the control of motion pictures. But he failed to convince the Court to go all the way in granting freedom from prior censorship.

Originally, in the *Mutual Film* case, the Supreme Court had left control of the movies in the hands of the "people," that is, in the legislative majorities which had been busy setting up prior-censorship systems. With such censorship, however, control passed to low-level administrators who, in time, tended to be responsive to certain active censorial groups. With the *Miracle* decision, control over the medium was, in part, removed from the censors by eliminating "sacrilegious" as a standard for censorship and, more significantly, by a necessary implication of First Amendment status —that of *de novo* review in the courts. This review, in turn, was to be exercised in a context where freedom of speech was the rule and restraint merely the exception.

Still, the institution of prior censorship remained, the Court having chosen not to deal with the issue of its constitutionality. This left unanswered the question of how the theory of free speech—essentially elitist in terms of the tolerance it assumes and requires—would be reconciled with a mass medium which, except for a relatively brief period in its history, was neither distinguished for its self-restraint nor subject to any collaborative restraint by advertisers. Would the theory of free speech undergo a kind of mutation that would allow the limited prior censorship of motion pictures? Or on the other hand, would the *Miracle* decision be, in effect, only the first stage of a complete transition of status for motion pictures that eventually would see them entirely freed of official prior censorship?

The importance of the *Miracle* case was not limited to the question of

prior censorship. To a degree, the decision recast the entire role of government in accommodating demands for restriction of the medium. Though the
extraordinary Catholic effort to bar the film in New York involved pressure
at a number of points, the suppression actually came about through lawful
processes. The Supreme Court's decision, on the other hand, represented a
failure of government to satisfy demands for restriction. This failure was a
spectacular one not only because a case had been lost at the highest levels,
but also because the capacity of government to respond lawfully to censorial protests had been significantly and permanently impaired. Unsurpris-
ingly, the decision did not succeed in stilling much of the protest. Catholics
were called upon, anew, to stay away from the film and to complain directly
to exhibitors who showed it. The National Council of Catholic Men said
that now "the only effective bulwark against pictures which are immoral,
short of being obscene, is public opinion manifested through such organizations as the Legion of Decency."[57] The entire *Miracle* controversy indicated
that the task of safeguarding and augmenting free speech in motion pictures
would necessarily be a more complicated one than that of merely restricting
the censors.

The *Miracle* decision also had an impact on motion picture content. The
new freedom it provided helped to stimulate a maturity in the medium that
eventually saw greater sophistication of subject and treatment and less dependence on the "family" film. In the words of a leading film critic, the decision "cut through what has been an inhibition for thirty-seven years—to
wit, the reactionary notion that movies are but childish 'spectacles'."[58]
There were, of course, other factors in this change—the decentralization of
the film industry and competition from television, for example—but the
protection of the movies as speech was a key legal and psychological step.
More sophisticated and "adult" films were being made in 1952, but they
were mainly European, and an American audience for them had not yet developed. The *Miracle* decision not only gave freedom to one of these films,
but it bestowed status on the entire genre.

Yet it was also true that the freedom which would allow maturity would
also allow abuse. The doors open to art would not be easy to close against a
host of threatening representations, some of which would fairly raise the
question of obscenity. It appeared in 1952 that this was a risk a free
speech society might afford to take and probably should take. Even so, this
free speech society was also a mass democratic society, and if the two communities were to exist side by side, responsibilities would have to be exercised. This raised anew the very old question of whose responsibilities they
were to be.

3

Procedures: Pragmatic Assessment

An Interim Period

The fundamental questions raised by the *Miracle* decision were not dealt with immediately by the Supreme Court, and the law of prior censorship developed somewhat haphazardly following that case. It was not until *Times Film Corp.* v. *Chicago,* in 1961, that the Court ruled on the constitutional status of licensing, while the problem of permissible licensing procedures was not considered until *Freedman* v. *Maryland,* in 1965. Nonetheless, six licensing cases were heard by the highest court in the interim period, and the power of the censors was cut back in each one. In five of these, all decided *per curiam,* censorship orders were reversed, apparently because of faults in the substantive licensing standards or in application of those standards to particular films.[1] In the sixth case, *Kingsley International Pictures* v. *Board of Regents,* involving an adaptation of the D. H. Lawrence novel *Lady Chatterley's Lover,* the Court held that a licensing standard of "sexual immorality," having been construed to ban a film depicting adultery as a desirable way of life, was in effect a bar to the discussion of ideas.

The Court's clear anticensorship persuasion in these cases, coupled with its failure to be more definitive, left the constitutionality of prior censorship in doubt. In the mid-1950's the highest courts in Ohio[2] and Massachusetts,[3] in what were to prove to be poor guesses, did invalidate licensing laws in their respective states and held that prior censorship itself violated the First Amendment. And in Kansas, the legislature at one point actually repealed the state censorship law in the belief that the Court, in effect, had found prior censorship to be unconstitutional.[4]

Though the *Kingsley Pictures* case and the five rather cryptic *per curiam* decisions failed to provide clear guidelines, the Supreme Court may actually have done all that it was capable of doing under the circumstances. It seems clear now that use of the *per curiam* method was forced by lack of essential agreement among the Justices on the constitutional issue, particularly since oral argument was heard on the cases. The extent of this disunity was later obvious in *Kingsley Pictures,* where six opinions were filed in a unanimous decision. And still later, when the constitutional issue was finally drawn in *Times Film* v. *Chicago,* the Court was divided five to four. In the ten years following the *Miracle* case, it was much easier for nine Justices to repair an abuse of prior censorship than to agree upon a theory for doing so.

The lack of definition in these interim decisions cannot obscure the fact that they were many—six in seven years—and that they were unanimous. They indicated the Court was willing to build upon the constitutional base it had established for the medium in the *Miracle* case, and to exercise a judicial supervision over censors that had been so conspicuously absent in the *Mutual Film* period. The Court's failure to address itself to the fundamental constitutional issue and to the question of procedural requirements was the price of a strenuous and salutary effort to provide judicial supervision at a time when judicial consensus was seemingly unobtainable.

The *Times Film* Case of 1961

The alternative to simply finding all prior censorship unconstitutional is some kind of "pragmatic assessment of its operations in particular circumstances."[5] Such less-than-absolute approach allows a number of values besides that of free speech to be taken into account. In particular, it permits a flexibility in the face of two unknowns: the future content of motion pictures and the capacity of the medium for harm. On the other hand, a pragmatic approach, allowing the exercise of a reasonable censorship, requires a difficult balancing of interests, which in turn demands a continuing judicial review of not only the procedures and objectives of censorship, but also of the challenged motion pictures themselves. Moreover, at some point the pragmatic approach requires an affirmation of censorship itself. For some members of the Supreme Court, these disadvantages were too high a price to pay, particularly in the light of previous abuses of licensing. For other members, none of whom it may safely be said has had any love for censorship, the task of pragmatic assessment has ranked as a difficult and unpleasant one at best.

Four years before the *Times Film* case, a majority of the Court had held back from the absolute position in considering a type of prior restraint on magazines and other printed matter. In *Kingsley Books* v. *Brown,* a New York statute providing for postpublication injunction of the distribution of obscene publications was held not to violate the First Amendment. Justice

Frankfurter, speaking for the majority of five, indicated that the Court would make a "particularistic analysis" of such censorship: "the term 'prior restraint' is not a self-wielding sword, nor can it serve as a talismanic text." There was instead a "duty of closer analysis and critical judgment in applying the thought behind the phrases." At the same time, Frankfurter seemed to imply that the Court would not uphold licensing as a prior restraint, at least not on printed media. Prior restraint was an exception to the general rule of free speech, and thus "it is to be closely confined so as to preclude what may fairly be deemed licensing or censorship."[6]

It was against the background of this case and the six movie censorship decisions of the 1950's that the Times Film Corporation, a distributor of foreign films with headquarters in New York, challenged Chicago's licensing system and the constitutionality of all prior censorship of motion pictures. The company had tendered a license fee to the city's board of censors, but refused to submit the film itself, claiming that the city, if it wished to act against objectionable films, could do so through the criminal process *after* exhibition. Though the film, *Don Juan,* based on Mozart's opera *Don Giovanni,* was apparently innocent of any matter that would have raised a censorship question, the city censors refused to issue a permit.

Five members of the Court—Justices Frankfurter, Clark, Harlan, Whittaker, and Stewart—voted to uphold the city's power to license films. In an opinion written by Clark, they saw Times Film's argument as involving the claim that constitutional protection "includes complete and absolute freedom to exhibit, at least once, any and every kind of motion picture."[7] Against such a claim, the city's ordinance requiring submission of films before their public exhibition was not void on its face.

Reviewing freedom of speech cases beginning with *Near* v. *Minnesota,* Clark pointed out that the freedom was not an absolute right even as to the protection against prior restraint. He noted that obscenity was one of the limits to free speech enumerated in *Near.* To accept the Times Film argument against prior censorship would be to strip a state of "all constitutional power to prevent, in the most effective fashion, the utterance of this class of speech."[8] It would also mean ignoring the fact that motion pictures might have a greater capacity for harm than other methods of expression. Here Clark repeated a dictum of the *Miracle* case, that motion pictures were not "necessarily subject to the precise rules governing any other particular method of expression. Each method . . . tends to present its own peculiar problems."[9]

Moreover, it was not the Court's business to limit a state in its selection of the remedy it deemed "most effective to cope with such a problem, absent, of course, a showing of unreasonable strictures on individual liberty resulting from its application in particular circumstances."

Taking care to limit the scope of the Court's ruling, he pointed out that the Court was not holding that a censor could be granted the power to prevent exhibition of any film he found distasteful, nor was it evaluating the particular standards of the Chicago ordinance; and, finally, it was dealing only with motion pictures and not with other forms of expression.

Four members of the Court—Chief Justice Warren and Justices Black, Douglas, and Brennan—took issue with the decision in a long dissenting opinion written by the Chief Justice. By binding itself to the more extreme implications of Times Film's argument, the majority had formulated the wrong issue, according to Warren. The real issue in the case was whether any organ of government "may require all motion picture exhibitors to submit all films to a police chief, mayor, or other administrative officials for licensing and censorship prior to public exhibition. . . ."[10] That being so, Warren believed, the Court's ruling did two things of serious consequence: it approved unlimited censorship of motion pictures, and risked the danger of eventual censorship of every form of communication.

Acknowledging that protection of First Amendment liberties from prior restraint was not unlimited, the Chief Justice claimed that licensing or censorship was never considered to be within the "exceptional cases" discussed in *Near*. The Court, in *Times Film,* had sustained prior restraint "without requiring any demonstrations that this is an 'exceptional case' . . . and without any indication that Chicago has sustained the 'heavy burden' which was supposed to have been placed upon it."

What was the impact of such a prior restraint? Here Warren discussed *Kingsley Books* and the narrowly upheld New York statute which provided that obscene literature could be enjoined from distribution after a judicial hearing. By comparison, the Chicago ordinance, he said, offered no such procedural safeguards. There was no trial on the issue before restraint became effective. There was no requirement of showing some cause to believe a film obscene before restraint could be imposed. There were no provisions for a speedy trial on the issue of obscenity. And if the exhibitor chose to show the film without a permit, nonobscenity was no defense.

Though admitting that an exhibitor or distributor could seek judicial remedies if he believed the censor had abused his authority, Warren claimed this was no answer to the possibility of irreparable damage resulting from the sort of delay usual in the adjudicatory process; he pointed out that the present litigation had consumed almost three years. Rather than undertake costly and lengthy litigation, it was far more likely the film proprietor would simply capitulate. Here the Chief Justice said Chicago had chosen a "most objectionable" course to attain its goals "without any apparent attempt to devise other means so as not to intrude on the constitutionally protected liberties. . . ." Since the majority had in no way explained why films should be treated differently from other forms of expression, it "comes perilously close to holding that not only may motion pictures be censored but that a licensing scheme may be applied to . . . every other medium of expression." Even if motion pictures had greater impact than other media, this fact provided no basis for subjecting them to greater suppression. The "peculiar problems" a medium of speech may present are only those concerning the conditions surrounding delivery and have nothing whatever to do with the content of speech.

In a separate dissenting opinion, Justice Douglas, with Justice Black, restated his view that censorship of films by governmental licensing was unconstitutional because it was a prior restraint on free speech.

So divergent were the majority and minority opinions that a dialogue between them is not easily joined. Nominally, the disagreement resulted from the majority deciding the extreme issue which Times Film had conveniently placed before it—whether constitutional protection includes absolute freedom to exhibit a film at least once—while the minority asked whether a state could require submission of all films for licensing without having to show that exhibition in a particular case would impair some vital public interest. Yet the breach was more fundamental, and involved at least three other issues: interpretation of the *Near* rule against prior restraints, the procedural safeguards that should accompany use of a prior restraint, and the differentiation of motion pictures from other media of speech.

The majority interpreted the *Near* doctrine to allow a licensing system. A method of control requiring systematic examination of all films was permissible for the purpose of *discovering* as well as for suppressing obscenity and other types of "exceptional" speech. The majority would not require the state to show that licensing was the *only* effective way to control such speech. On the contrary, a state would be limited in its choice of method only upon a "showing of unreasonable strictures on individual liberties resulting from its application in particular circumstances." In effect, this seemed to say that as long as the state's intention was to control or discover "exceptional" speech, the method it chose would have the presumption of constitutionality.

The minority, on the other hand, saw the *Near* rule as allowing prior restraint only where an utterance had *already* been shown to be "exceptional" speech. Thus a licensing system which required submission of all films— only a few of which would ever be shown to be "exceptional"—and at the same time penalized exhibition of unsubmitted films, would never be a permissible prior restraint.

As for the procedural requirements of prior restraint, the majority was uncomfortably silent except for the single "unreasonable strictures" phrase. For Chief Justice Warren, however, a permissible prior restraint would have to include certain definite procedural safeguards. The most important of these appeared to be the requirement that the state show some cause to believe a film "exceptional" before a restraint could be imposed. And even then, the issue would have to be subject to a speedy adjudication. Yet just how a state could make such a showing without first requiring submission of all films for its own examination, and at the same time still not allow a questionable film to be shown publicly beforehand, was a question the Chief Justice did not answer. He did leave the door open, however. Unlike his fellow dissenters, Douglas and Black, he was opposed to a licensing system rather than to all forms of prior restraint.

Central to the majority's position was the idea that movies may have a special capacity for harm. This fear, which can be traced back through Justice McKenna's opinion in *Mutual Film* to the first prior-censorship case, *Block* v. *Chicago,* made a state's resort to licensing reasonable. Such a fear also implied a possible rationalization for constitutionally distinguishing movies from other media of speech.

Yet, as Warren pointed out, nowhere in his opinion did Clark attempt to state why or how films might have a greater impact than, say, newspapers, magazines, or television. For the minority, there was no problem on this point at all. For the purposes of controlling content, one medium within the First Amendment could not be constitutionally distinguished from another. Greater impact, even assuming such could be proven, could not mean greater suppression.

These differences put a great distance between the majority and minority opinions. The majority avoided the easy absolutism of declaring all licensing unconstitutional, but it was not willing to say much more .about the case. It was the minority, instead, which actually posed pragmatic questions on the operation of prior censorship. The majority—with the help of Times Film's either-or type of argument—had framed the issue in such a way as to force the great problems involved in the licensing of a medium of speech into what appeared to be an almost trivial perspective. For in the protection of free speech there would seem to be only slight value and certainly no particular warranty in a "freedom to exhibit at least once." Even if the great advantage of freedom of speech is conceded to be the opportunity for truth or wisdom to win acceptance over error or poor judgment in the "marketplace of ideas," absolute freedom for a single exhibition would hardly seem crucial. The struggle of the "market place" is more apt to be measured by many advances and retreats over years and even decades than by, say, the outcome of one-night stands.

Nevertheless, as the minority was willing to recognize, there was something very substantial behind the claim of freedom to exhibit at least once. The claim implied that control of free speech must be through the criminal law and not through licensing. This perhaps should have induced an evaluation of the differences between licensing and criminal prosecution—in the main, who will carry the burden of going to court and, once there, the burden of proof. But these points were not discussed by the Court.

For these reasons it may be asked whether the case should have been heard at all. One student of the Court, Alexander Bickel, himself not opposed to all prior restraints, has argued that *certiorari* should have been denied.[11] Times Film's design, Bickel contends, was to force the Court's hand by framing the type of case in which the main issue was whether all prior restraints were improper under all circumstances. As such, the case deprived the Court of choice, because the facts and pleadings were ill-suited for any consideration of the actual workings of prior censorship and, therefore, of the prudence of licensing. As a result, "only one outcome on the merits was open to the Court on principle—legitimation; and this was unwise in its tendency," since it would "encourage majoritarian forces of order which speak for themselves readily enough when they feel the need."[12]

It may be conceded that the case was a poor one for a pragmatic assessment of prior censorship. Yet whether the Court should have heard it at all must be weighed against the need for a degree of certainty in the law. Another case, the facts of which might have allowed a fuller and tidier consideration of many of the important dimensions of prior censorship, would perhaps have been preferable, but awaiting this advantage would have meant prolonging the uncertainty already manifest among lower courts, legislators, and administrators. Moreover it is doubtful, given the evident disagreement on the Court over prior censorship, that the nine Justices could have decided the constitutional issue and set out procedural requirements all in the same case.

The possibility of legitimation—reflecting as it does Warren's misgiving and that of several respected journalistic sources as well[13]—was a reasonable concern in view of the questions left unexplored in the majority opinion. But actual developments following the decision do not bear out these fears. For one thing, it did not result in lower courts upholding censors. In fact, the very opposite occurred. In eleven appellate decisions between *Times Film* and the Supreme Court's next movie censorship case, *Freedman* v. *Maryland,* in 1965, the censors were not once upheld on the merits. In four of these cases, licensing itself was invalidated under free speech provisions of state constitutions.[14] In two others, procedural deficiencies were found in licensing laws,[15] and in two more, licensing standards were held misapplied to particular films.[16] Finally, in three cases in which the censors prevailed, two turned on the fact that the film proprietor had proceeded improperly,[17] and the third on the appellate court's refusal to consider the obscenity issue or to view the film, thereby letting stand an adverse decision in the trial court.[18]

Nor did the *Times Film* decision spur the creation of a host of new censorship bodies. On the contrary, the number of functioning licensing boards actually declined following the case. In January, 1959, two years before the decision, five states and forty-eight municipalities had prior-censorship boards active in one degree or another.[19] In January, 1963, two years after the decision, only four state and twenty-seven municipal boards were active. New review bodies had been formed in only two cities—Columbus, Ohio, and Sumter, South Carolina—in the interim. In a third city, Abilene, Texas, an already active board was given new powers. But in the meantime six municipal boards had become inactive and twelve municipalities had dropped prior censorship altogether.[20]

If *Times Film* was a spur to censorial energies, one would also expect to find large-scale increases in the activity of the licensing boards themselves. Yet figures taken from the annual reports of the four state boards—Kansas, Maryland, New York, and Virginia—lead to mixed findings. Comparison of a two-year period before the decision with a two-year period afterward (Table 1) reveals that the number of films denied permits altogether increased in three of the four states, but the number of films in which deletions were required actually declined in two of the four states.

TABLE 1   *Censorship by State Licensing Boards in Two-Year Period Before* Times Film *Decision, January 23, 1961, Compared with Censorship by Same Boards in Two-Year Period After the Decision*[a]

Licensing board	Films approved with deletions		Films rejected		Total censorship	
	before	after	before	after	before	after
Kansas	235[b]	69[b]	15	5	250[b]	74[b]
Maryland	36	85	0	16	36	101
New York	67	51	2	3	69	54
Virginia	30	42	8	14	38	56

Table is based upon the annual reports of the licensing boards of the states of Kansas, Maryland, New York, and Virginia.

[a] Where the fiscal years of the boards began July 1, as they did in Kansas, Maryland, and Virginia, the pre-*Times Film* period was taken as July 1, 1958, to June 30, 1960, and the post-*Times Film* period as July 1, 1961, to June 30, 1963. The fiscal year July 1, 1960, to June 30, 1961, was eliminated from the comparison. In New York, where the fiscal year began April 1, the pre-*Times Film* period was taken as April 1, 1959, to March 31, 1961, and the post-*Times Film* period, from April 1, 1961, to March 31, 1963.

[b] Figures include the number of prints of censored films distributed in the state, since the Board of Review, unlike other boards, did not compile merely the number of individual productions censored.

Affirmation of the licensing power in *Times Film,* a necessary step toward any pragmatic consideration of prior censorship, did not revitalize the censors or result in "unlimited censorship" as Chief Justice Warren had feared. Legitimation of the licensing power may have been distasteful, but it did not prove to be dangerous.

An interesting by-product of the *Times Film* decision, and one further allaying libertarian fears, were the findings by the highest courts of three states—Pennsylvania,[21] Oregon,[22] and Georgia[23]—that motion picture prior censorship violated the free speech provisions of their respective state constitutions. These decisions, all within fifteen months of *Times Film,* were by the mid-1960's the only outstanding appellate authority that prior censorship was unlawful per se. (Presumably the fact that earlier invalidation of licensing in Ohio and Massachusetts had been based on the First Amendment would not stand in the way of a revival of prior censorship in those states.)[24]

The provisions of the three constitutions are remarkably alike. Pennsylvania's[25] and Georgia's[26] differ only in minor phrasing from Oregon's, which declares,

No law shall be passed restraining the free expression of opinion, or restricting the right to speak, write, or print freely on any subject whatever; but every person shall be responsible for the abuse of this right.[27]

The key phrase "responsible for the abuse" is identical in all three, and each of the state courts relied upon it to distinguish these free speech provisions from the First Amendment. In none of the cases, however, was any authority cited for this interpretation. The Pennsylvania Supreme Court thought it "clear enough that what it was designed to do was to prohibit the imposition of prior restraint."[28] The Oregon Supreme Court said it was "self-evident that the draftsmen of Oregon's basic charter wanted no censorship in Oregon."[29]

Yet the explanation for these three quick and somewhat surprising decisions probably lies less in differences in phraseology between the state constitutions and the First Amendment, or in the possibility that the former were regaining their late-eighteenth century status as chief guardians of individual liberties, than in the impact of Chief Justice Warren's dissent in *Times Film* and in the considerable antilicensing swell that had been mounting in American courts since the *Miracle* case. To many libertarians, it seemed that a fitting resolution of this trend would have been a finding by the United States Supreme Court that licensing was unconstitutional per se. This nearly occurred in *Times Film,* and the fact that it did not drew the forceful protest from Warren and three other members of the Court. This protest appeared to lash the anticensorship surge, supplying it with the powerful rationalization, if not the decision, that it had previously lacked. It was Warren's dissent from which the three state courts drew their inspiration. One of the three even cited the dissent, at the same time making no mention of the majority decision anywhere in its opinion.[30] The three decisions represent a kind of high-water mark in antilicensing doctrinal development.

The *Freedman* Case of 1965

If the prior censorship power was not invalid per se under the First and Fourteenth Amendments, were existing licensing systems constitutional? Using Justice Clark's dictum in *Times Film,* that no "unreasonable strictures on individual liberty" should result from prior censorship, one lower court found the Chicago licensing ordinance procedurally deficient.[31] Chief Justice Warren had answered this question more sweepingly in his *Times Film* dissent, by viewing as unconstitutional any prior censorship which required submission of all films and at the same time gave the state power of administrative suppression. By either of these measures, the typical licensing system of the early 1960's—largely unchanged in its procedural character from the *Mutual Film* period—appeared to be of doubtful standing.

In *Freedman* v. *Maryland* in 1965, the Supreme Court dealt with the procedures of licensing for the first time. The case involved the conviction and $25 fine of a Baltimore theatre manager for showing a film without first obtaining a license from the Maryland Board of Censors. With the backing of the Times Film Corporation, the distributor, Freedman had notified the board of his intention to exhibit without a permit. He was arrested after the first performance. The film itself, *Revenge at Daybreak,* a story of the Irish Revolution, presented no question of obscenity. The litigation was thus carefully designed to challenge the submission requirement of prior censorship in a concrete statutory context, and thereby to overcome not only the abstract quality which marked *Times Film* but the holding in that case as well. The right claimed was freedom from criminal prosecution for showing a constitutionally protected film—that is, a film free of obscenity. The real aim, of course, was nothing less than the elimination of licensing as a practical matter. Freedman argued that authority of the state to exclude certain films in advance, and its cognate authority to punish for exhibiting an unlicensed film, were both "exhausted when the legitimacy of the film sought to be exhibited is conceded." The *Times Film* holding did not stand in the way since "all it could conceivably mean, compatibly with the First and Fourteenth Amendments . . . is that a system of prior censorship, containing appropriate procedural safeguards, may be permissible with respect to films which are demonstrably outside the scope of constitutional protection."[32]

In deciding for Freedman, the Supreme Court was unanimous. Yet the theory of seven Justices, in an opinion written by Justice Brennan, was not that criminal punishment for showing an unlicensed-yet-innocent film was itself invalid. Rather, the state's requirement that all exhibited films first be licensed failed because it operated as part of a larger statutory scheme that did not "provide adequate safeguards against undue inhibition of expression."

Times Film did not mean that a challenge to the censorship statute was limited to its submission requirements. The only question in *Times Film,* Brennan said, was "whether a prior restraint was necessarily unconstitutional *under all circumstances*"[33] (emphasis in original). The decision in that case did not uphold specific features of the Chicago licensing ordinance. Here the film proprietor was not arguing that submission was "unconstitutional simply because it may prevent even the first showing of a film whose exhibition may legitimately be the subject of an obscenity prosecution." Instead, he was claiming submission to be invalid because "in the context of the remainder of the statute it presents danger of unduly suppressing protected expression."[34] Brennan then called attention to the hazards licensing systems presented to free speech:

The administration of a censorship system for motion pictures presents peculiar dangers to constitutionally protected speech. Unlike prosecution for obscenity, a censorship proceeding puts the initial burden on the exhibitor or distributor. Because the censor's business is to censor, there inheres the danger that he may well be less responsive than a court—part of an independent branch of government—to the constitutionally protected interests in free expression. And if it is made unduly onerous, by reason of delay or otherwise, to seek judicial review, the censor's determination may in practice be final.

Applying the settled rule of our cases, we hold that a noncriminal process which requires the prior submission of a film to a censor avoids constitutional infirmity only if it takes place under procedural safeguards designed to obviate the dangers of a censorship system.[35]

The Maryland censorship apparatus failed by these measures. In summary, its deficiencies were three: first, it failed to provide for prompt judicial review of the censor's ruling; second, it failed to provide that the censors must either license a film or take the matter into court where they, themselves, would carry the burden of proving the film unprotected expression; and third, it failed to provide for prompt judicial determination on the merits.

Finally, the Court went out of its way to suggest what prior-restraint procedures might be permissible. "A model is not lacking," Brennan said, in a specific reference to the New York injunction procedure upheld by the Court in *Kingsley Books.* Then, repeating the dictum that "films differ from other forms of expression," he added that the nature of the motion picture industry may suggest different time limits for judicial determination. One possible scheme would be to

allow the exhibitor or distributor to submit his film early enough to ensure an orderly final disposition of the case before the scheduled exhibition date—far enough in advance so that the exhibitor could safely advertise the opening on a normal basis. Failing such a scheme or sufficiently early submission under such a scheme, the statute would have to require adjudication considerably more prompt than has been the case under the Maryland statute.[36]

In a concurring opinion Justice Douglas, joined by Justice Black, again restated his view that all prior censorship of speech was unconstitutional. He would admit no distinction between motion pictures and other protected media. He was also opposed to the New York injunction procedure which "substitutes punishment by contempt for punishment by jury trial."

The *Freedman* decision, four years after *Times Film,* represents a kind of reconciliation of the majority and minority positions in the earlier case. The Court dealt with some of the procedural questions the *Times Film* minority had raised and which the majority in that case had left unanswered. In its holding and tone, the *Freedman* decision is in the line of Chief Justice Warren's dissent in *Times Film.* The requirements that the entire licensing process be speeded up, that judicial participation be built into it, and that the burden of proof be shifted to the censors, were not rationalized in terms of Justice Clark's "unreasonable strictures" limit to licensing in *Times Film.* In fact, that phrase appears nowhere in Brennan's opinion. The spirit of the holding and its reasoning are that of the minority's dissent in *Times Film.* Brennan made no effort to conceal a distaste for licensing as an institution. His opinion can be searched in vain for a single kind word about prior censorship or even about a state's interest in barring obscene motion pictures.

Neverthless, the Court made its decision within the framework of a licensing system and, in doing so, recognized the exercise of licensing power. The Court's aim was reform rather than liquidation. Freedman had based his attack on the submission requirement in the Maryland law. This requirement, when coupled with the criminal sanction for exhibiting without a permit, is the essence of a licensing system. Yet the Court refused to consider the submission requirements at all, except to acknowledge that procedural deficiencies in the licensing apparatus could be challenged by ignoring them. The Court went no further than this, even though eliminating the criminal penalty for showing an unlicensed film would not necessarily have meant an overruling of *Times Film.* In an *amicus* brief the American Civil Liberties Union had offered a rationalization:

As to Section 17's requirements that Maryland's Board of Censors be provided with a copy of each film to be shown, this much may not be repugnant to Constitutional requirements, *and* this may be all that *Times Film Corp.* v. *Chicago* . . . was meant to, or need, stand for [emphasis in original].[37]

The Court declined to take this opportunity to reduce the task of censors to, in the words of the ACLU, the "residual prerogative to offer advisory opinions." Whether in the future—under a licensing system the Court would find acceptable—a film proprietor would be allowed to prove nonobscenity as a defense in a prosecution for exhibiting without a license, was a moot point. *Freedman* nullifies the *Times Film* implication that the method a state uses to control "exceptional" speech has the presumption of constitutionality. Yet by letting the coercive element in the submission requirement stand, the Court stopped short of eliminating licensing.

The *Freedman* decision did not deal directly with the third issue dividing the Court in *Times Film*—the distinction of motion pictures from other media of speech. Brennan did say that the prior submission requirement sustained in the earlier case was "consistent with our recognition that films differ from other forms of expression." But the Court ignored entirely Freedman's argument that since "99.5 per cent of films examined were approved without incident" by the Maryland censors, the film medium did not present "any such distinctive hazard as would tend to justify the special burden" of prior censorship.[38] A theory upon which motion pictures could be constitutionally distinguished was again left unarticulated.

However, it is significant that the decision—the first on film licensing since *Times Film*—found the Court unanimous. This may merely indicate again that consensus was easier to reach on the ways in which censors are to be constrained than on the principle of censorship itself. Or it may indicate that the Court, with two new members since *Times Film,* was in generally wider agreement on censorship problems. Here Justice Douglas and Black apparently failed to win over to their absolutism either of the new Justices, White and Goldberg, who had replaced two members of the *Times Film* majority, Whittaker and Frankfurter.

Some Immediate Results

Little time was wasted in using the *Freedman* requirements to attack existing licensing systems. Within nine months of the decision, all four state boards and those in several cities were challenged in the courts, and the requirements were used to attack the Bureau of Customs' inspection of imported films. Although other claims were involved in some of the cases, procedural deficiencies were the central target in all.

In New York, licensing had first been declared unconstitutional by the United States Supreme Court in a *per curiam* decision[39] based on the *Freedman* case. The state Board of Regents, with supervisory power over the Motion Picture Division, then attempted to repair the licensing procedure administratively. The Regents' new rules required the division to grant or deny a license within five days of receiving a film. If the division refused a license, the commissioner of education was to rule on the denial within seven days. If the denial was upheld, the education department was to begin court proceedings "forthwith." These new arrangements were declared unconstitutional by the state Court of Appeals, which held that procedural reforms, to satisfy the *Freedman* requirements, would need to go much further.[40] The court said:

> there will have to be provided at the very least: (1) authority for the Board of Regents to institute "Within a specified brief period" judicial action "to restrain showing the film" in the event that a license is not issued administratively, since the "burden of proving that the film is unprotected expression must rest on the censor" and not upon the applicant. . . . and (2) a judicial procedure to "assure prompt final judicial decision, to minimize the deterrent effect of an interim and possibly erroneous denial of a license." . . . This latter safeguard would seem to require that definite time limits be specified for court determination of the appropriate proceedings. Such a requirement, it can be argued, may only be imposed by the Legislature.[41]

Prior censorship in Kansas,[42] Virginia,[43] and Memphis[44] was also found to be procedurally deficient under the *Freedman* requirements. In fact, the Kansas board was declared to be without power to amend its own rules to meet procedural inadequacies in the censorship statute. The legislatures in New York, Virginia, and Kansas, and the city council in Memphis, all failed to re-enact licensing laws; thus, for the present at least, the post-*Freedman* decisions have terminated prior censorship in those jurisdictions.

A different result came about in Maryland, where the *Freedman* case itself had arisen. In the wake of that decision the state legislature had enacted a new licensing law requiring the Board of Censors to view a film within five days after submission, to file a complaint in the Circuit Court for Baltimore within three days should a license be denied, and then to carry the burden of proving the film objectionable. The circuit court, in turn, was required to set a hearing within five days and hand down a ruling within two days.[45] In all, the new rules would furnish a film proprietor with a judicial determination not more than fifteen days after presenting a film to the board. These reforms were upheld by the state Court of Appeals as meeting the *Freedman* requirements.[46]

However, later decisions by the state's highest court indicated that the board of censors' obligation of proving obscenity would be an arduous one. The court ruled against the board's denial of a license to *Lorna* on the ground that the obscenity question could not be determined merely by a viewing of the film in court. Except where a film "screams out for all to hear that it is obscene," the censors must produce supporting evidence in the form of testimony by experts or other witnesses.[47] In a subsequent case, the court held that the trial judge had erred in asking a panel of petit jurors to view *This Picture Is Censored* and fill out a questionnaire on whether or not it was obscene. According to the court, the licensing law places the burden of proof on the board of censors and this burden could not be assumed by the trial judge.[48] On remand, the film was again found obscene, with the state producing a number of witnesses, including film critics, columnists, and civic leaders, to support its allegations of obscenity. On the appeal, however, the Court of Appeals held that obscenity was not proven merely by the testimony of witnesses who do not qualify as experts. A witness must be shown to possess some special and sufficient knowledge and information which would elevate his opinion above the realm of conjecture, speculation, or personal reaction, before being allowed to offer expert testimony on obscenity, according to the court.[49]

In Chicago, the city licensing ordinance, redrafted in 1961, was amended by the city council shortly after the *Freedman* decision in an attempt to meet the new procedural requirements. The new provisions allowed an exhibitor seven days in which to appeal denial of a license by the police Film Review Section to the city's Motion Picture Appeal Board. The Appeal Board had fifteen days in which to review the film and another fifteen days in which the film proprietor was given opportunity to present evidence in support of granting a license. Within five days of such hearing the Appeal Board was required to rule on the appeal. If the board denied the license, it had to file for an injunction in the Circuit Court of Cook County within ten days.[50] The ordinance had already required the Film Review Section to view and rule on a film within three days of receiving it.

In Dallas, a licensing system set up after the *Freedman* decision and limited to the classification of films as suitable or unsuitable for "young persons" was at first successfully challenged by a group of local exhibitors.[51] Even though the licensing ordinance provided that an order of the Classification Board was to be suspended unless the board obtained an injunction within fifteen days of receiving an exhibitor's notice of nonacceptance of the order, the ordinance was found to be lacking in "sufficient procedural safeguards to obviate the dangers of a censorship system."

Within a month of this ruling the city council amended the ordinance and set up what were probably the most elaborate procedural obligations ever required of a prior censorship agency. The ordinance provides that the

Classification Board must make application for an injunction to a district court of Dallas County within three days of receiving notice of nonacceptance of its order from an exhibitor (such a notice itself must be filed within two days of the board's order). The board must then have its application for injunction set for a hearing within five days after filing. If the injunction is granted and the exhibitor appeals to the Court of Civil Appeals, the board is required to file a reply brief within five days of receiving a copy of the exhibitor's brief and to request the Court of Civil Appeals to "advance the cause upon the docket and to give it a preferential setting the same as is afforded an appeal from a temporary injunction or other preferential matters." If the Court of Civil Appeals affirms the trial court's judgment for the board, and the exhibitor appeals to the Texas Supreme Court, the board must file a reply brief within five days of receiving a copy of the exhibitor's application for writ of error, and "be prepared to submit the case upon oral submission or take any other reasonable action requested by the appealing exhibitor to expedite the submission of the case to the Supreme Court." A similarly detailed set of requirements is imposed upon the board if it appeals the district court's denial of its application for an injunction.[52]

These provisions were upheld as meeting the minimum procedural safeguards set out in the *Freedman* decision.[53] A procedural timetable in which the Classification Board's application for an injunction was filed in the trial court on February 14, trial held February 18, appeal taken March 28, and decided April 5, was also upheld.

The *Freedman* requirements have had three immediate effects. Directly they have been the means for upsetting licensing systems in operation at the time of the decision. Indirectly they have resulted in either a reforming of licensing procedures, as in Maryland, Chicago, and Dallas, or a lapsing of prior censorship where state or city legislative bodies have been unwilling or unable to reform the licensing procedures. On the other hand, none of the lower courts hearing post-*Freedman* cases found licensing itself to be unconstitutional. In fact, most of the decisions contain dicta that prior censorship is not unconstitutional per se.

Procedural requirements are, of course, only one dimension of the prior-censorship problem. Assuming that the United States Supreme Court does not hold prior censorship itself to be unconstitutional, the shape of licensing in the future will depend on developments in the law of obscenity and on the striking of a new balance of bargaining power between censors and film proprietors, as well as on procedural refinements. Yet it is clear that the censors, who had already been receiving fairly close judicial supervision of a sort altogether lacking during the *Mutual Film* period, will have the courts looking over both shoulders in the future. The *Freedman* rules mean that the legal doctrine of prior censorship is now equipped to hold censors in various jurisdictions to unusually high standards of procedural fairness.

The Federal Bureau of Customs

Any film or other matter that is obscene or that urges treason, insurrection, forcible violation of the law or threatens to take life or inflict bodily injury is barred from importation by the Tariff Act of 1930.[54] The same law empowers the Bureau of Customs to seize films or other matter its agents deem to fall within the above descriptions. With the increased popularity of foreign films in the 1950's, the bureau came to exercise what is today a more or less systematic examination of all imported motion pictures.

When a collector of customs at any port of entry detains a film, he is required under the Tariff Act to transmit such information to a United States attorney who, in turn, is directed to bring forfeiture proceedings against the film in a federal district court. In such an action any party of interest may demand a jury trial and has the right of review by a higher court. Before the bureau places the information in the hands of the federal attorney, it usually allows an importer opportunity to execute an "assent to forfeiture" or to request permission to reexport the film.[55]

Admission of a film by the bureau, however, does not exempt it from state or local licensing. In a licensing statute a state is considered to exercise police power *after* the film has lost its character as an import.[56]

Though the bureau's exercise of prior restraint on media of speech has been sustained in lower federal courts, the Supreme Court itself has not ruled on the point. And though there have been many challenges to state and local motion picture licensing in the years following the *Miracle* decision, no court had been called upon to consider the constitutionality of Customs censorship of movies until the *491* case in 1965.[57]

This case, inspired by the *Freedman* decision, involved a forfeiture proceeding against the Swedish film *491,* which the bureau had seized as obscene. The Second Circuit Court of Appeals sustained Customs procedures under the Tariff Act of 1930 at the same time that it found the film itself not obscene. Provisions for the seizure of obscene matter and, thereupon, transmission of information on it to a United States attorney for a forfeiture action were held to provide sufficient safeguards against unreasonable delay in obtaining final determination on the obscenity question. Where admissibility of a film is questioned by the examining Customs official, the court sustained the bureau's practice of having it rescreened by his superior and, if still believed to be inadmissible, of having it sent to the Washington office for a final administrative ruling. Furthermore, Customs procedures were not improperly applied to the handling of *491* itself. Although nearly five and a half months elapsed between the arrival of the film at the port of entry and the forfeiture action, the court noted that most of the delay was occasioned by the importer and not by Customs officials. Likewise, the subsequent judicial action of nearly seven months was not unconstitutionally protracted where, as in the case of the administrative proceedings, the importer was largely responsible for any major delays which occurred.

Though Customs censorship, pragmatically assessed, has thus been upheld in its current procedure, exactly how much delay is permissible in administrative and in judicial review is not yet clear. In an obscenity trial involving Customs seizure of *The Adventures of Father Silas* and several other books, a federal district court held that the *Freedman* requirements were not met by an administrative review of three and a half months in one instance and five and a half months in another, where apparently much if not all of the delay was due to Customs actions rather than those of the importer.[58]

4

Objectives: Obscenity and Classification

A Process of Elimination

The great majority of movie-censorship decisions since the *Miracle* case have involved either questions of permissible objectives of prior censorship —the substantive standards set out by state legislatures and city councils— or the application of these objectives by the censors to particular films. In almost all of these contests the movie interests have prevailed, and the ground upon which censors stand has been steadily cut away. So effective has this judicial limitation been that when the Supreme Court set out the minimum procedural requirements of prior censorship in *Freedman* v. *Maryland* in 1965, it was dealing with an institution that in its substantive powers bore little resemblance to the one that prospered during the *Mutual Film* period.

As a practical matter there is only one permissible censorship objective in licensing for a general audience today—obscenity. Oddly enough, the Supreme Court has never ruled on this point. Perhaps the lack of consensus among the Justices on prior-censorship theory has prevented a definitive statement. Nevertheless, the Court has not hesitated in eliminating other censorship standards that were frequently used in the *Mutual Film* period. At the same time, it has repeatedly issued dicta that obscenity would be a permissible standard.

The process of dispatching other standards, of course, began with the *Miracle* decision, in which the Court found "sacrilegious" to be an unconstitutional licensing criterion. In the next five years, the Court, using the *per curiam* method, reversed a number of censorship orders. The statutory standards involved in these decisions were (1) "prejudicial to the best interests of the people" under which Marshall, Texas, censors denied a license to *Pinky*;[1] (2) the requirement that a license be issued only to films "of a moral, educational, amusing or harmless character," under which Ohio had refused to license *M* "on account of being harmful";[2] (3) "immoral or tended to corrupt morals" under which New York State refused to license *La Ronde;*[3] (4) "cruel, obscene, indecent, or immoral, or such as tend to debase or corrupt morals," under which Kansas denied a license to *The Moon is Blue;*[4] and (5) "immoral and obscene", under which Chicago denied a license to *Game of Love.*[5]

As might be expected, these *per curiam* decisions provoked a great deal of judicial and scholarly speculation. For example, it was not clear whether the Court was engaged in eliminating licensing altogether,[6] or whether the censorship standards involved were, like that of "sacrilegious" in the *Miracle* case, merely "not the business of government," or whether the standards were unconstitutionally vague.[7] In retrospect it is doubtful that a majority of the Justices agreed on any single theory. And in the light of later cases the exact meaning of these cryptic decisions is less important than the fact that they signaled a willingness of the Court to build upon the *Miracle* decision and closely supervise the prior censorship of motion pictures.

In 1959, in *Kingsley International Pictures* v. *Board of Regents,* the Court held censorship for thematic or "ideological" obscenity unconstitutional. New York censors, and later the state Board of Regents, had refused to license *Lady Chatterley's Lover,* the film version of the D. H. Lawrence novel, on the grounds that the film was immoral in presenting adultery "as a desirable, acceptable, and proper pattern of behavior." The censors and the Regents acted under a censorship statute which defined an immoral film as one which "portrays acts of sexual immorality, perversion, or lewdness, or which expressly or impliedly presents such acts as desirable, acceptable or proper patterns of behavior."[8] In sustaining the censorship order, the New York Court of Appeals had held that the state could refuse a license to a film that portrayed adultery as desirable for certain people under certain circumstances.[9]

The Supreme Court was unanimous in reversing, though the Justices were not in agreement on the reasons for doing so. Five members of the Court, in an opinion by Justice Stewart, ignored the questions of vagueness and obscenity entirely, and dealt only with the New York court's construction of the statute. That construction, according to Stewart, gave the term "sexual immorality" a meaning entirely different from the one embraced in words like "obscenity" and "pornography."

Moreover, it is not suggested that the film would itself operate as an incitement to illegal action. Rather the New York Court of Appeals tells us that the . . . law requires denial of a license to any motion picture which approvingly portrays an adulterous relationship, quite without reference to the manner of its portrayal.

What New York has done, therefore, is to prevent the exhibition of a motion picture because that picture advocates an idea—that adultery under certain circumstances may be proper behavior.[10]

Since the "First Amendment's basic guarantee is a freedom to advocate ideas," such a construction could not stand. Thus for the majority of the Court, speech dealing with sex at the level of ideas did not lose its protection merely by attractively portraying behavior that offended conventional moral standards. Apparently such speech could be proscribed only if it actually incited to illegal action or was presented in an obscene manner.

This last possibility was expressly stated by Justice Clark, who, concurring separately, believed the New York court's construction too vague to meet the requirements of due process. Yet had the statute been construed to "ban 'pornographic' films, or those that 'portray *acts* of sexual immorality perversion, or lewdness' " it would have met the requirements of due process (emphasis in original).[11] Three members of the Court—Harlan, Frankfurter, and Whittaker—while agreeing that mere abstract expressions of opinion could not be censored, believed the state court *had* construed the statute to require obscenity or incitement to crime. Therefore the statute was valid; the fault lay in improper application of it to *Lady Chatterley's Lover,* a film "lacking in anything that could properly be termed obscene or corruptive of public morals by inciting to the commission of adultery."[12]

With the *Kingsley Pictures* case, the Supreme Court had decided seven movie censorship appeals in seven years. Taken together, these decisions narrowly limited the objectives of prior censorship. No longer were censors to have the kind of statutory authority that in the *Mutual Film* period had allowed them to ban or cut films containing unconventional political, social, or religious ideas, or themes of sexual immorality.

This process of elimination has left obscenity as the chief permissible objective of licensing. Although other standards remain in censorship laws, they are now probably unenforceable or, as a practical matter, inapplicable to motion pictures. Most state and local licensing laws, for example, still have provisions for withholding permits from "immoral" films. The decision in *Kingsley Pictures,* however, would seem to bar use of this standard as one substantively distinct from that of obscenity or incitement to crime. Such a standard might also be unconstitutionally vague—at least it seems no more lucid than "harmful," which the Supreme Court has found unconstitutional.

In Chicago, the city's licensing ordinance still provides for denial of a permit to a film depicting "a lack of virtue of a class of citizens of any race, color, creed or religion and exposes them to contempt, derision or obloquy . . . or purports to represent any hanging, lynching or burning of a human being."[13] In Fort Worth, the municipal licensing ordinance provides for denial of a permit where a film is "calculated to promote or encourage racial or sectional prejudice."[14] Though these standards appear not to have been challenged in court, their constitutionality now seems dubious.

On the other hand, incitement to crime—a provision in nearly every licensing law—is unquestionably a valid standard. What is doubtful about it is its applicability to the type of motion picture produced for commercial exhibition and profit. To be applicable at all, the connection between the film and criminal behavior would have to be close. As the Supreme Court pointed out in *Kingsley Pictures,* mere advocacy of proscribed conduct is insufficient if there is nothing to indicate that such advocacy would be immediately acted upon. Conceivably, the standard could apply to a film entirely lacking advocacy but which, nonetheless, dealt with an emotionally charged theme or circumstance. Yet even in such a case, the inciting effect would probably depend upon a highly particularized audience situation. It is hard to conceive of a commercial motion picture content that could generally incite American audiences to illegal behavior.

Two lower courts have ruled on the applicability of incitement-to-crime subprovisions of two state licensing laws.[15] Both cases involved the identical statutory provisions—that a license be denied to a film which "advocates or teaches the use of, or the methods of use of, narcotics or habit-forming drugs."[16] In *Broadway Angels* v. *Wilson,* the New York Supreme Court ordered that a license be issued to *Teenage Menace,* which depicted a teenager's gradual addiction to heroin and the details of administering the drug. The court said "as a matter of speculation, one could not predict that no person viewing the film would ever commit the crime of possessing or using drugs, but we fail to find any sufficient evidence of the picture's tendency to corrupt morals or incite to crime."[17] The Maryland Court of Appeals reached a similar conclusion with respect to *The Man With the Golden Arm.* Though the film depicted the mechanics of heroin addiction, it was held not to "advocate or teach" the use of narcotics. Thus as a practical matter, the questions of how obscenity is to be determined and what actually constitutes cinematic obscenity have become the outstanding ones in the law of movie censorship.

The Obscenity Standard

Obscenity is at once the most familiar and most elusive of concepts in law and in social life. On the one hand, it is widely supposed that nearly everyone has a notion of obscenity and would consider certain utterances or materials to be, for one reason or another, proscribable. On the other hand, the concept has an ambiguity that prevents the sort of precise formulation that is desirable in framing a reference for meting out criminal penalties or for limiting freedom of speech. Zechariah Chafee, Jr., once despaired that a satisfactory solution to the problem could ever be found because "the law likes to be logical, whereas it is impossible to be wholly logical in dealing with relations between the sexes. The subject by its very nature includes a large element of irrationality."[18]

The obscenity phenomenon raises three general questions which can be noted only briefly here. Why is obscenity bad? What are the actual effects of obscenity? To what degree should obscenity be restricted as a matter of governmental policy?

Obscenity is usually considered bad or harmful for one or more of three reasons. It may be viewed as temptation, as an appeal to the prurient interest; or as offensive, and therefore essentially traumatic in character; or as subversive, that is, jeopardizing moral values and teachings through its idea and attitude content. This typology, in turn, suggests a fuller consideration of values that might be protected by proscribing obscenity. These might include prevention of criminal or injurious behavior in "average" adults, or in "susceptible" persons, that is, youth or sexually maladjusted individuals; prevention of emotional disturbance in average adults or in youth; prevention of the formation of attitudes corruptive of the existing moral order in average adults or in youth; etc.[19]

The obscenity question would be simplified, though probably not resolved, were the effects of specific exposure known. Unfortunately, evidence of a conclusive nature is still unavailable.[20] This informational vacuum, however, is not accompanied by indifference to the question. In support of one side or the other is a considerable amount of opinion and "common sense" evidence, beliefs held all the more strongly, perhaps, for the absence of objective proof.[21]

The question of control of obscenity through public policy raises the problem of protecting countervailing values—namely those associated with freedom of speech and due process of law—from excessive governmental action. Conclusions about where a balance should be struck result in a great variety of proposals. For example, at one extreme, some students would eliminate all legal controls over obscenity.[22] Others would require that proscribable erotica be shown to cause or to "be so closely brigaded with illegal action as to be inseparable from it."[23] At another extreme are those who would proscribe so-called thematc obscenity, that is, immoral ideas.[24] A more restrictive balance is sometimes advocated where the consumers of the utterance are children or adolescents.[25]

An Emerging Doctrine

The Supreme Court dealt with the problem of obscenity for the first time in 1957, in the companion cases *Roth* v. *United States* and *Alberts* v. *Cali-*

fornia. It took what may be termed a middle position. Obscenity was held to be outside the protection of the First Amendment because it is "utterly without redeeming social importance." Yet the Court lost no time in adding that "sex and obscenity are not synonymous . . . The portrayal of sex, e.g. in art, literature and scientific works . . . [is entitled to] the constitutional protection of freedom of speech and press." To determine the obscenity of an utterance, the test must be "whether to the average person, applying contemporary community standards, the dominant theme of the material taken as a whole appeals to the prurient interest."[26]

Seemingly straightforward enough at this rather high level of abstraction, the *Roth-Alberts* test has actually provided only limited guidance for deciding concrete cases. Recognizing this, the Court has tried to clarify various elements of the test. Yet these attempts have revealed views so widely divergent and so numerous that it is now difficult to speak with confidence of a majority position on the particulars of the obscenity equation.

For at least three Justices—Brennan, Warren, and Fortas—the *Roth-Alberts* test now requires, in addition to a finding of prurient appeal, a determination that the utterance is "patently offensive because it affronts contemporary community standards relating to the description or representation of sexual matters and . . . is utterly without redeeming social value."[27] In addition, there can be no weighing of social value against prurient appeal or patent offensiveness. An utterance is not obscene unless it is "*utterly* without redeeming social value"[28] (emphasis in original).

For two members of the Court, Clark and White, social importance is not by itself controlling.[29] According to Clark, it "does not constitute a separate and distinct constitutional test. Such evidence must be considered together with evidence that the material in question appeals to the prurient interest and is patently offensive."[30]

Several of the Justices have tried to clarify the "community standards" element of the *Roth-Alberts* test. For Brennan, such standards refer to a national rather than local community. The concept of obscenity may vary from period to period but "not from county to county, or town to town."[31] On the other hand, Warren has claimed that "community standards" do refer to those of the local community. According to the Chief Justice, there is "no provable 'national standard' and perhaps there should be none."[32]

Closely related to the question of community standards is that of the Court's review in obscenity cases. On the one hand, Brennan would have the Court make a *de novo* review of the obscenity issue. In cases involving First Amendment rights, the Court "cannot avoid making an independent constitutional judgment on the facts of the case as to whether the material involved is constitutionally protected."[33] On the other hand, Warren would limit the Court's review to a "sufficient evidence" standard where a proper application of the *Roth-Alberts* test had been made in the lower courts. This is the only way "to obviate the necessity of this Court's sitting as the Super Censor of all the obscenity purveyed throughout the Nation."[34]

Harlan's views appear to be divided between the Brennan and Warren positions. Long the Court's champion of a case-by-case development of the obscenity doctrine, Harlan would allow greater power to the states than to the federal government in obscenity control. Where federal power is involved Harlan favors complete *de novo* review of the obscenity issue.[35] In cases involving state restrictions he would limit this review and "would not prohibit them from banning material which, taken as a whole, has been reasonably found in state judicial proceedings to treat with sex in a fundamentally offensive manner, under rationally established criteria for judging such material."[36] In a third position are Black and Douglas. For them any governmental control of obscenity, short of some showing of clear and present danger, is unconstitutional.[37] Apparently, in the absence of such a showing, they would review only in order to overturn criminal convictions or censorship orders. Black has long been a critic of case-by-case *de novo* review in obscenity litigation, an approach he believes makes the Court a "Supreme Board of Censors."[38]

Given the indefiniteness of the *Roth-Alberts* test and of the divergent views among the Justices on it and on the Court's obscenity review, it is hardly surprising that there is only a small inventory of opinion in the highest tribunal to indicate what exactly is or is not obscene in particular utterances. Within a year of the *Roth* and *Alberts* decisions, the Court reviewed four cases in which lower federal courts had made findings of obscenity. In each instance, the Supreme Court reversed *per curiam,* citing only the *Roth* or *Alberts* cases.

In *One, Inc.* v. *Olesen,* the Court upheld the mailability of issues of *One —The Homosexual Magazine.* In its finding of obscenity, the Court of Appeals for the Ninth Circuit had held that the magazine failed to realize its claimed purpose of "dealing primarily with homosexuality from the scientific, historical and critical point of view—to . . . promote among the general public an interest, knowledge and understanding of the problems and variation." The court noted one story in which a "young girl gives up her chance for a normal married life to live with the lesbian," and a poem "about alleged homosexual activities of Lord Montague and other British peers."[39]

The mailability of two nudist publications, *Sunshine and Health* and *Sun Magazine,* was also upheld.[40] The district court had found obscenity in photographs of nude men and women showing the genital and pubic areas. The court described one photograph of an obese woman:

She has large elephantine breasts that hang from her shoulder to her waist. They are exceedingly large. The thighs are very obese. She is standing in the snow in galoushes. But the part which is offensive, obscene, filthy and indecent is the pubic area shown. . . . The hair extends outwardly virtually to the hip bone. It looks to the Court like a retouched picture.[41]

In *Times Film Corp.* v. *Chicago* (not the 1961 challenge to the Chicago licensing system, already noted) a movie-censorship order which had found *Game of Love* "immoral and obscene" was reversed. (Parts of the film which the state court had held obscene are described on page 62, below.)

In the fourth case, a finding of obscenity against a collection of imported nudist and art-student magazines was reversed and remanded after the Government made a "confession of error" that the test used by the Court of Appeals for the Ninth Circuit was "materially different from the *Roth* test."[42] The court had found nothing offensive in the text, but held the publications obscene because of photographs emphasizing the front view of nude men and women and showing the genital and pubic areas.[43]

It has been argued that the Court made an independent examination of the materials in the three absolute reversals and therefore that the Justices had actually found the materials themselves not obscene.[44] Whether or not this was in fact the case, the only occasion in which at least a majority of the Court has ruled expressly on the obscenity or nonobscenity of particular utterances was in three 1967 cases disposed of in a single *per curiam* opinion.[45] There, seven members of the Court held that two paperback books, *Lust Pool* and *Shame Agent,* and ten popular "girlie" magazines, *High Heels, Spree, Gent, Swank, Bachelor, Modern Man, Cavalcade, Gentleman, Ace,* and *Sir,* were not obscene. However, the Court admitted that there was no single theory upon which the majority could agree. Two Justices, Harlan and Clark, dissented on the ground that the obscenity of the publications was not an issue the Court had agreed to review.

In several cases individual Justices have given their opinion that utterances involved were not obscene. This was one of Harlan's conclusions in his *Roth* dissent. In that case, convictions were based on an issue of *American Aphrodite* which contained selections of several established writers, including Pierre Louys and Henry Miller, and on advertisements for the book and for other publications. Concurring in *Kingsley Pictures,* Harlan, joined by Frankfurter and Whittaker, found the film *Lady Chatterley's Lover* not obscene. (Elements of the film found obscene by the lower court are described on page 62.) In *Manual Enterprises* v. *Day,* Harlan and Stewart found three magazines—*Manual, Trim,* and *Grecian Guild Pictorial,* all slanted toward homosexual interests—not to be obscene. The publications consisted mainly of photographs of nude or nearly nude male models with particular emphasis on their genitals and buttocks. According to the Government's description,

. . . although none of the pictures directly exposed the model's genitals, some showed his pubic hair and others suggested what appeared to be a semi-erect penis . . .; others showed male models reclining with their legs (and sometimes their arms as well) spread wide apart. . . . Many of the pictures showed models wearing only loin cloth, "V" gowns, or posing straps . . .; some showed a model apparently removing his clothing. . . . Two of the magazines had pictures of pairs of models posed together suggestively. . . . There were also pictures of models posed with chains or of one model beating another while a third held his face in his hands as if weeping. . . .[46]

In *Jacobellis* v. *Ohio,* Brennan and Goldberg found the film *The Lovers* not obscene. (Parts of the film cited in the lower court's finding of obscenity are described on page 63.)

In only a few instances has a member of the Court been willing to affirm the obscenity of an utterance on independent examination. In the *Fanny Hill* case, Clark found the novel obscene. He described it as

nothing more than a series of minutely and vividly described sexual episodes. . . . These scenes run the gamut of possible sexual experience such as lesbianism, female masturbation, homosexuality between young boys, the destruction of a maidenhead with consequent gory descriptions, the seduction of a young virgin boy, the flagellation of male by female, and vice versa, followed by fervid sexual engagement, and other abhorrent acts, including over two dozen separate bizarre descriptions of different sexual intercourses between male and female characters. . . . In each of the sexual scenes the exposed bodies of the participants are described in minute and individual detail. The pubic hair is often used for a background to the most vivid and precise descriptions of the response, condition, size, shape, and color of the sexual organs before, during and after orgasms.[47]

In the *Alberts* case, Harlan found sado-masochistic photographs, commonly known as bondage or torture pictures, proscribable under state obscenity laws. Dissenting in the *Jacobellis* case, he was willing to affirm the obscenity of *The Lovers,* and in the *Fanny Hill* case he voted to uphold a finding of obscenity against the novel. Both of these cases involved state prosecutions; whether he would have held the same view had federal power been involved is not clear.

The Court's reluctance to find obscenity or to uphold lower court findings of obscenity has led a number of observers to conclude that the constitutional standard of proscribable erotica is now, or eventually will come to be, that of so-called hard-core pornography.[48] Indeed, two members of the Court have spoken favorably of such a limitation. Harlan would limit federal obscenity control, which he sees as more restricted than that of the states, to hard-core pornography.[49] Stewart would go even further and limit both state and federal power over obscenity to such a standard. Admitting the difficulties of defining hard-core pornography, Stewart has nonetheless claimed "I know it when I see it."[50] A general description of hard-core pornography given by the Solicitor General in the *Roth* and *Alberts* cases follows:

> Some of this pornography consists of erotic objects. There are also large numbers of black and white photographs, individually, in sets, and in booklet form, of men and women engaged in every conceivable form of normal and abnormal sexual relations and acts. There are small printed pamphlets or books, illustrated with such photographs, which consist of stories in simple, explicit words of sexual excesses of every kind, over and over again. No one would suggest that they had the slightest literary merit, or were intended to have any. There are also large numbers of "comic books," specially drawn for the pornographic trade, which are likewise devoted to explicitly illustrated incidents of sexual activity, normal or perverted. . . . It may safely be said that most, if not all, of this type of booklets contain drawings not only of normal fornication but also of perversions of various kinds.
>
> The worst of the "hard-core" pornographic materials now being circulated are the motion picture films. These films, sometimes of high technical quality, sometimes in color, show people of both sexes engaged in orgies which again include every form of sexual activity known, all of which are presented in a favorable light. The impact of these pictures on the viewer cannot easily be imagined. No form of incitement to action or to excitation could be more explicit or more effective.[51]

In contrast to the hard-core pornography standard, several Justices have been willing to give weight to the manner in which an utterance is promoted, advertised, and exploited, in determining obscenity. A striking application of this principle was made in *Ginzburg* v. *United States*. Five members of the Court—Brennan, who delivered the opinion, Warren, Clark, White, and Fortas—held that material dealing pervasively with erotica, but not necessarily obscene in the abstract, was obscene when promoted by "pandering." Exploitation of such materials by an open and sole appeal to the prurient interest of their consumers could justify a conclusion that the material was without redeeming social importance.

Along somewhat similar lines in an earlier case, Warren, with Clark, rejected the hard-core pornography guide, claiming that such a concept could not be defined with any greater clarity than that of obscenity. Instead, he stressed the uses to which an utterance was put. For example, "a technical or legal treatise on pornography may well be inoffensive under most circumstances but, at the same time, 'obscene' in the extreme when sold or displayed to children."[52] This "variable" concept of objectionable erotica, in which not only the nature of the utterance itself but also its promotional context is considered, has considerable scholarly support.[53]

Whether or not the obscenity doctrine eventually evolves to a standard of hard-core pornography or to one of "variable" obscenity, or to some combination of both, the Supreme Court has clearly taken a narrow view of proscribable erotica. The divergency of views so evident in the foregoing cases currently obscures the finer lines of this emerging doctrine. Yet the outcome of the cases leaves little doubt about the general direction of its development. It is clear that American judge-made law is now more permissive in the matter of the depiction and discussion of sex than it has been at any time in the past.

The Movies: A New Freedom

Since the *Miracle* decision, the radical procedural limitation of the censors' powers has been more than matched by a narrowing of the permissible objectives of censorship. Not only were various censorship standards eliminated in the 1950's so that, as a practical matter, only obscenity remains, but the application of the obscenity standard itself has been narrowed as a result of a very close judicial supervision of the substance of censorship rulings. With greater freedom in the law for portrayal of erotica and nudity, it was hardly surprising that movie censors should come to lose some notable legal battles on the obscenity issue. The results of this litigation are, perhaps, even more spectacularly one-sided than the outcome of the contests over censorship standards and censorship procedures.

In all, there appear to be seventeen movie-censorship cases since the *Miracle* decision in which there was a finding of nonobscenity at trial or on final appeal.[54] In contrast, there appears to be only one reported appellate case in which a finding of obscenity was allowed to stand, and in that instance the court refused to consider the obscenity issue because it had not viewed the film, which was not put into the record by the distributor.[55] There is apparently no outstanding finding of obscenity at the appellate level in a prior censorship case—a truly remarkable pattern of libertarian supervision.

Before giving closer attention to some of the problems raised by application of the obscenity standard to motion pictures, it may be useful to recapitulate what American courts have found *not* to be obscene in the film medium. In the cases noted in the preceding paragraph, the original findings of obscenity were based generally on one of four types of depiction: immoral sexual behavior, with or without nudity; nudity without sexual behavior; indelicate or "dirty" words; and sex education.

Immoral sexual behavior with or without nudity. In the *Times Film per curiam* decision of 1957, the Supreme Court made an independent review of *Game of Love* and apparently found it not obscene. It reversed the Seventh Circuit Court, which had found obscenity and which described the film as follows:

The thread of the story is supercharged with a series of illicit sexual intimacies and acts. . . . [A] flying start is made when a 16-year-old boy is shown completely nude on a bathing beach in the presence of a group of younger girls [as a result of a boating accident]. On that plane the narrative proceeds to reveal the seduction of this boy by a physically attractive woman old enough to be his mother. Under the influence of this experience and an arrangement to repeat it, the boy thereupon engages in sexual relations with a girl of his own age. The erotic thread of the story is carried, without deviation toward any wholesome idea, through scene after scene. The narrative is graphically pictured with nothing omitted except those sexual consummations which are plainly suggested but meaningfully omitted and thus, by the very fact of omission, emphasized.[56]

Though a majority of the Court has never ruled expressly on the obscenity or nonobscenity of a motion picture, a number of the Justices have stated their individual views on particular films. In *Kingsley Pictures,* Harlan, Frankfurter, and Whittaker thought *Lady Chatterley's Lover* not obscene, though New York state censors and the state Court of Appeals had ruled it "immoral." The Justices could not "regard this film as depicting anything more than a somewhat unusual and rather pathetic 'love triangle.' " In contrast, the New York censorship order had required the following deletions:

Reel 2D: . . . all views of Mellors and Lady Chatterley in cabin from point where they are seen lying on cot together, in a state of undress, to end of sequence.

Reel 3D: . . . all views of Mellors caressing Lady Chatterley's buttock and all views of him unzipping her dress and caressing her bare back. Eliminate following spoken dialogue [in French] accompanying these actions:

But you're nude. . . . You're nude under your dress, and you didn't say so. . . . What is it?
Eliminate accompanying English superimposed titles:

You have nothing on. . . . And you didn't say so. . . . What is it?
Reel 4D: . . . entire sequence in Mellors' bedroom showing Lady Chatterley and Mellors in bed, in a state of undress.[57]

In the *Jacobellis* v. *Ohio*—which involved a conviction for showing an obscene film, rather than a censorship order—Brennan and Goldberg thought *The Lovers* not obscene. The film involves a woman bored with her life and marriage who abandons her husband and family for a young archeologist with whom she has fallen in love. There is an explicit love scene in the last reel of the film, and the state's objections are based almost entirely upon that scene.[58]

Yet Harlan, also viewing the film, thought the state had acted within permissible limits in condemning it. Warren and Clark did not think "the courts below acted with intemperance or without sufficient evidence in finding the moving picture obscene."[59] It was not clear whether these two members of the Court saw the film.

On the other hand, the trial court had described *The Lovers* as follows:

. . . the dominant theme of sex is brought into sharp focus early in the film. After the stage has been set and the characters have assumed their relationships to each other, there is evident a calculated, concentrated, and determined effort to portray the sexual theme basely and wantonly. In a tantalizing and increasing tempo, the sexual appetite is whetted, and lascivious thought and lustful desires are intensely stimulated. The apex is reached when the wife of the publisher and the itinerant archeologist engage in protracted love play, give full vent to their emotions, and indulge themselves in sexual activity. Very little, if anything, is left to the imagination. Lurid details are portrayed to the senses of sight and hearing. After the narrative has reached this carefully built up and long anticipated climax, it scurries to a hasty conclusion.[60]

In a case terminating in the lower courts, the French film *Twilight Girls,* involving lesbianism in a girls' school, was held not obscene by the New York Court of Appeals in a memorandum opinion.[61] In refusing a permit for the film the state Board of Regents had given the following description:

The authors of the production devote most of the sequences to girls in the dormitory while they are going to bed, sleeping and getting up. . . [the story] revolves around two girls who are lesbians. Contrary to an order by the supervisor, they take their pajamas off; then there are various scenes in which the lesbians embrace and show their interest in this type of sex perversion. There is further exhibition of nudity and the girls take shower baths. From the beginning of this sequence, the type of presentation taken together clearly appeals to the prurient interest of the public.[62]

In 1957 an Illinois appellate court found *The Miracle* not obscene, observing that

it is not at all probable . . . that *The Miracle* would arouse sexual desires in the "average normal" individual . . .; it appears unlikely that even the salaciously inclined individual would be so affected by a film whose central character is clothed only in rags and whose personality is devoid of any charm; there is no gloss or glamour anywhere in the film.[63]

The Danish-made *A Stranger Knocks,* which has two scenes of sexual intercourse between unmarried persons, one with the woman astride the man, was found not obscene by the Maryland Court of Appeals. According to the court,

the weight of the testimony—including the film itself—establishes that the film is a serious work of art. . . the film begins with a quotation from Holy Writ and ends with the death of the man, with the woman facing a possible murder charge. This is not calculated to indicate approval of sexual relations outside of wedlock, but rather the contrary. . . . the implied sexual relations are by no means presented as desirable, acceptable, or proper patterns of conduct, but rather the contrary is presented.[64]

The Swedish *491*, dealing with the orgiastic experiences of several delinquent boys and detailing a variety of abnormal sexual behavior, was found to be "repulsive, revolting, and disgusting" by the Second Circuit Court of Appeals, yet the court said:

If *491* is viewed solely as an exhibition on the screen of a series of sexual acts (1) sodomy (buggery); (2) intercourse with a prostitute; (3) a homosexual act; (4) intercourse between the prostitute and a dog; and (5) of self-mutilation then the picture might well be characterized as "utterly without redeeming social significance" or "utterly devoid of social value." . . . But to attribute to this two-hour picture, attempting to deal with social problems which in 1966 are not only on our own doorstep but very much over the threshold such a purpose is completely to misunderstand and misview the picture and its message.[65]

The Swedish film *The Virgin Spring*, involved in the only censorship case in which a finding of obscenity has been allowed to stand on final appeal, was held obscene by the trial court because of the film's long and vivid rape scene.[66]

Nudity without sexual behavior. Portrayal of nudity in a nudist camp, even where activities are fictionalized, has been held not obscene in two decisions involving *Garden of Eden.* According to one of the courts, the film had

nothing sexy or suggestive about it. It has been shown in 36 states and in many foreign countries. In it the nudists are shown as wholesome, happy people in family groups practicing their theory that clothing, when climate does not require it, is deleterious to mental health by promoting an attitude of shame with regard to natural attributes and functions of the body.[67]

In the second case it was noted that the film "did not expose the private parts of adult characters."[68]

The Maryland Court of Appeals found depiction of nudism outside the environs of a nudist camp to be not obscene in the film *Have Figure, Will*

Travel, which portrayed the vacation cruise of three girls on their own boat. "It is conceded that no sexual activity or awareness was presented and that while on the boat the girls were seen unclothed only by each other."[69]

Likewise, depiction of aboriginal nudity in a documentary film has been held not obscene. In 1957 the Maryland Court of Appeals reversed denial of a license to *Naked Amazon,* pointing out that

None of the scenes portray any action which is even suggestive of sexual activity. The natives are quite unaware that they are without clothing and the narration accompanying the scenes in no manner suggests that they are sexually excited or exciting, rather, the photography and narration dwell on their unusual customs and rituals which seemingly give the appearance of rather child-like games.[70]

The court also noted that "the pubic areas of the body were either not photographed or were shadowed out so as not to be visible."[71]

Indelicate or "dirty" words. Two appellate courts have reversed censorship orders based solely on the use of particular words. The infrequent mention of "rape" and "contraceptive" in *Anatomy of a Murder* was held "not likely to so much arouse the salacity of the normal and average viewer as to outweigh its [the film's] artistic and expert presentation."[72] In *The Connection* the use of the word "shit" several times as slang for heroin was held not to be obscene.[73]

Sex education. The film *Mom and Dad,* consisting of three parts—a family drama, instruction on sex and the process of birth, and discussion of venereal disease—all unconnected dramatically, was held not obscene by the Seventh Circuit Court of Appeals. According to the court, the film "combined straightforward instruction on sex with drama illustrating the necessity for sex instruction."[74] Earlier, a New York State Board of Regents' refusal to license the film on the ground that the human birth sequence was "indecent" had been reversed by the Appellate Division of the State Supreme Court. The sequence, "which constituted a small part of a long narrative film, and which was a biological demonstration, scientific in level and tone, portraying under restrained and controlled conditions a human birth," was not "indecent."[75]

The foregoing cases reveal a willingness of the courts to review the censors' application of the obscenity standard. Whether the amount of this review is to be *de novo* or that of "substantial evidence" is not yet clear. In either case, however, the censors will have been taken ashore from still another "boundless sea" of the *Mutual Film* period.

The cases also reflect an increasing judicial permissiveness in the portrayal of erotica and nudity, and in this, they are in keeping with those obscenity decisions involving printed media. From these cases it would appear that the great majority of films produced for commercial public exhibition today—including many that have been the object of extralegal restraint and group pressures—have little to fear from the law of obscenity as it is now developing. In fact, not only has this new permissiveness made possible an entirely new genre of films—the exploitation feature—but it has also opened the door to the inclusion of nudity in major productions.

In contrast, these decisions say very little about what *is* obscene in movies. Here, the major frame of reference still appears to be the "stag" film. This type of movie, clandestinely exhibited, is the cinema equivalent of hard-core pornography in the printed media and accordingly is clearly proscribable. There is still a very large gap between stag films and those exonerated in the cases above. Yet, just as the latter films have helped to close what was once an even greater distance, future productions can be expected to enter the remaining unoccupied territory. In doing so, they may go a long way before the element of "social importance"—to say nothing of profit—is exhausted, if, indeed, it will ever be for the enterprising film maker.

Exactly where and how the obscenity standard will apply to movies, then, is still unclear. An application confined to films approaching the "stag" type would ignore the very factor that has made the movies the most politically controversial of all media of speech in the portrayal of erotica— the notion that they have a special impact or "capacity for evil." For its part, the Supreme Court has repeatedly stated in dicta that the movies are not necessarily subject to the same rules governing other media of speech. Yet these statements—upon which the Court has never expanded—have been made in cases in which the main issue was the censorship power itself rather than the standard of obscenity.

A Double Standard?

With the obscenity doctrine yet to be definitively applied to motion pictures, many film proprietors and not a few civil libertarians contend that the movies should have all the freedom accorded other media of communication, including books and magazines. This claim, which tends to ignore the movies' unusual communicative power, necessarily raises questions about the comparative thresholds of objectionable erotica, and particularly whether the level in the movies may be reached before the element of social importance is exhausted.

Comparisons between obscenity decisions involving the printed media and those dealing with the movies are difficult, because of the small number of cases and because of the many procedural distinctions among them. Yet, taking the decisions discussed in the preceding pages as a point of departure, it can be seen that the movie cases have clearly involved subjects and the treatment of subjects considerably more subdued than those in the book and magazine decisions. It is unlikely that any of the plots, dialogue, or physical action in any of the films would have stirred the slightest controversy had they been dealt with through the printed media. Yet it is doubtful that this proposition could be reversed, and in this sense there is no one-to-one relationship between films and the printed media. The story *Lady Chatterley's Lover* provides a striking example, since it has been found not obscene by American courts in both its original novel form[76] and in its movie adaptation. One glance at the specified deletions in the New York Board of Regents' censorship order (page 62) reveals how temperate an adaptation the film version was. Perhaps the movie case, *Kingsley Pictures,* would have been decided the same way had the Supreme Court been dealing with a film more faithful to the novel—one that gave honest and serious representation to D. H. Lawrence's detailed descriptions of sexual intercourse, the state of sexual organs, etc., and his use of four-letter words, for example. But at least the matter is doubtful.

A sensible distinction between motion pictures and the printed media could rest on the reasons why exhibition of a movie completely faithful to *Lady Chatterley's Lover* is hard to imagine, while publication of the book is not. The contrast appears to lie in the differences between the two media in terms of their communicative power and the level upon which their communication takes place. The natural constituents of the camera are material objects, behavior, events, etc., rather than discussion or exposition. Thought and ideas themselves cannot be photographed; to be effectively or dramatically communicated on the screen, they must be revealed through something physical, often something in motion as well, be it only the raising of an eyebrow. A movie dealing expressly or extensively in rational discussion would probably be judged a poor one by that measure, and its creators blamed for not making greater use of the peculiar gifts of the medium, particularly its power to deal with visible reality. Almost anything materially manifest in three-dimensional space can be unerringly simulated in two-dimensional lights and shadows, themselves projected several times larger than life. This capacity for literal realism has been the special force and attractiveness of the movies since their nickelodeon days. Visibility and movement are the essence of a medium whose aim is the reproduction of the real world rather than its abstraction.

When these characteristics of the film are joined to the viewing situation, the communication is likely to be received on a level largely subrational and subcritical. The viewer can assume a position of relative passivity and receptiveness, with little or nothing required of him intellectually. The plung-

ing of the theatre into darkness may signal a radical switching off of every-
day reality, to absorb without effort the "other" reality of the screen. In
many instances the viewer is watching performers with whom he has already established strong emotional ties. The subrational, subcritical impact
of the communication may also be reinforced by the social context in which
the viewing takes place. What is seen on the screen may seem more authoritative or acceptable because of the public character of the theatre and the
attitudes manifested by the audience.

These circumstances set the films off from books and magazines in degree, if not in kind. Yet it is not easy to make this distinction operational in
the control of obscenity. Recently the New York Court of Appeals attempted to draw the line at the simulation of an act of sexual intercourse.
The court's theory was that where the state had power to forbid "public
and semipublic sex displays" it had the power to prevent similar conduct
portrayed on the screen. This comparison was carefully limited:

In most instances, the real conduct is illegal because of what is accomplished
by the person, as in murder, forgery, or adultery. In such cases, the filmed
dramatization obviously does not share the evil aimed at in the law applicable
to the real thing. Where, however, the conduct is illegal, not because of what
is accomplished by those involved, but simply because what is done is shocking,
offensive to see, and generally believed destructive of the general level of
morality, then a filmed simulation of it shares . . . the evil of the original.[77]

In trying to separate permissible advocacy of ideas from the nonpermissible,
this theory relies entirely upon an analogy to a distinction made in criminal
law. In doing so, it seems unusually and unnecessarily restrictive, since apparently it would not take into account anything about the advocacy—for
example, the content, treatment, seriousness of purpose, or artistry of presentation.

The key to distinguishing motion pictures from the printed media would
seem to lie less in the portrayal of certain kinds of acts, such as sexual intercourse, than in the amount of "distance" placed between the viewer and
the simulated reality.[78] In dealing with events or behavior, the movies can
sweep away the ordinary technical barriers—words, pictorial stillness, dimi-
nution—that stand between the viewer and physical reality depicted by the
printed media. Thus, because the movies are far less "handicapped" than
the printed media, it would not be unreasonable to require them to erect
substitute barriers—those of indirection, stylization, absence of detail, vis-
ual remoteness, etc. The capacity of a medium to simulate reality, and the
amount of intellectual effort required to comprehend the representation,
might determine the degree of descriptive freedom that could be allowed in
the portrayal of erotica. By this measure, the mere presence of an idea or

the slightest element of "redeeming social importance" in a movie would not rule out obscenity as a matter of definition. An idea would not itself be proscribable, but its manner of presentation might be if it failed to establish enough "distance" between the viewer and the simulated reality. Such a requirement would bar a literal cinematic adaptation of *Lady Chatterley's Lover*, a film that would have considerable "redeeming social importance" (as does the novel) by any commonly understood meaning of that term. Treating the film medium in this way would mean that the constitutional status of an allegedly obscene movie would be determined by a kind of balancing process, in which "social importance" would be a prominent but not necessarily decisive factor.

Just as an undiscriminating standard of obscenity for all media ignores the peculiar character and capacity of the movies, a single standard for all film-viewing situations will itself often yield uncomfortably rigid results. In many instances "social importance," "patent offensiveness," and "appeal to the prurient interest" are likely to vary with the audience and with the manner in which the film itself is presented or advertised. In its "dominant theme" a movie may advocate an idea to one audience and appeal to the prurient interest of or be patently offensive to another. This differential result is most likely where the dominant theme is fairly ambiguous and therefore determined largely by the viewer's expectations of the film. In turn, these expectations may themselves be the product of advertising and other promotion of the movie. In an attempt to win the widest possible audience, it is not uncommon for distributors to outfit a film with a "split personality" promotionally. In some instances the two advertising campaigns can hardly be recognized as referring to the same motion picture. When the award-winning documentary *The Sky Above and the Mud Below* opened in New York, it was given what *Variety*, in its characteristic way, termed the "class pitch" in ads in three of the city's newspapers, the *Times*, the *Herald Tribune*, and the *World-Telegram and Sun*. Ads in the city's other papers were "on the lurid side."[79] Many of the aboriginals shown in the film were naked or nearly naked, and the film contained footage of love rituals. When luridly exploited, these elements were well suited to changing the image of the movie and its anticipated "dominant theme" for prospective viewers.

Few films portraying erotic behavior are likely to be so unambiguous as to present a clear "dominant theme" that would be unaffected by expectations a viewer brought with him. The importance of the state of mind of the viewer or reader was aptly noted several years ago by Judge Curtis Bok in a celebrated description of *l'homme moyen sensuel*:

. . . If he reads an obscene book when his sensuality is low, he will yawn over it or find that its suggestibility leads him off on quite different paths. If he reads the Mechanics' Lien Act while his sensuality is high, things will stand between him and the page that have no business there.[80]

When expectations of moviegoers are largely conditioned by advertising and other promotion preceding exhibition, such presentation might be considered an extension of the communication itself.[81] The concept of "dominant theme," then, may be thought of more realistically as being variable rather than constant.

Similarly, the "average person" factor, which in the *Roth-Alberts* test means the "normal" adult rather than the weak or susceptible adult or the young person, may not be an entirely satisfactory measure for a medium more than half of whose audience is formed by teenagers and children.[82]

For these reasons the concept of obscenity as a variable phenomenon, depending not only on words and pictures themselves but also on the way in which the materials are advanced, may be an especially apt one for motion pictures.

Age Classification

Age classification is the labeling of movies as suitable or unsuitable for children and youth on the theory that some films, though not harmful to adults, may be injurious to the less mature. Such ratings may be either governmental or nongovernmental, or they may be advisory or compulsory, depending on whether or not unaccompanied youth are actually barred from films classified as unsuitable. Advisory nongovernmental classification is the most common form in the United States, and includes ratings of the Film Board of National Organizations' "Green Sheet," the National Catholic Office for Motion Pictures, and other private sources, such as magazines and local organizations. A few exhibitors—mainly operators of so-called art theatres—and an occasional producer restrict audiences to adults. However, the United States remains the only major Western nation without some form of systematic compulsory classification of movies. Today governmental classification exists in only a few cities—Chicago and Dallas, for example. Accordingly, the great majority of films now shown in this country—including many foreign films designed for adults-only exhibition in their country of origin—are allowed unrestricted audience.

In American law there is ample precedent for denying youth certain privileges—driving automobiles, purchasing alcoholic drinks, and so forth—which are allowed adults. Nevertheless, movie classification raises a question of the child's First Amendment rights. Though the Supreme Court has not yet defined these rights, some members of the Court have recognized "the legitimate interest and indeed exigent interest of States and localities throughout the Nation in preventing the dissemination of material deemed harmful to children."[83] Yet this interest cannot justify the total suppression of material.[84]

In an early case, *Prince* v. *Massachusetts,* the Court upheld a child-labor law which prevented juveniles from selling religious pamphlets from door to door. The statute's interference with the parent's right to bring up his child or with the child's First Amendment freedoms was held not so great as to overcome the state's interest in the welfare of children. Thus

The state has a wide range of power for limiting parental freedom and authority in things affecting the child's welfare and this includes to some extent, matters of conscience and religious conviction.[85]

As yet there have been few reported cases involving classification.[86] However, the power to classify has been upheld in litigation involving the Dallas licensing ordinance. Classification of films was found to be a reasonable means to the end of preventing incitement to crime, delinquency, and sexual promiscuity on the part of young persons. Designating some films as not suitable for youth did not violate constitutional guarantees of free expression. Nor did the court believe the city had to show evidence of a causal relationship between certain films and criminal, delinquent, or promiscuous behavior. The legislative inference of a causal connection from data available to the city council was not "so unreasonable or arbitrary as to be invalid."[87] Thus it would appear that doctrinal problems presented by classification are less likely to involve the power to classify than the particulars of classification such as objectives and standards, age limits, and the enforcement of restrictive orders.

Obviously, standards used in classifying films will be more restrictive than those used in general licensing, where the two powers coexist. Such classification standards may be confined to erotica and nudity and thus present, in effect, a "variable" concept of obscenity, or they may go further and include new subject areas. The classification provision of the Chicago censorship ordinance is of the former kind, limited to erotica and nudity where

the picture, considered as a whole, has the dominant effect of substantially arousing sexual desires in any person less than seventeen years of age, or if the picture is indecent, or is contrary to contemporary community standards in the desciption or representation of nudity or sex.[88]

An example of the broader kind of classification is found in a New York State Board of Regents proposal introduced in the 1965 session of the New York legislature but not acted upon. The state Motion Picture Division would have been authorized to classify a film as acceptable for children under sixteen unless it contained scenes of nudity, sexual relationships, violence, terror, horror, brutality, sadism, drug addiction, lewdness, lasciviousness, physical torture, scenes which are disgusting, scenes which engender disregard for law or other scenes which are destructive of proper social relationships, in a manner, or to an extent which would be detrimental to the health, morals, safety and well-being of a minor under the age of sixteen years.[89]

Another example of far-ranging classification is that contained in a proposal of Dr. Henry Rago, a member of the Chicago Motion Picture Appeal Board, to revise Chicago's licensing ordinance. The proposal appears to be less an attempt to set out operational legal standards than a philosophical statement of the ideal of classification. As such, it reflects the wide gap that must inevitably lie between these two goals. A film would be unsuitable for children if

taken as a whole in its treatment of sex, violence, or any other areas of human concern to which such children or juveniles in their characteristic stages of emotional immaturity are peculiarly sensitive, such film tends, to an important and dangerous degree, to be disturbing, or precipitous of latent impulses toward destructive or anti-social acts.[90]

American law has no tradition that defines terror, horror, violence, sadism, or most other standards of the type contained in the New York Regents' proposal. Yet, because age classification does not directly place an added burden on adult freedom of expression and because a child's First Amendment rights are not as great as those of an adult, more latitude may be allowed in setting standards for classification than is allowed in general licensing.[91]

In an early case, a classification provision of Chicago's former licensing ordinance was held to be unconstitutionally vague for failing to give censors a rational guide.[92] Under the provision, a film was to be given an adults-only permit if it tended "to create a harmful impression on the minds of children where such tendency as to the minds of adults would not exist if exhibited only to persons of mature age."[93]

However, in the Dallas litigation, the Fifth Circuit Court of Appeals held that the general standard "not suitable for young persons," which proscribed "brutality, criminal violence, or depravity" along with certain types of erotica, was limited to the control of obscenity. So restricted, the general standard was not unconstitutionally vague. Moreover, the test for obscenity itself in classification was whether or not a film was

one which, to the average young person, applying contemporary community standards, the dominant theme of the material taken as a whole appeals to the prurient interest, substantially goes beyond the customary limits of candor in description or representation of such matter to the average young person, and is utterly without redeeming social importance.[94]

Thus the fact that certain films are free of obscenity under the *Roth-Alberts* definition would not necessarily render them not obscene when viewed by an audience of young persons.

The designation of "children" may also raise a constitutional question. Though any age line establishing a minor's incompetence in adult activity is bound to be arbitrary to a degree, such a line for movie viewing obviously cannot be set too high. In the Chicago case, the classification provision was found unconstitutional on the alternative ground that an age limit of twenty-one was unreasonable. Under it "a 20-year-old married serviceman would be prevented from seeing a film that might not be suitable for a girl of 12."[95] Most existing or proposed classification systems today set an age limit of sixteen or seventeen years. Most systems also provide for exemptions if a "child" is accompanied by a parent or guardian. A charge of unnecessary arbitrariness could probably be avoided by providing exemptions for married persons, servicemen and servicewomen, and high school graduates, etc.

Liability of exhibitors in the enforcement of classification decisions presents an additional problem. Responsibility for determining the age of youthful customers is not new for proprietors, having been borne for many years by owners of bars, clubs, and restaurants selling alcoholic drinks. The constitutional requirement of *scienter* could probably be extended to protect an exhibitor who admitted a child in the honest but mistaken belief that he was over the age limit.[96] In Chicago, for example, issuance of an adults-only permit means that "it shall be unlawful for any person exhibiting said picture to *knowingly* allow any persons under the age of 17 years" to see the film (emphasis in original).[97]

Penalties imposed on exhibitors committing offenses under a classification ordinance may present a free speech question if they impair the showing of films that would not be obscene to an adult audience. A provision in the Dallas ordinance for revocation or suspension of a special exhibitor's license to show films "not suitable for young persons," in the event that the exhibitor violated terms of the classification ordinance, was held to abridge guarantees of the First Amendment. According to the court, the provision failed to give adequate protection for exhibition of nonobscene films to an adult audience.[98]

Obscenity and classification are the two objectives of prior censorship today. The former standard has itself been confined in the law in recent years, though its definition is still uncertain and its exact application to movies unclear. Standards in classification are only now beginning to undergo doctrinal review. Assuming the classification power itself is upheld, permissible restriction will no doubt embrace more than obscenity, at least as obscenity is now defined in the law. However, whether it will go beyond a concern with erotica is still unclear.

III

PRIOR CENSORSHIP
IN OPERATION

5

Boards, Procedures, and Decisions*

Prior Censorship Establishments

In one form or another, prior censorship of movies in the United States has operated at all three levels of government: national, state, and local. Federal authority is vested in the Bureau of Customs and extends only to imported films. State censorship is performed by a licensing board which makes systematic prior examination of all films, foreign and domestic, intended for exhibition within the state. At the time of the *Freedman* decision, in 1965, four states—Kansas, Maryland, New York, and Virginia—censored motion pictures. However, in 1967 only the Maryland board was still in operation. The New York, Virginia, and Kansas licensing systems had been declared unconstitutional in their procedural arrangements on authority of the *Freedman* decision, and were not reformed by the respective state legislatures.

Municipal censorship bodies have always been more numerous and considerably more varied in form than state licensing boards. Since there are many more censorship ordinances on municipal code books than there are censorship bodies enforcing them, the exact number in operation at any one time is difficult to gauge. Many of the ordinances are inactive, though even these may have occasional enforcement where a particular film has become

---

* Much of the data on prior-censorship operations used in this chapter and in Chapter 6 was obtained from interviews with the following censor board members, government legal counsel, and Federal Bureau of Customs personnel: Marvin Aspen, Assistant Corporation Counsel, City of Chicago; William P. Bagwell, Jr., Assistant Attorney General, State of Virginia; Irving Fishman, Director, Division of Imports Compliance, Bureau of Customs, New York; Elwood Gebhart, Executive Secretary, Maryland Board of Censors; Mrs. Margaret K. Gregory, member, Virginia Division of Motion Picture Censorship; Mrs. Eva Holland, Reviewer, Maryland Board of Censors; Mrs. Polly Kirk, Chairman, Kansas Board of Review; Sgt. Robert Murphy,

the source of local complaints or has had well-publicized censorship problems elsewhere.

A recent study by the Motion Picture Association of America (MPAA) found thirty-eight cities and towns with motion picture censorship laws.[1] Of these, however, apparently only ten were engaged in active censorship. The study classifies the censorship ordinances into three groups: (1) those requiring submission of all films to a censorship agency for licensing before exhibition; (2) those requiring that a censorship agency be given notice of films scheduled for exhibition, and authorizing the agency to view, before exhibition, a film that it believes may be objectionable, and then, if necessary, to order deletions or the ban of the entire film; and (3) those which authorize a censorship agency to view films during the regular local engagement, and where one is found objectionable to order deletions or the withdrawal of the film. Active and inactive ordinances, as well as those held unconstitutional in recent years, are listed for each of the three groups in Table 2.

The MPAA compilations do not include unofficial citizen-advisory committees which function in several cities. Though these groups have no legal powers, they may, as in the case of the Milwaukee Motion Picture Commission, exercise an effective censorship, largely through voluntary compliance by local exhibitors.

Head, Chicago Film Review Section; Louis Pesce, Director, New York Motion Picture Division; Dr. Henry Rago, member, Chicago Motion Picture Appeal Board; Ptl. Stanley Russell, member, Detroit Police License Bureau; Kenneth W. Sain, Assistant Corporation Counsel, City of Chicago; Miss Eleanor Suske, Division of Imports Compliance, Bureau of Customs, New York; Valentine Wells, Executive Secretary, Milwaukee Motion Picture Commission; and Mrs. Lollie C. Whitehead, member, Virginia Division of Motion Pictures.

Other useful data on state and local censorship operations was obtained from interviews with the following persons: Miss Hildegarde Albrecht, Metro-Goldwyn-Mayer Film Exchange, Milwaukee; Felix Bilgrey, Esq., New York; Richard Brandt, Trans-Lux Distributing Corp., New York; Vincent Canby, *New York Times;* Howard Clark, Standard Theatres, Milwaukee; Bosley Crowther, *New York Times;* Elmer Jancke, Universal International Film Exchange, Milwaukee; Edward Johnson, Theatre Service Booking Agency, Milwaukee; Henry Kratz, Allied Theatre Owners of Wisconsin, Milwaukee; Ephraim London, Esq., New York; Charles E. McCarthy, Congress of Motion Picture Organizations, New York; Michael F. Mayer, Independent Film Importers and Distributors of America, New York; Radley H. Metzger, Audubon Films, New York; Carl Peppercorn, Peppercorn-Wormser Film Enterprises, New York; Martin Quigley, Jr., Quigley Publications, New York; George Regan, George Regan Film Distribution, Chicago; Donald S. Rugoff, Cinema V, New York; Miss Barbara Scott, Motion Picture Association of America, New York; Edward Solomon, Embassy Pictures Corp., New York; Irving Wormser, Peppercorn-Wormser Film Enterprises, New York.

TABLE 2   *Analysis of Municipal Censorship Ordinances*

Active	Inactive	Invalidated 1961–1966

Ordinances requiring submission of all films to censorship agency for licensing before exhibition

Active	Inactive	Invalidated 1961–1966
Chicago, Ill.	Evanston, Ill.	Atlanta, Ga.
Detroit, Mich.	Kansas City, Mo.	Portland, Ore.
Fort Worth, Tex.	Mt. Clemens, Mich.	
Providence, R.I.	Pasadena, Calif.	
	Sacramento, Calif.	
	San Angelo, Tex.	
	Waukegan, Ill.	
	Wichita Falls, Tex.	
	Winnetka, Ill.	

Ordinances requiring that censorship agency be given notice of scheduled films and authorizing it to preview any it believes may be objectionable and to order deletions or ban

Active	Inactive	Invalidated 1961–1966
Abilene, Tex.	Gary, Ind.	Birmingham, Ala.
Dallas, Tex.[a]	Lansing, Mich.	Memphis, Tenn.
	Spokane, Wash.	
	West St. Paul, Minn.	

Ordinances authorizing censorship agency to view films during regular local engagement and to order deletions or withdrawal

Active	Inactive	Invalidated 1961–1966
Columbus, Ohio	Bellingham, Wash.	Seattle, Wash.
Houston, Tex.	Bridgeport, Conn.	
Little Rock, Ark.	Denver, Colo.	
Seattle, Wash.[a]	Greeley, Colo.	
	Greensboro, N.C.	
	Highland Park, Ill.	
	New Haven, Conn.	
	Oklahoma City, Okla.	
	Palo Alto, Calif.	
	Rockford, Ill.	
	San Diego, Calif.	
	Sioux City, Iowa	
	Tacoma, Wash.	
	Trenton, N.J.	
	Waco, Tex.	

Table is based in part upon compilations of the Motion Picture Association of America in Appendix to Brief of American Civil Liberties Union and Maryland Branch, ACLU, Amici Curiae at 3a–13a, *Freedman* v. *Maryland*, 380 U.S. 51 (1965).

[a] Classification only.

Surveys of municipal censorship ordinances by two other sources are both somewhat at variance with the MPAA's. The *1964 Film Daily Yearbook,* which makes no distinction between active and inactive ordinances, omits several noted by the MPAA study, but includes ten which are not on the MPAA list.[2] The ten are those in Bessemer, Alabama; Chester, South Carolina; Geneva, Illinois; Glendale, California; Milwaukee, Wisconsin; Port Arthur, Texas; San Jose, California; Tampa, Florida; Valdosta, Georgia; and Waterloo, Iowa. Likewise, the *1965 International Motion Picture Almanac,* whose compilations have not changed since 1962, also omits some ordinances the MPAA has noted, while at the same time including in its own list seventeen omitted by the MPAA.[3] In six of these latter seventeen, the *Almanac* notes, the ordinances are inactive: in Bessemer, Alabama; Council Bluffs, Iowa; Decatur, Illinois; Valdosta, Georgia; Waterloo, Iowa; and Worcester, Massachusetts. In four of the seventeen, active censorship is exceptional: Corvallis, Oregon; Eugene, Oregon; Minneapolis, Minnesota; and Sumter, South Carolina. The *Almanac* gives no indication of the status of censorship in the remaining seven cities: Hartford, Connecticut; Lynn, Massachusetts; Madison, Wisconsin; Milwaukee, Wisconsin; Oak Park, Illinois; Taunton, Massachusetts; and St. Joseph, Missouri.

The four states with licensing at the time of the *Freedman* case and the ten cities listed by the MPAA as having active censorship have a total population of nearly 33,000,000, according to 1960 census figures. Although this was only about 19 percent of the national population, the censorship has often been effective beyond its territorial lines. For example, active licensing boards in large cities like Chicago and Detroit influence smaller censorship bodies in nearby suburbs. These smaller bodies are ordinarily inactive, but they may occasionally "come to life" to examine a film that has been censored in the larger city and is scheduled for local exhibition in uncensored form. In at least one city, Mt. Clemens, Michigan, the censorship ordinance itself prescribes this practice by expressly barring films "not approved by the Detroit Police Department."[4]

Prior censorship can also have extraterritorial effect through voluntary compliance of exhibitors outside the censorship jurisdiction. When, for example, the Milwaukee Motion Picture Commission finds a film objectionable, a distributor may have difficulty booking it in its uncensored form in several other Wisconsin cities as well. In the case of art or foreign films, the Chicago licensing process has long been regarded as a kind of moral weathervane by Midwest exhibitors, including those as far away as St. Louis and Minneapolis. Where prior censorship has extraterritorial effect through voluntary compliance, it is probably less a mark of the power of licensing than of the local informal pressures—including extralegal acts by public officials and direct action by private groups—that can be brought against exhibitors.

Prior censorship may also have extraterritorial result for purely technical reasons. A rushed booking schedule may make it difficult to restore cut footage before the film is shipped out of the licensing jurisdiction. And, quite apart from haste, the likelihood that a particular print may come back into the licensing area sometime in the immediate future may cause cut footage to be left out as a matter of convenience. Although some exhibitors, particularly those dealing with nudist or "nudie" films, often demand a print in its uncensored form, such insistence in the case of other types of films appears to be exceptional.

There are also some well-known exceptions to the extraterritorial effect of prior censorship. A few municipalities near cities with censorship have actually become havens for uncensored films. For several years the city of Highland Park, Michigan, encircled by Detroit, has profitably allowed exhibition of uncensored films that were cut or banned in the larger city. When Memphis had censorship, uncensored films were shown in West Memphis, Arkansas, a community of 19,000 across the Mississippi. These situations are, nevertheless, exceptions to the general rule that the effect of municipal prior censorship does *not* stop at the city limits.

The Licensing Process

A closer examination of the work of seven major state and municipal censorship bodies and of the Federal Bureau of Customs will serve to illustrate the operation of prior censorship. The four states—Kansas, Maryland, New York, and Virginia—had licensing systems at the time of the *Freedman* decision. (The licensing systems of New York, Virginia, and Kansas were discontinued after the *Freedman* decision.) The cities—Chicago, Detroit, and Milwaukee—are the three largest cities censoring films.

Operations of the seven major state and municipal censorship bodies considered here were and are variously organized. Maryland has a three-member board, as Kansas and Virginia did when their boards were functioning. In New York, however, the censorship system was supervised by the state Board of Regents, though licensing itself was in the hands of the board's Motion Picture Division, which included a director, an assistant director, and four reviewers. In the Chicago licensing system, first examination is made by the police department's Film Review Section, which is supervised by a police sergeant though its six reviewers are civilians. Appeals from their action are referred to the Motion Picture Appeal Board, which has independent status within the city administration. In Detroit, the licensing authority is a nine-man Police Licensing Bureau also charged with the scrutiny of books, magazines, and live entertainment in the city. In Milwaukee, where there is no official censorship, the Motion Picture Commission, consisting of nine members, makes censorship recommendations.

Typically, the official licensing boards are authorized to examine all movies intended for exhibition in the licensing jurisdiction. In addition to features, this includes short subjects, serials, cartoons, and, in at least one jurisdiction, advertising materials. Newsreels and current-events films are exempt from examination, by law, in Chicago, as they were in New York, Kansas, and Virginia. In Maryland and Detroit these films are not examined as a matter of practice. In the case of films of a scientific, educational, or religious character that are not intended for commercial exhibition, each of the state boards was authorized to issue permits without examination.

Initial Examination. Initial viewing procedures have not varied greatly from one board to another. In Kansas and Virginia, films were seen by at least two board members. In Maryland, two reviewers make the examination. If they recommend censorial action, the film is screened in the presence of at least one board member, who decides whether or not to issue a censorship order. When no board member is immediately available, the board's executive secretary sits in his place, and apparently makes the decision himself. In New York, examination was ordinarily made by two of the Motion Picture Division's four reviewers, unless it was clear beforehand that a particular film was likely to present a censorship question. Often, in that event, the entire reviewing staff of the division, including the director and assistant director, viewed the film, with the director having final authority.

In Chicago, films are viewed by three or more members of the Film Review Section. The police sergeant supervising the section takes part in the examination process only when the section members are evenly divided. Films in Detroit are sometimes viewed by a single member of the Police Licensing Bureau, though more often than not two members make the initial examination, especially when it appears that a censorship question might arise. Ten of the bureau's thirteen members view films from time to time in order to "keep everyone in tune with what is going on." Usually, however, one or two of the bureau's members have become "specialists" in motion pictures.

The situation in Milwaukee differs again from that of the other boards. Only a small percentage of films are viewed in advance of exhibition. These are ones which the Motion Picture Commission's executive secretary, who is also a commission member, has thought likely to present censorship problems. His findings are based on the reading of advance notices in the trade press, reviews in other cities, advertising, the distributor's failure to give assurances of the character of the film, etc. Such films are viewed by at least five members of the commission before exhibition. All others are viewed by a commission member or commission "aide" (of which there are fifteen, chosen by the members) at the opening night performance. If, at that point, the member or aide makes a censorship recommendation, at least five members of the commission view the film later in a special session.

Ordinarily both the film proprietor and the public are excluded from the initial viewing and deliberation. Occasionally boards have sought outside advice (other than that from government legal counsel) before making their decision on a film. These instances have usually involved invitation to police narcotics specialists to view films depicting drug addiction. During the racial crisis in Cambridge, Maryland, in 1964, the state Board of Censors invited representatives of the National Association for the Advancement of Colored People and the Congress on Racial Equality to view a film dealing with violence in race relations.

The Maryland and Chicago boards have their own projection facilities. In most cases, a reviewer or board member has a bell or buzzer apparatus at his side which he sounds when a questionable series of frames is noted. This footage is then either rerun immediately or "marked" by the projectionist, usually by slipping a piece of paper in the reel, and rerun at the conclusion of the film. In Detroit and Milwaukee, where special projection facilities are lacking, the screening has been provided by the film proprietor —usually the distributor—at his own expense. Sometimes this censorship examination takes place at the same marketing screening the distributor has arranged for local exhibitors. However, special screenings are often arranged for the censorship authorities alone.

When a board has had its own projection facilities, the initial examination and licensing decision normally have taken place within two or three days after receipt of the film—in many cases on the same day. A film presenting a censorship question, however, may require much more time (in the case of New York, for example, it was as much as two weeks). Before the *Freedman* decision only one board, the Chicago Film Review Section, was statutorily required to make initial rulings within a specified period of time—in its case, five days. The censorship statutes in Virginia and New York required the respective state boards to make initial examination "promptly." Under Maryland's new licensing law, redrafted after the *Freedman* decision, the Board of Censors must make the examination within five days of submission of the film. Though instances of intentional delay by a board have been known, they appear to be relatively uncommon.

Notice. When the distributor has arranged the screening at which the first examination is made, he is usually told of a censorship finding immediately after screening or after deliberation, which in most cases follows the screening. If a censor board has used its own projection facilities, the distributor is notified of a censorship order formally by letter. In most cases the information is also given informally beforehand by telephone, though in many instances this is done only when the distributor himself has called the board.

Review. A censorship order found unacceptable by a distributor may be reviewed administratively and judicially. Normally, the administrative review is an occasion for negotiation and compromise between the censors and the distributor. In most instances, a representative from the office of the state attorney general or, in the case of a municipal board, the city corporation counsel is present as legal counsel for the censors. Frequently, legal counsel for the distributor also takes part in these proceedings.

Administrative review may be either formal or informal. In the case of Detroit it is a highly informal, one-step process. Usually the film is rescreened the next day in the presence of the film proprietor, an assistant corporation counsel, and the one or two members of the Licensing Bureau who viewed the film originally. In Kansas the procedure was more drawn out. Upon request, the board rescreened the film and reconsidered its original order. This process took about a week. If the distributor was still not satisfied he then, according to the board chairman, "threatened to sue the board." This maneuver resulted in another screening at which counsel for both sides were usually present.

Before its censorship system was declared unconstitutional, New York had the most formal and attenuated administrative review procedure. A distributor's first step was to ask for a rescreening by the director of the Motion Picture Division, a proceeding at which the distributor was allowed to be present. If he was still dissatisfied, he could then appeal to the state Board of Regents itself, or what was, in effect, a three-man committee of the Regents chosen by the full body to hear motion picture appeals. The committee received briefs and heard oral argument from both sides, and also viewed the film. The hearing was open to the public at the distributor's request. On the average, an appeal to the Regents consumed about two or three months if it was taken during the school year, when apparently the committee could be more readily assembled. If the summer months were involved, an appeal might take as long as five or six months.

At present, only the Chicago licensing system has a separate administrative body to review the original censorship order. The rescreening takes place before the five-member Motion Picture Appeal Board. Under an amendment to the city's licensing ordinance following the *Freedman* decision, the Appeal Board now has fifteen days in which to view the film. Fifteen more days are allowed for a hearing, at which the film proprietor or his representative can present evidence on why the original censorship order should not be affirmed. The board is required to rule on the appeal within five days of this hearing. Formerly, there was no time requirement for the rescreening, hearing, or ruling on the appeal, and the review process often required more than two months—particularly during the summer when, as in the case of the New York Board of Regents subcommittee, it was more difficult to convene the appellate body.

Before the *Freedman* decision, judicial review of the administrative appeal depended entirely on the initiative of the distributor. Crowded court calendars made it likely that several months or even a year or more might pass before the case came to trial. Under the Maryland system, out of which the *Freedman* case developed, the distributor was merely given the statutory right to appeal a decision of the board to the Baltimore City Court. Two or three months usually elapsed between the time of filing the suit and trial. Under the new Maryland censorship law enacted after the *Freedman* decision, the Board of Censors, in denying a permit, must itself file a complaint in the city court, and do so within three days. The court, in turn, is required to set a hearing within five days of the filing of the complaint, and hand down a ruling within another two days. The Board of Censors is also charged with proving the film objectionable. Chicago's amended ordinance provides that if the Motion Picture Appeal Board upholds a censorship order, it must file a petition for an injunction in the Circuit Court of Cook County within ten days.

The unofficial status of the Milwaukee Motion Picture Commission bars any opportunity for formal official review. Yet, since the commission's informal authority rests in large measure on the willingness of city officials to prosecute an uncooperative exhibitor for showing an allegedly obscene film or to revoke his theatre license, some form of official review does operate in the rare instance of a completely recalcitrant exhibitor. In other instances, a quasi-appellate agency has been set up. Twice in the last ten years an *ad hoc* liaison committee of three commission members, three exhibitors, three distributors, and the party of grievance has been formed to try to mediate a dispute in question.

Inspection. All licensing boards have auxiliary inspection systems, to check on whether films are being shown without permits and whether specific cuts required by censorship orders have actually been made. Instances of films shown deliberately without having been submitted for examination have apparently been rare, and are likely to occur only in order to develop test litigation. On the other hand, cases of distributors or exhibitors failing to make required cuts are not uncommon. In Detroit, where members of the Licensing Bureau could not recall a single instance of exhibition without prior submission of the film, four full-time inspectors check films in theatres during their regular exhibition. Inspectors in Milwaukee are the fifteen aides attached to the Motion Picture Commission. Kansas had a single full-time salaried inspector who covered the entire state. In contrast, inspectors in Virginia were low-level patronage appointees of each state legislator. They received passes instead of pay, and, whenever they happened to go to the movies, they merely looked for the censor board's perforation. Apparently they had no knowledge of specific cuts required by the board.

Penalties. Violation of a licensing law is a misdemeanor in every jurisdiction and is punishable by fines ranging from $25 to $100, depending on the particular censorship law, with each exhibition in violation considered a separate offense. In Detroit, failure to comply with a censorship order results in the issuance of an ordinance violation ticket which, like a traffic summons, requires the exhibitor to appear in court the next day. In addition, an inspector discovering a violation may enter the projection booth and demand that the proper cuts be made on the spot. Failure of the exhibitor to comply at this point has resulted in seizure of the print in question. If the exhibitor should be convicted of the ordinance violation, the penalty may be as high as $500 or ninety days in jail or both.[5] In addition, the corporation counsel may initiate theatre-license revocation proceedings before the city council. Needless to say, few exhibitors have been willing to carry resistance to such a point, and use of these extraordinary measures has been infrequent over the years.

In Milwaukee, deliberate failure to comply with the Motion Picture Commission's recommendations may be met by the threat of city or county authorities to prosecute for showing an obscene film, or to revoke the exhibitor's theatre license. But, as in the case of Detroit, where the responsibility for challenging the censorship system also has rested with the exhibitor rather than the distributor, few disputes have reached the point where these penalties are actually invoked. The last instance of a theatre license suspension in Milwaukee involved exhibition of *The Outlaw,* in 1947.

Standards: Prescribed and Applied

The Licensing Laws

Licensing laws, active as well as inactive, contain many criteria other than that of obscenity. In fact, obscenity accounts for perhaps only 10 to 20 percent of the censorship standards specifically set out in licensing laws, and for only about the same percentage of space taken up in the elaboration of standards in those laws. Yet censorship for any reason other than obscenity is rarely applied today. The major reason for this, of course, is the effect of the emerging legal doctrine which, as we will see, has made the application of many of the standards still in licensing laws "unthinkable" in the minds of today's censors. In addition, some standards, such as that of "incitement to crime," have never been readily applicable to the content of the commercially exhibited motion picture. Further, many of the more unusual or more vaguely phrased standards are found in licensing laws that are inactive.

Though the various standards other than obscenity thus have little practical significance today, they are worth noting because they indicate the extent to which authority of movie censors has been narrowed from that originally granted to them by legislative bodies. They also indicate the sorts of harm American communities have believed they needed to fear from motion pictures.

Most licensing laws in recent years have contained one or more of the familiar triad of prohibitions: obscenity, indecency, and immorality. (See Table 3.) Some laws augment these three by proscribing specific cinematic content. For example, the Kansas City, Missouri, ordinance, one of the most detailed, forbids

human nudity or simulation thereof, partial nudity which is sexually immoral or offensive to public decency, dances suggesting or representing sexual action or indecent passion or emphasizing indecent movements, lewd poses and gestures, lustful embraces, or other acts, representations, or expressions of erotic or pornographic nature calculated to stimulate sexual desire or lascivious thoughts; or present acts related to sex which constitute felonies or misdemeanors under the state laws of Missouri; or . . . scenes portraying sexual hygiene, sex organs, abortion, methods of contraception, veneral diseases, or scenes of actual human birth.[6]

Other laws are detailed to such a degree that if they were to be strictly enforced, they would probably have kept many, if not most, films of the 1960's from local exhibition. For example, the Birmingham, Alabama, ordinance forbade portrayal of

any female in a drunken state, unless reduced to a flash, or any rape or attempt at rape, or any childbirth or any domestic or conjugal infidelity of an immoral nature upon the part of either husband or wife, or any bawdy house transaction therein, or the plying of the trade of a procurer, procuress, cadet or other person who profits directly from prostitution of one or more females, or the seduction or attempted seduction of any person, or immoral or unlawful sexual conduct or relations.[7]

Several licensing laws authorize censorship of scenes which are likely to induce unlawful behavior, usually phrased as "incitement to crime" or "disturbance of the public peace or order," while others proscribe the mere portrayal of crimes or criminal behavior. For example, the Oklahoma City ordinance forbids the showing of "any ex-convicts, outlaw or outlaws, bandit

TABLE 3   *State and Municipal Censorship Laws: Proscriptive Standards, 1965*

Jurisdiction	Obscenity	Indecency	Immorality	Incitement to crime	Disturbance of the peace	Portrayal of criminal behavior	Racial, religious, or class prejudice
Kansas	X	X	X				
Maryland	X		X	X			
New York	X.	X	X	X			X
Virginia	X	X	X	X			
Abilene, Tex.	X						
Birmingham, Ala.	X	X	X			X	
Bridgeport, Conn.		X	X				X^a
Chicago, Ill.	X		X		X	X^b	X
Columbus, Ohio						X	
Dallas, Tex.	X^c		X^d	X^d			
Denver, Colo.		X	X				
Detroit, Mich.		X	X				
Fort Worth, Tex.	X	X	X^e				X
Gary, Ind.	X^f		X				
Greeley, Colo.	X^f	X	X				
Greensboro, N.C.	X		X				
Highland Park, Ill.			X			X	
Houston, Tex.	X	X	X		X		X
Kansas City, Mo.	X	X	X	X		X^g	
Lansing, Mich.					X		X
Little Rock, Ark.	X	X	X				
Memphis, Tenn.	X^f		X	X^h			
Mt. Clemens, Mich.			X				
New Haven, Conn.	X^f	X				X	X^a
Oklahoma City, Okla.	X^f	X	X			X	
Palo Alto, Calif.	X	X	X		X		
Pasadena, Calif.	X	X					
Providence, R.I.	X		X				
Rockford, Ill.	X		X			X	

Table is based in part upon excerpts from licensing laws compiled by the Motion Picture Association of America in Appendix to Brief for American Civil Liberties Union and Maryland Branch, ACLU Amicus Curiae, *Freedman* v. *Maryland*, 380 U.S. 51 (1965).

  [a] Blasphemy.

  [b] Hanging, lynching, or burning of a human being.

  [c] Prurient interest of youth.

  [d] Of youth.

  [e] Also of youth.

  [f] Lewdness or lasciviousness.

  [g] "Acts related to sex."

  [h] Overthrow of the national government.

TABLE 3, *Continued*

Jurisdiction	Ob-scenity	Inde-cency	Immor-ality	Incite-ment to crime	Distur-bance of the peace	Portrayal of criminal behavior	Racial, religious, or class prejudice
Sacramento, Calif.	X	X	X				
San Angelo, Tex.	X	X	X				
Seattle, Wash.	Xⁱ						
Sioux City, Iowa		X	X			X	
Spokane, Wash.	X						X
Tacoma, Wash.	X	X	X	X	Xʲ		
Trenton, N.J.		X	X	X			
Waco, Tex.		X	X				
Waukegan, Ill.	X	X					
W. St. Paul, Minn.	X	X	X			X	
Wichita Falls, Tex.		X	Xᵈ	X		X	
Winnetka, Ill.	X	X		X	X		

ⁱ For persons under eighteen.
ʲ Glorification of crime.

or bandits, engaged in the commission of their former crimes or in any crimes in which said ex-convicts, outlaw or outlaws, bandit or bandits, are made the feature of said show."[8] In its proscriptions, the Sioux City, Iowa, ordinance includes depiction of "illegal acts, burglaries, safe-cracking, hold-ups, stagecoach or train robberies . . ."[9]

Material that casts reproach or derision on class, race, or religion, or which encourages racial, religious, or sectional prejudice is also censorable under several laws. Particularly shocking scenes are forbidden under three ordinances: Palo Alto, California ("gruesome, revolting, or disgusting scenes or subjects"); Rockford, Illinois ("unduly horrible"); and Tacoma, Washington (brutality).

Several laws contain very general standards. The Evanston, Illinois, and Greensboro, North Carolina, ordinances ban material that is "objectionable," while the Highland Park, Illinois, ordinance proscribes that which is "questionable." The Spokane, Washington, ordinance bars films that have a "harmful influence on the public," and under the Rockford, Illinois, law, a film which "touches false ethics" may be barred.

Finally, two laws defer to rulings or ratings elsewhere. The Mt. Clemens, Michigan, ordinance proscribes films "not approved by the Detroit Police Department."[10] In Waukegan, Illinois, the licensing ordinance authorizes censorship of films not "passed upon by the National Preview Committee."[11]

Today, movie censorship based expressly on any grounds other than obscenity is unusual. Yet with the ambiguity still surrounding obscenity as a philosophical notion and a legal concept, use of that standard may occasionally hide the conscious or unconscious resort to other standards, which in some instances may not yet be quite as "dead" as they appear.

The Censors and the Legal Doctrine

The narrowing of permissible licensing objectives to the proscription of obscenity, and the reform of the obscenity doctrine itself, have had emancipating consequences for the content of movies, particularly in the portrayal of erotica and nudity and the use of language. Yet in turning to actual prior-censorship rulings one must be prepared for certain negative discoveries. For example, the censors are generally unsympathetic with the doctrinal developments, and their understanding of the law is often imperfect. Some censorship orders—at least in their initial sway—appear to disregard obvious doctrinal requirements; and where there seems to be a reasonable choice, the censors often prefer the more restrictive ruling. The censors do tend to censor, as their more severe critics have contended. Yet for task-oriented administrators the tendency is not surprising, nor is it morbid or sinister. Rather, it is the sort of behavior that might be expected from administrators who have found their powers steadily cut away at the same time they have been led by their constituents to believe that their duties are increasingly urgent.

On the contrary, what is surprising and impressive is the degree to which the legal doctrine has affected the behavior of the censors. The great changes in the law of prior censorship and obscenity in the last dozen years have developed out of conflict rather than consensus, with the censors defeated in open battle, not won over by persuasion or bargaining. Under these circumstances it would hardly be surprising if they were unreconciled to the doctrinal changes. Nevertheless, much reform has actually taken place. Older hands recognize that the days of freewheeling censorship are over, while newer censors have never known such times. Accordingly, much that was allowed in the past is now seen by the same censors or their successors as "unthinkable." Because of the doctrinal changes, the censors have acquired a degree of built-in self-restraint, and to this extent a major battle for freedom of speech in movies has been won.

Yet the ordinary censor can hardly be expected to resolve all his doubts in favor of free expression. The protection of free speech in movies still depends in part on conflict. This means that where reconstruction of the censors leaves off, freedom of speech rests upon a dynamic relationship between adversaries: the censors and the film proprietors. In this contest, the *probable* outcome of litigation is often, though not always, decisive. Developments in the legal doctrine have made defeat for the censors in court a likely event, and at the same time have fashioned instant civil libertarians out of many film proprietors. In a sense, then, the film proprietor enforces the doctrine on the censors. In this, however, he is not alone. He usually has a powerful "ally" in the person of government counsel in the censors' own administration. An attorney general or a corporation counsel, though usually critical of the film proprietor, has no desire to undertake an unsuccessful legal defense of a censorship order. In effect, then, legal departments exercise a continuing check on censorial authority. If this were all there was to the adversary relationship there would be, for better or worse, much less censorship. Yet the relationship is not this simple, for two reasons. The law of obscenity is not so clear, particularly as applied to the new frontiers of portrayed erotica, that the film proprietor and the government counsel will always agree on what the probable outcome of a court contest might be. Furthermore, in many instances a film proprietor may be reluctant to undertake litigation even when he stands a good chance of winning.

Censors on all the major licensing boards today know that prior censorship, for practical purposes, is constitutionally limited to obscenity, regardless of what statutory provisions may authorize. Even in Detroit, where obscenity is not mentioned in the licensing ordinance, "indecent" has been given an interpretation which confines its effect largely to that of obscenity. Most censors are aware of the *Roth-Alberts* test, at least by its provisions, if not by name. In fact, a certain homely orthodoxy has grown up about the matter. According to one member of the Detroit Police Licensing Bureau, "The first thing we do with a magazine or movie, is give it the *Roth* test."

Most censors also appear to be aware that the frame of reference for general censorship cannot be that of protecting children from harm. At least two censors interviewed indicated an awareness of *Butler* v. *Michigan,* and its holding that reading material cannot be denied to adults on the ground that it might incite minors to violent or immoral acts. Familiarity with the legal doctrine beyond this level varies considerably from censor to censor. Some censors have been briefed on the Supreme Court's movie-censorship decisions by government counsel, while others have actually read some of the opinions. Where Virginia censors could give only a garbled version of detailed points of the law, members of the Chicago Motion Picture Appeal Board, one of them a lawyer, were familiar with the outstanding litigation and even with the positions of the various Justices. Louis Pesce, director of the now defunct New York State Motion Picture Division, has a detailed and balanced knowledge of the relevant Supreme Court and state court decisions on movie censorship and obscenity.

Awareness of the legal doctrine is attended in many instances by concern and uncertainty. Many censors are unsure not only of their authority, but also of their jobs. At the same time, many feel strongly that the courts, particularly the Supreme Court, have erred in "allowing" the types of films with which the boards now find themselves embattled. Most censors are willing to admit that, were their own views controlling, their decisions and orders would be more restrictive than they tend to be at present.

The Substance of Censorship

Analysis of censored motion picture content is difficult for two reasons. First, movie censorship has been and continues to be in flux, because of changes in the legal doctrine of prior censorship and obscenity and because of an increasing boldness in the content of movies themselves. Second, systematic analysis of censorship orders is not possible because files of the licensing boards—which in most cases contain detailed records of every film ever examined—are closed to the public and to researchers. This policy, which sometimes seems sinister to libertarians, is actually largely for the economic benefit of the film proprietor, since public disclosure of required deletions can undermine the profit potential of a film. Most information on the substance of censorship orders, then, is obtained from the censors directly, and only in general terms. In some measure, the representativeness of this data can be checked, again in general terms, by questioning film proprietors and such more or less disinterested observers as trade journalists. I found that, in large measure, these persons concur with the information provided by the censors themselves on the substance of censorship. Also, the pattern of censorship as described by the censors is remarkably similar from one board to another.

The information thus obtained reveals two striking facts. First, the vast majority of censorship orders today are confined to erotica. Second, the entire scope of censorial action falls within far narrower limits than in the past. Nearly all censorship orders today are based upon one or more of seven categories of depiction: nudity, eroticism without nudity, profanity or indelicate words, sex education, shocking or offensive material not necessarily related to sex, use of narcotics, and unflattering or unconventional portrayal of religion, race, or race relations.

These categories not only reflect the vast changes that have marked prior censorship, but they also offer a chance to compare actual censorship today with the popular stereotype of the censorial interest. Unhappily, this stereotype, founded on the antics of censors during the *Mutual Film* period, still has wide currency. One of the best known descriptions, Chief Justice Warren's dissenting opinion in the *Times Film* case of 1961, lists twenty-five instances of censorship; yet, by the most generous assessment, only seven of these would fall into the categories of current censorship above. Moreover, it is doubtful that any of these seven—the duration of a kiss (*Carmen*) or a Negro "passing" for white (*Lost Boundaries*), etc.—would be repeated anywhere today. The remaining seventeen examples—for instance, scenes of poverty among southern tenant farmers or the portrayal of gangsters—are species of censorship now long extinct.

Going back to one of the few quantified studies of censorship orders in the *Mutual Film* period, the contrast is no less impressive. In their book *Censored—the Private Life of the Movie*, Morris Ernst and Pare Lorentz used nineteen categories to analyze 2,960 deletions ordered by state licensing boards in 1928. Of these nineteen categories, only five, at most, correspond to the seven categories above. These five accounted for 1,115 deletions, or 37.7 per cent of the total made in 1928.[12] Judging from Ernst and Lorentz' description of some of the deletions in these categories, few, if indeed a single one, of the 1,115 would be made by present-day censors. Ernst and Lorentz' other categories—for example, "display of dangerous weapons" (528 deletions), "reference to drinking" (56 deletions), or "derogatory reference to countries" (50 deletions)—are not relevant to censorship today.

Before examining each of the seven current categories, several general points should be noted. First, a censorship order can either contain directions that certain specific changes be made in the film before it is acceptable, or it can reject a film entirely. Also, where boards are empowered to classify films, an order may be limited to issuance of an "adults only" permit. The distinction between required deletions and an outright rejection of a film is really one of degree. Some boards in practice do not reject any film entirely, but merely list the changes that would make it acceptable. The Detroit Licensing Bureau, for example, once required 6,000 feet of deletions in a film 8,000 feet long. Needless to say, the film was not shown. In another instance, the New York Motion Picture Division is said to have required so many changes in the seventy-minute "nudie" *Not Tonight, Henry*, that the film would have been transformed into a twelve-minute short with even the credits cut out![13] Other boards, in rejecting a film outright, in effect have concluded that so many changes would be necessary, no coherent work would remain. Today, films that are rejected entirely or required to be so altered that they cannot be shown are the exception rather than the rule. Most films involved in censorship have few deletions, often only one, and in most instances the cuts are relatively short, sometimes only a few feet or seconds in length.

A change required by a censorship order may not necessarily require a deletion. In some instances, technical changes are made in the film by its proprietor. For example, the New York Motion Picture Division was reported to have licensed *Les Liaisons Dangereuses*, which contained nudity in an erotic context, after the film's producer agreed to "darken" two scenes.[14]

Finally, censorship of a film can go through the several procedural stages that have been discussed, at any one of which the original censorship order may be modified. Most of the following censorship orders were, in effect, final ones; that is, they were either not changed as a result of protest from the film proprietor, or they are themselves the modified censorship order. Those instances where the censorship order mentioned was not final— where it was later changed in the course of an administrative appeal—are pointed out.

Nudity. Without doubt the main traffic of prior censorship today is nudity, or as a member of the Detroit Licensing Bureau has described the chief concern of his work, "a matter of too much woman showing." The nudity is generally one of three types: documentary, nudist, or erotic. The typical documentary of this sort—*The Sky Above and the Mud Below* or *Naked Amazon,* for example—features aborigines who are nude by habit. In this context the nudity is almost always nonerotic. This type of film, once the subject of frequent litigation, is seldom involved in censorship today unless it contains ribaldry.

The nudist film usually is set in a nudist camp or in some way proclaims the nudist "philosophy," however unrelated that may be to the plot, if indeed there is a plot. The nudity presented is ostensibly nonerotic, and, to all appearances, is meant to present the physical and spiritual advantages of a way of life. With such "advocacy" clearly aimed at claiming free speech protection, nudism has become the most extensively expounded idea in the entire history of motion pictures. Though the nudist film, like the documentary, has been vindicated through litigation, censors have been reluctant to give this type of movie their automatic approval. Unlike the case of some of the documentaries, exposure of genitals or of pubic hair is not allowed. Exposed breasts—the *raison d'être* of all nudist films—are permitted by most boards today, however. The Maryland board, for example, allows breast exposure when it is clear that there is a nudist camp in the film. The Detroit Licensing Bureau, adopting a rule from its regulation of burlesque shows, does not permit "a fully exposed breast," which in the bureau's analysis usually means exposure of the nipple. An example of Detroit censorship of a nudist film is contained in the following set of notes made by a member of the bureau during examination of *The Phantom Peeper*.

10:55—start of movie.
11:08—girl at dressing table, cut bare breast.
11:24—girls with nude breasts in dressing rooms.
11:26—scene in nudist camp, cut all shots of bare breast.

11:33—cut all closeups of girl undressing in office.
11:34—cut all pool scenes showing bare breasts.
11:42—cut scene of girl in dressing room—bare breast.
11:50—girl in bathtub, cut shot of bare breasts.

The seven deletions amounted to 400 feet, or about four and a half minutes, in a film 5,000 feet long. With only one board—Kansas—was there a policy of rejecting nudist films. The Milwaukee Motion Picture Commission, though having no formal policy on the matter, usually finds itself rejecting nudist films, since it allows no unusual breast exposure.

Erotic nudity is more varied and usually more imaginative than documentary or nudist-camp nudity, and in some of its forms reaches what is probably the hard core of censorial determination today. Aside from the near-universal rule against genital exposure, and the occasional rule against complete breast exposure, most of the boards do not appear to have any general policy on erotic nudity. The Detroit Licensing Bureau is apt to be more permissive if erotic nudity is in the context of comedy. Likewise, there is usually no censorship when exposure is merely suggested, and left to the imagination. The Milwaukee Motion Picture Commission, which until the mid-1960's rejected any film in which there was *any* nudity, now confines its proscription to nudity designed "solely for shock value or for the purpose of arousing the prurient interest." Maryland censors bar erotic nudity which has "no connection with the story and issued the following censorship order for *The Candidate:*

In bedroom sequence between Angie and Frank Carlton, eliminate all views of them from a point where Frank turns out the light, down to a point where Frank is shown sitting up in bed. This will include all views of them apparently nude together in bed embracing, views of Angie as she rolls over, her body on top of his and subsequent views of Angie with breast exposed, lying in bed beside Frank.

On the other hand, the board approved *Woman in the Dunes,* a Japanese film of considerable artistry, in which there was breast exposure in a non-erotic context at first, and then in an erotic one.

The success of the documentary film in the courts, and later in getting an almost automatic license from the censors, has given rise to the pseudo-documentary film, which features erotic nudity, often in the form of burlesque footage or stock footage of nude women inserted in what is usually purported to be either a social or cultural study or a travelogue. A typical movie of this sort is *Europe in the Raw,* which in 1964 became the first film rejected entirely by the Chicago Motion Picture Appeal Board. The board contended that the film was not what it was held out to be—a documentary on prostitution and exotic dancing in Europe—but rather that its "producer . . . is preoccupied with presenting nudity and sex for the sole sake of such."[15] The measure used by the board is similar to one used by the New York Motion Picture Division, which cut nudity where it appeared to be the subject of "morbid interest," but approved it where it appeared to be presented in the context of advocating an idea.

Another common type of erotic nudity is that presented in a sado-masochistic context. An example of censorship of such a film is the following order of the New York Motion Picture Division for a feature, the name of which the division withheld:

Delete views of girl lying on dungeon floor with her breasts exposed. 98 feet.

In scene in which woman expresses erotic interest in girl as latter lies nude before her, eliminate view of woman caressing girl's leg. 9 feet.

In sequence which follows of woman removing her own blouse and pants, delete all views of her with breasts and buttocks exposed. 37 feet.

In scene of girl injecting herself with drugs, delete all views of her with breasts exposed. 147 feet.

In scene in which girl is tortured while hanging by hands, eliminate all views of her with breast exposed. 39 feet.

The director of the division believed that his agency was powerless to censor sadism except where it was connected with nudity.

Eroticism without Nudity. After nudity, eroticism alone probably accounts for the greatest number of censorship orders made by licensing boards today. A few years ago, when nudity was all but absent from the screen and when censors still widely applied an "immorality" standard— that is, when they still censored so-called thematic obscenity—plain eroticism probably accounted for most censorship orders. Today, censorial objections to erotica without nudity are confined almost entirely to physical familiarities, dances or other bodily movements, and dialogue.

Generally speaking, there has been a great relaxation of restrictions on the showing of physical contact between the sexes. At one time, not long ago, all censor boards cut any scene of a man and woman in bed together. Now, as the Detroit Licensing Bureau expresses it, "it all depends on how the scene is handled." On the one hand, most boards are reluctant to approve fondling of breasts or caressing of thighs or buttocks. The Maryland board cut a scene from *Passionate Demons* "in which a man ran his hand up a woman's leg while she rested her leg on his." On the other hand, Detroit censors claim that a familiarity like "a man swatting his wife on the rear" would be approved if it were "done as a joke."

As one might expect, it is the representation of intercourse that causes the greatest censorial consternation. Though suggested intercourse off-screen has been allowed almost since the beginning of motion pictures, suggested intercourse before the camera meets with objections. According to Detroit censors, "if a man and woman are beneath blankets and it is apparent what they are doing, even if there is no nudity at all, we will cut it." Thus the Danish film *A Stranger Knocks* was a trial for most boards. A serious work which received several awards and respectable reviews, the film appeared almost diabolically contrived to embarrass movie censorship. With no nudity, intercourse was portrayed in two scenes, the second of which—perhaps the most explicit shown in this country until that time—was also undeniably the dramatic climax of the film. The movie was originally censored by most boards, but was eventually released intact in many areas after New York lost an appeal of its censorship order before the United States Supreme Court.[16] Deletions ordered in the film by the Maryland board appear below.

Reel 3A—In beach sequence between man and Vibacka eliminate all views from a point where he places his hand on her bare knee down to and including fadeout of sequence.

This will include all views of his caressing her bare knee and thigh, views of his body over hers and views of her erotic facial reflexes.

Reel 4B—Eliminate all views revealing act of sexual intimacy between man and Vibacka, while on couch, from point where she is seen straddling his body, down to point at which time she notices scar on his arm.

Short of a court ruling to the contrary on the merits, it seems likely that boards of censors will continue to try to cut scenes of intercourse, regardless of the artistic merits of the film.

Extremes in erotic dances, usually of the bump and grind sort, or what the director of the New York Motion Picture Division referred to as "unilateral coitus," are normally cut by all boards. The New York board, however, made exceptions for foreign or exotic dances performed in their cultural context. Other movements of the female body not connected with dancing are sometimes the object of censorship, as in the case of the Kansas board's objections to "the extreme bobbling of nearly bare breasts of the billboard girl [Anita Ekberg] as she runs" in *Boccaccio 70*.[17] This particular order was later rescinded, after the distributor threatened to take the issue to court. A more typical instance of censorship of female bodily movements is found in a New York order involving a foreign film whose name the Motion Picture Division withheld.

In dance sequence delete all obscene and pelvic movements of unidentified performer. Include all front and rear views of her as she holds and straddles chair, as she removes garter belt, and as she assumes kneeling position on floor.

Dialogue—excluding expletives and other specific words which will be discussed in a category of their own—is another area in which censorship standards have been markedly relaxed, even in the last two or three years. It is also an area about which it is hard to generalize, since objections appear to vary considerably from board to board. Discussion of sex in clinical terms, *double entendres,* or bawdy talk may be cut on occasion. The Kansas and Virginia boards, each of which was made up of women, appeared to be the most squeamish. The former at first ordered—only later to rescind under pressure—that the line "They build temples to whores" and the phrase "not like animals in heat" be cut in *Boccaccio 70.*[18] In what was for them an unusual disclosure of a specific censorship order, Virginia censors told me of two deletions in *Black Like Me,* a film in which the white hero masquerades as a Negro in the South. According to a board member, deletions were ordered in a scene in which a white truckdriver and the protagonist "talk about the size of a man's organs," and a second scene in which there is a discussion with a Negro woman about the necessity of Negro women "putting out" when they go to work for white men. Here the board rescinded its order of the first cut after the distributor complained. It is probably with dialogue that the boards reveal the greatest idiosyncrasy today. For example, the Detroit Licensing Bureau, which has professed a general lack of concern with dialogue, ordered a cut in a scene of *The Pumpkin Eater* in which James Mason, in an unusual closeup shot which fills the entire screen with his mouth, says, "he can't even lay a broad without telling the world about it." As far as I know, this footage and dialogue have been passed by all other boards.

Today nearly all boards are more permissive with erotica if a film has artistic merit than if it is obviously of the so-called exploitation variety. The boards also tend to be more permissive when erotica is set in a particular cultural or historical context. For example, *Tom Jones,* adapted from the eighteenth-century Fielding novel, and perhaps the most ribald major film ever seen in this country, had few censorship problems.

Profanity and Indelicate Words and Phrases. According to the director of the New York Motion Picture Division, the decision in *Connection Co.* v. *Board of Regents* precluded mere words from being an element in obscenity. In that case, New York censors were overruled in their attempt to cut the word "shit," which was used several times in the film as slang for heroin. While the Motion Picture Division functioned, its director believed that for expletives or any other particular words to be censored as obscene they must be part of a description of an act which is obscene. This attitude was a more permissive one than most other boards of censors have been willing to take. The only "strong" words that are assured of getting by censors everywhere are "hell" and "damn." "God damn" met with objections in Kansas, and still does in Detroit, and sometimes in Chicago. The Ernst and Lorentz category "improper reference to women," which accounted for thirty-three deletions in 1928, is still a concern of some censor boards today, with "bitch," "whore," and "slut" the leading offenders. Detroit has allowed "whore" in films limited to art theatre exhibition. But Kansas cut the reference as a matter of policy, and ordered the word removed from even the adaptation of Eugene O'Neill's *Long Day's Journey into Night.* Generally speaking, the Kansas board seemed the strictest in objections to particular words or phrases. It cut "bitch" and "bastards" from *The Caretakers,* and "tell him to scratch my ass" and "no bastard insults me" from *Viridiana.* The Detroit Licensing Bureau and the Chicago Film Review Section appear to be somewhat more flexible, often taking the context of the word or phrase into account. The Chicago censors, for example, pointed with a certain pride to the fact that they did not object to "bastard" in *Becket* because it was used in its "historical sense." The Maryland board has maintained that particular words are no longer censored at all.

There was a time, perhaps not more than a dozen years ago, when not a single one of the questionable words or phrases mentioned in the preceding paragraphs, including "hell" and "damn," could be heard from the screen. And, in fact, relaxation would seem marked even since 1959, when the Chicago police censors unsuccessfully tried to cut the words "rape" and "contraceptive" used in a courtroom scene in *Anatomy of a Murder.*[19] The occasional indifference to the context of censored words that is indicated by rulings like that of the Kansas board in the Eugene O'Neill film appears to be one of the few residual habits of the *Mutual Film* era. Even so, the entire matter of expletives can rank as no more than a trivial aspect of movie censorship, or of film production, for that matter. They are rarely, if ever, central to the communication of ideas. In fact, it is believed that some film proprietors, aware of the objections of certain boards, use expletives— which are almost as easily inserted as they are deleted—deliberately in order to make "concessions" to the boards.

Sex Education. Films of an informational nature on sex account for only a very small fraction of censorial action or concern. One reason for this is that, until now at least, such films have been few in number. Another is that exhibitors have often restricted their showing to adults. Yet the matter is a potentially explosive one because of the absence of classification in most licensing jurisdictions, and because of the films' unquestioned traffic in ideas. The dilemma is illustrated by an unusual statement of the Maryland Board of Censors explaining its reluctant approval of *The Wondrous World of Birth,* a short color film showing the delivery of a child by natural process and by Caesarean section.

. . . The Birth of a child is a mysterious and wonderful process, and even though the detailed motion picture study of this procedure necessarily involves intimate exposure of the human body, the Board could not classify these scenes as obscene. Since obscenity, and not bad taste or vulgarity, is the only ground on which the Board may refuse to license a motion picture, this film has been licensed.

The Board, however, has the gravest reservations concerning the exhibition of this motion picture to the public at large, and especially to persons of tender years. The proper forum for such an exhibition, in the Board's opinion, would be in classes of Biology and kindred subjects in the schools, or under similar proper supervision. We do not, however, have the authority to so limit exhibition of any film. . . .

The Board is greatly disturbed by the fact that films of this nature have in the past been exhibited in drive-in theatres and other theatres catering to the juvenile trade. It is our feeling that an appeal has been made in the past to the prurient interest of the young people of this State, under the guise of educational or instructional films. In some cases the exhibition of films of this nature has been accompanied by sales in the theatre of books purporting to deal with sex hygiene and instructions, aimed at the teenage citizen. . . .[20]

With fingers unmistakably crossed, most censors are reluctant to say how such films would be treated should they become more common. Two boards, however, have been outspoken in their attitude toward such films. For Virginia censors, birth scenes were "for medical students, not for general entertainment." Kansas ordered cuts in a birth scene that had considerable gore and in another scene which showed the ravages of venereal disease, though these orders were later rescinded on advice from the state attorney general's office. The distributor is said to have removed the venereal disease scene voluntarily. The film, not named, was, in the view of the board chairman, "a good instructional film of the kind that might be shown to servicemen, etc., but not the kind for a general audience in Kansas."

Shocking and Offensive Material. Films of excessive violence and brutality, like those of sex education, account for a very small percentage of censorial orders today. This is due more to a lack of statutory censorship authority, though, than to a want of such films. Of the four states and three major cities censoring films in 1965, only in Chicago were censors equipped by law to deal with extremes of brutality or violence. The city's ordinance, however, proscribes only the portrayal of the "hanging, lynching, or burning of a human being." The Milwaukee Motion Picture Commission generally objects to "prolonged and excessively gruesome torture or death scenes." The commission, without official status, uses certain provisions of the Motion Picture Production Code as its guide.

Most censorship of violence is aimed at representation having a sexual connotation. The classic example of recent years involved the vivid, ninety-second rape scene in the widely acclaimed Swedish film *The Virgin Spring.* Several boards censored the scene, though it was obviously designed more to revolt than to stimulate erotically. Similarly, another shocking but far less explicit rape scene in *Two Women* was cut by some boards. The same scene and film were approved by the Maryland board which censored *The Virgin Spring.* The board attempted to distinguish between the two films, terming the scene in *Two Women* less overt, with "concentration on facial expression."

Censorship of violence or brutality unconnected with sex is unusual. One such case was Kansas' objections to *Blood Feast,* a film which included the drawing and quartering of a man among its highlights. The board ordered the following cuts:

Reel 2B—Scenes of amputation of Bea Miller's thumbs and arm.

Reel 3A—Scenes of horses pulling severed leg of John Miller.

Reel 3B—Scene of girl after teetering rock falls on her.

Representation of excretion or of the excretory processes is also objected to by most boards. However, exceptions are sometimes made when the subjects are babies or very young children.

Use of Narcotics. Portrayal of drug traffic or addiction is the subject of some determined but quantitatively insignificant censorship. A film which is detailed in its portrayal of addiction, or which appears to make addiction attractive, is likely to have censorship difficulties in Maryland, Detroit, and Milwaukee. In Maryland, local police, and occasionally federal narcotics officials, may be asked to sit in on the review of such films. The same was true in Virginia. The Maryland board, which lost an attempt to censor the original "addiction film," *The Man with the Golden Arm,* in 1956,[21] cut several scenes from *The Narcotics Story* after consulting local and federal officials. The film had shown how drug-yielding plants were grown, the extraction and preparation of drugs, and how injections were administered. Detroit appears to be somewhat less restrictive and, as in the case of female nudity, has in effect "drawn a line." The Licensing Bureau has allowed any aspect of drug traffic or addiction to be shown except "the needle entering the arm." The Kansas board, which had been active in most of the other areas of censorship, professed no interest in "addiction films."

Unflattering or Unconventional Depiction of Religion, Race, or Race Relations. Race and religion are two areas of censorship in which there is not only far less activity today than in the past, but also far less in relation to other censorship concerns. Objections today usually involve the association of race or religion with sex in some way. In these instances it appears that the proscribed material would not have been censored for its erotic content alone.

The two Chicago censorship boards are alone among the major licensing systems studied in having statutory authorization to censor because of the treatment of religion. The Chicago ordinance proscribes films exposing religion to "contempt, derision, or obloquy," but censorial objections under it appear to be infrequent and limited. One instance of such censorship was the Film Review Section's refusal of a permit to *Joan of the Angels* because it was thought the film suggested "the involvement of nuns in sex." This decision was never appealed to the Motion Picture Appeal Board. But since the board has had a reputation for overruling the Review Section, it is unlikely that many of the Review Section's censorship orders based on treatment of religion would be upheld on appeal.

Censorship of the treatment of race or race relations seems to be more common than that involving religion. There appear to be three major concerns in such censorship: the possibility of incitement to violence or riot; offensiveness to the Negro group image; and the possibility of undermining institutions of segregation. Most race or race-relations censorship in the past was apparently based on the third consideration. Today such censorship appears to be more concerned with the first and second, though of course the protection of segregated institutions (and the Negro group image, for that matter) can often be rationalized in terms of preventing incitement to violence. The Virginia board, which ordered dialogue cuts in *Black Like Me,* admitted occasionally censoring scenes which "might have a bad effect on Negroes." The Maryland board was recently concerned about a film showing Negroes as victims of racial violence. Though members of the board believed the film would present no problem if a Negro viewer sat through to the end, which depicted "retribution," they thought there might be danger if the Negro viewer walked out in the middle! The board's solution was to invite representatives of the NAACP and CORE to view the film. When members of these groups raised no objections, the film was licensed. Since release of the film in the state came shortly after racial demonstrations in Cambridge, it is not clear whether the board would manifest so jittery a concern with the treatment of race or race relations in calmer times.

The Milwaukee Motion Picture Commission has regularly objected to the word "nigger," and to any other material it believes will "cast aspersions" or "stir ill-feeling." In Chicago the six women, including one Negro, who make up the Film Review Section are described by their supervisor as being "very touchy on race." They have been known to give "adults only" classification to films they feared might incite youth in the city's Negro areas. Yet use of the word "nigger" has been approved by the Review Section and by its Negro member. The Detroit Licensing Bureau has appeared to be unconcerned with the treatment of race or race relations. The same had been true of the New York and Kansas boards.

With the chances of racial violence greater now than in the past, it is likely that censor boards, or at least some censor boards, will continue to look closely at the portrayal of race and race relations. This may sometimes afford opportunity for censorship that is based on the desire to preserve segregated institutions or to avoid an offense to a group image. Nonetheless, it is clear that censorship based expressly on a segregationist view of race relations is now almost entirely a thing of the past.

Classification—A Middle Ground

Because it only prevents exhibition to children or adolescents, classification is often considered a kind of middle ground between general censorship and no censorship at all. For this reason it appears to be receiving increasing attention from legislatures (including those in jurisdictions where general censorship has been invalidated), censors, and not a few civil libertarians. The Dallas Motion Picture Classification Board, which was set up after the *Freedman* decision, has been the prototype of municipal licensing limited to classification. However, among the major general-licensing systems examined here, only those of Chicago and Milwaukee classify or have classified films. Censors on boards not authorized to classify have found themselves in the quandary of being under increasing pressure to protect children, and at the same time being constitutionally forbidden to use children as a frame of reference for general censorship. This embarrassment has been met in part by development of substitutes for classification. Detroit, for example, has limited certain films to "art theatres" which have no children's admission. The Licensing Bureau's permits for films shown at these theatres have been conditional, requiring that the film must be resubmitted if it is later scheduled for general exhibition. Board members in Virginia occasionally put pressure on exhibitors to advertise particular films as "for adults only." However, this kind of advertisement often has little to do with actually limiting the audience to adults, since many exhibitors who proffer such notice make no attempt to enforce it. In such cases, the advertisement is widely thought to be one *for* a youthful audience.

There seems to be little doubt that censors would be less restrictive in general censorship were they also equipped to classify films. The director of New York's Motion Picture Division, for example, would have favored dropping general censorship altogether had his agency been authorized to classify films. Though few have been ready to say so publicly, censors on several other boards have appeared willing to actually substitute classification for general licensing.

An immediate problem in classification is the lack of precision in standards to be used. Censors are considerably less articulate about classifying films than they are about censoring them. They can express certain abstract substantive considerations, but these are usually no more informative than their abstract descriptions of censorable obscenity. According to Sgt. Robert Murphy, head of the Chicago Film Review Section, films are given "adults only" permits when children would tend to misunderstand or misinterpret the film. This standard is apparently not confined to erotica, since the Film Review Section on at least one occasion has given a restricted permit to a film which was feared might have an adverse effect on Negro youth. According to Dr. Henry Rago of the city's Motion Picture Appeal Board, films classified have been those that would tend to be emotionally disturbing or "precipitous of latent impulses toward antisocial conduct." On the other hand, Marvin Aspen, assistant city corporation counsel and legal counsel for the Appeal Board, maintained that classification criteria are the same as those for obscenity, except that a more restrictive measure is used.

In Milwaukee, the Motion Picture Commission, which has been classifying films since 1956, has had three categories of ratings—"general audience," "mature entertainment," and "adults only"—in addition to the "recommended not be shown." Technically the commission's decisions have been only advisory, but an exhibitor is expected to observe an "adults only" rating as much as he would the "recommended not be shown" decision, and he is usually under the same informal extralegal pressures to do so. "General audience" means that the film will "harm no one." "Mature entertainment" is intended merely to caution parents that the film "may not be understood by children." The "adults only" rating is given when a film has "sex scenes, sex dialogue, or scanty clothing," and signifies that the film is unsuitable for persons under eighteen.

Movies that received the commission's "adults only" classification in recent years included a number of foreign and art films like *Blow Up, Ulysses, A Man and a Woman, The Pawnbroker,* and *Dear John,* all of which received some degree of critical acclaim; "nudie" films like *Not Tonight, Henry;* general exploitation films like *The Garbage Man, Orgy at Lil's Place, Malamondo,* and *Shock Corridor;* and general circulation films of foreign and American origin like *Alfie, 8½, The Trip, Mondo Cane, The Memoirs of Fanny Hill, Tom Jones, The Group,* and *Who's Afraid of Virginia Woolf?* A few of these "adults only" films may also have carried cuts to save them from the "recommended not be shown" category. In contrast, films given "recommended not be shown" ratings in recent years have been, with few exceptions, nudist films like *Paradiseo* and *Nature's Sweethearts*, "nudie" films like *Promises! Promises!* and *Mr. Peter's Pets*, or sado-masochistic features.

The Dallas classification board has been authorized to rule a film unsuitable for persons under sixteen if it portrays "nudity beyond the customary limits of candor in the community, or sexual promiscuity or extramarital or abnormal sexual relations in such a manner as . . . to appeal to their [the young person's] prurient interest." Prurient interest is appealed to if the calculated or dominant effect of the film "on young persons is substantially to arouse sexual desire."[22] With the creation of the board, the city's exhibitors have themselves voluntarily classified an increasing number of films. Many, though not all, of these films have been of the exploitation variety, particularly "nudies." The board has classified others, including some major American productions, over the objections of exhibitors—*The Sandpiper, The Amorous Adventures of Moll Flanders, The World of Suzie Wong, Wild Angels,* and *Sadist!,* for example.

Quantitative Aspects

Measuring the amount of censorship of the major licensing boards is difficult for two reasons. First, board files are not open to public inspection. Second, though most boards compile annual totals of various sorts, their interest in such statistical intelligence is limited, and the quantitative records they do keep are often inconsistent and seldom systematic. The best available sources of information on the amount of censorship, then, are the very general totals that appear in annual board reports. Only the state boards, however, file public annual reports. In various forms these reports usually provide totals for films examined, those approved without changes, those approved with changes, and those rejected. These figures usually are not broken down.

In Table 4, annual figures are compiled for each of the state boards for the five-year period 1960–1964. A word of caution is necessary, however. The figures indicate nothing about the character or the degree of censorship in the films that were censored. Another variable not reflected is the changing content of movies, with nudity, eroticism, and sadistic violence having increased markedly in the last four or five years. These two hidden factors —the qualitative aspect of censorship and the changing content of films— impair the usefulness of the figures for comparative purposes.

Yet, having said this, several general observations are possible. First, the number of films involved in censorship of some kind—measured either by

TABLE 4   *Films Examined and Films Censored by Four State Boards of Censors, 1960–1964[a]*

Fiscal year ending	Licensed without changes	Licensed with changes	License denied	Total examined	Total censored	Per cent censored
		Kansas				
June 30,						
1960	455	15[b]	8	478	23	4.8
1961	449	9[b]	6	464	15	3.2
1962	454	4[b]	1	459	5	1.1
1963	427	43	4	474	47	9.9
1964	431	19	0	450	19	4.2
	2,216	90	19	2,325	109	4.7
		Maryland				
June 30,						
1960	1,008	17	0	1,025	17	1.7
1961	1,122	13	2	1,137	15	1.3
1962	1,136	40	3	1,179	43	3.6
1963	1,255	45	13	1,313	58	4.4
1964	1,202	34	9	1,245	43	3.5
	5,723	149	27	5,899	176	2.9
		New York				
March 31,						
1960	1,052	41	1	1,094	42	3.8
1961	1,134	28	1	1,163	29	2.5
1962	1,111	29	0	1,140	29	2.5
1963	1,152	22	3	1,177	25	2.1
1964	1,226	26	4	1,256	30	2.4
	5,675	146	9	5,830	155	2.7
		Virginia				
June 30,						
1960	433	14	4	451	18	4.0
1961	444	17	4	465	21	4.5
1962	458	12	2	472	14	3.1
1963	455	30	12	497	42	8.5
1964	463	21	8	492	29	5.9
	2,253	94	30	2,377	124	5.2

TABLE 4, *Continued*

Fiscal year ending	Licensed without changes	Licensed with changes	License denied	Total examined	Total censored	Per cent censored
All state boards						
1960	2,948	87	13	3,048	100	3.28
1961	3,149	67	13	3,229	80	2.48
1962	3,159	85	6	3,250	91	2.80
1963	3,289	140	32	3,461	172	4.97
1964	3,322	100	21	3,443	121	3.51
	15,867	479	85	16,431	564	3.41

Table is based upon public annual reports of the censorship boards of the states of Kansas, Maryland, New York, and Virginia.

ᵃ Figures for each of the boards include shorts—cartoons, serials, short subjects—as well as features. Features accounted for 60–70 per cent of the films examined and about 95–100 per cent of the censorship orders. New York was the only one of the four states in which a separate analysis was made for shorts and features. In the 1960–1964 period, the Motion Picture Division ordered cuts in four shorts and 142 features.

ᵇ The totals represent adjusted figures. In the Board of Review's record-keeping for this category in 1960, 1961, and 1962, figures for the originally examined films were not separated from figures for duplicate prints. Unfortunately, then, the board had no record of the number of separate motion pictures approved with cuts during these years. The board's combined totals for each of the three years were 79, 53, and 23, respectively. These figures were adjusted to those in the table by multiplying each of them by the percentage of the total prints approved (that is, original and duplicate) that were original prints in each of the respective years. This adjustment may slightly underestimate the number of films approved with cuts, since the most widely circulating films—that is, the ones for which the most duplicate prints are submitted—were generally the films least likely to have censorship troubles.

deletions or by outright rejection—is small, slightly more than 3.5 per cent for the five-year period. Films rejected outright amount to only 0.5 per cent of those examined.

Second, it is probable that censorship, at least as measured by the percentage of films involved, has declined in recent years, and particularly since the *Miracle* case in 1952. For example, in a twenty-year period preceding that decision, the New York Motion Picture Division examined 33,084 films and approved 2,545 with changes, a percentage of 7.69, compared with 5,675 films examined and 146 approved with changes, or a percentage of 2.57, in the 1960–1964 period.[23] As indicated in Table 5, a similar contrast with the 1960–1964 period is revealed in the somewhat more detailed figures available for the five-year period 1943–1947.

TABLE 5 *Number of Films Censored by the New York State Motion Picture Division, 1943–1947 and 1960–1964*

	1943–1947[a]	1960–1964[b]
Films examined	8,024	5,830
Licensed without changes	7,487	5,675
Licensed with changes	510	146
Per cent	*6.36*	*2.56*
License denied	27	9
Per cent	*0.34*	*0.16*
Total censored	537	155
Per cent	*6.69*	*2.73*

[a] Figures are derived from a table in Samuel Beckoff, "An Inquiry into the Operative Principles Applicable to Licensing Motion Pictures in New York State," unpublished doctoral dissertation, New York University, 1959, p. 78.

[b] Figures derived from annual reports of the New York State Motion Picture Division.

On the other hand, figures available for the Virginia board for the thirty-six-year period 1922–1958 show a censorship percentage comparable to the percentage in the 1960–1964 period. In the earlier period the board examined 49,592 films, approved 2,308 with changes, a percentage of 4.65, and rejected 83, a percentage of 0.17.[24]

Third, though no year-to-year trends are apparent in the five-year 1960–1964 period, the fiscal year 1963 saw a marked increase in the number of films censored by three of the four boards. This increase may be accounted for, at least in part, by the fact that the nudity, nudist, and "nudie" vogue, which had been developing for some time, appeared to reach a new peak in the 1962–1963 release period.

Comparisons between and among individual boards are difficult for several reasons and, if made only on the basis of the figures in Table 4, may be misleading. First, some boards review more films than others. Of the 1,000–1,300 films released in the United States in any given year, probably all but fifty or fewer were examined by the New York Division of Motion Pictures. In contrast, the Kansas and Virginia boards saw far fewer films, largely because of marketing considerations, though perhaps censorship itself cannot be ruled out entirely as a factor. In the year ending March 31, 1964, for example, the New York board examined 909 features, of which 671 were foreign-made. The great majority of these foreign films were intended mainly for exhibition among foreign-language groups. Most of them were probably not shown outside of New York and perhaps two or three other large cities. On the other hand, it is unlikely that the Kansas board dealt with any of these films. In fact, Kansas and Virginia are not considered particularly inviting markets for even the more general foreign or art films.

Second, two boards which view a film may not, in fact, see the same film, since it is not uncommon for more than one version of a film to be in circulation. Some films are produced in "hot" and "cool" versions (and are so designated, without benefit of euphemism, on the cans in which the reels are shipped). A distributor who was turned down on a "hot" version in New York, for instance, may have submitted only the "cool" version to Virginia. Conversely, some distributors, having had a "cool" version licensed by New York, might submit the "hot" version to another board, maintaining that the film had been approved by New York. For these reasons it is possible that a film may be licensed by one board and censored by another without the two boards having used different measures. Another source of differential censorship impeding comparisons among the boards is the possibility that a film censored by one board may be shipped to another board in its censored state.

Third, there may be an element of anticipatory self-censorship in a distributor's failure to submit a film to a particular board. In the distributor's calculations, the area market prospects of a questionable film must be weighed against the chances of censorship and the costs in time and money of resisting a censorship order. For example, a distributor may have decided that since foreign and art films do not have a large market in Kansas, it was not worth submitting a film of this kind at all if it was a particularly controversial one. As a result of this kind of reasoning, some boards may not even see certain films that might present censorship questions.

Finally, not all films are submitted to all boards at the same time. Because of marketing imperatives, the New York Motion Picture Division was apt to receive films several months to even a year or more in advance of their submission to boards in some other areas. In addition, there was a three-month difference in the fiscal (and record-keeping) year between New York and other state boards.

The number of films involved in censorship is not by itself, then, a sound base for comparisons among state boards.

Though the city censor boards—Chicago, Detroit, and Milwaukee—have also compiled certain statistics, they tend to be even less systematic about it than the state boards. They also lack a tradition of making annual public reports. Quantitative analysis of their work is further obstructed by the fact that all three have practiced some form of classification. This is a complicating factor, because for some films an "adults only" rating is a substitute for deletions, while for others it is accompanied by deletions in order to allow the film to escape outright rejection. In their compilations, the city censors usually do not take such variables as these into account.

In Detroit, the Licensing Bureau has kept records only by footage. In 1964 the bureau examined 4,800,000 feet of film ("approximately 500" films) and ordered deletions amounting to 45,600 feet, a percentage of 0.95. According to the bureau, the ratio of cut footage to total footage has remained fairly constant in the last few years. No figures are available on the number of films given permits restricted to art theatre exhibition, a form of licensing that functions as classification.

The Milwaukee Motion Picture Commission has made pre-exhibition examination of only 15 to 20 per cent of the films it has rated—those that its executive secretary believes might be difficult to label. The remainder are evaluated on the basis of information obtained about them from the trade press, though only 40 to 50 per cent of these eventually play in the city. Those that do are viewed at the opening night performance. In the four-year 1963–1966 period, the commission rated 2,212 films by prior examination or "press review." (See Table 6.) Excluding those rated "adults only," there were 147, or 6.65 per cent of the 2,212, involved in censorship; seventy-four "recommended not be shown"; and seventy-three in which changes were required. With the "adults only" films included but subtracting those in which changes were also required, the commission was restrictive in the case of 420 films, or 19 per cent of those rated during the four-year period.

More than half of the films rated "recommended not be shown" or "adults only" in 1963–1966 were so rated on the basis of "press review." Though the general character of some films may be accurately assessed through information in advance advertisements and reviews, it is hard to see how any sensitive consideration can be given most films, for the various

TABLE 6   *Ratings of the Milwaukee Motion Picture Commission, 1963–1966*

	1963	1964	1965	1966	Total
Films examined	510	588	569	545	2,212
"General audience"	315	429	325	296	1,365
"Mature entertainment"	105	83	140	142	470
"Adults only"	62	53	97	91	303
"Recommended not be shown"	28	23	7	16	74
Number in which changes were made	7	20	21	25	73
Number "censored"ᵃ	35	43	28	41	147
Per cent "censored"	*6.9*	*7.3*	*4.9*	*7.5*	*6.65*

Table is based on figures obtained from Valentine Wells, executive secretary of the Milwaukee Motion Picture Commission.

ᵃ These figures include films "recommended not be shown" and those which received a less restricted rating after changes were made. The figures do not include films given "adults only" rating.

TABLE 7   *Number of Films Censored by the Chicago Film Review Section, 1964–1966*

	1964	1965	1966	Total	Per cent
Films examined	798	764	893	2,455	100
General permits	664	650	755	2,069	84.3
Adult permits without deletions	63	49	46	158	6.4
Adult permits after deletions	38	18	20	76	3.1
Rejected	33	47	72	152	6.2

Table is based on figures obtained from Sgt. Robert Murphy, head of the Film Review Section, and from Kenneth W. Sain, assistant corporation counsel.

ratings the commission has used, on the basis of anything but an actual examination of the film. Moreover, even though the commission may eventually examine films given advance ratings, a *restrictive* advance rating can affect the rental price and marketing arrangements for a film. On that account, the advance ratings may determine whether the distributor will find it profitable to have the film exhibited at all.

In Chicago, the Film Review Section examined 2,455 films in the three-year period 1964–1966 (see Table 7). Of these, 6.2 per cent were denied permits, and 3.1 per cent were given adult permits after deletions—a total censorship percentage of 9.3. When films given adult permits without deletions are included, then the Review Section was restrictive with 386 films, or 15.7 per cent of those examined. In the three years 1964–1966, appeals were taken to the Motion Picture Appeal Board on 152, or 39.4 per cent, of these restrictive rulings, most of them involving denial of permit. In the great majority of appeals, the Appeal Board modified or reversed the Review Section ruling, either by granting an adult permit (sometimes after deletions) in the case of films denied permits, or, in the case of an appeal of an adult permit, by granting a general permit. In the first two years following the *Freedman* decision, the Appeal Board upheld the Review Section's denial of permit in only twelve instances, all involving exploitation films. In all twelve cases, the films were found to be obscene by the Cook County Circuit Court.

6

Limits, Costs, Constituents, Personnel, and Customs Censorship

The Limits of Censorship

Censorship by Negotiation

Whether a film is censored or not, and how much so if it is, depends, of course, on how the censors judge its particular scenes, words, and so forth. But the extent of actual censorship is also determined in large measure by the film proprietor himself. In every instance of censorship, a film proprietor—usually a distributor—has a choice of accepting the restrictive order as given or contesting it. These decisions, made hundreds of times in a year, largely define the limits of movie censorship in the United States. The legal doctrine of prior censorship by which censors are confined today was itself the product of distributors' resistance. And, in turn, resistance today is partly the product of a favorably emerging legal doctrine.

The doctrine controls the censors at three levels. The most formal and exact of these is, of course, actual litigation resulting in specific court orders. Yet losses in court have become effective limits on the censors at two levels *outside* the courtroom, and have further removed censors from the "boundless sea" of the *Mutual Film* period. One of these informal levels is internal. The censors are self-restrained in the degree to which they themselves have assimilated the legal doctrine. This internalization is a "floor" under freedom of speech in motion pictures, and it is reflected in the development of several "unthinkable" areas of censorship, such as those involving political ideas or "sacrilegious" expression.

Between court orders and assimilation of the legal doctrine is an intermediate level of limitation that will be examined in this section. This third level of control is the *anticipation* of litigation and of the likelihood of an eventual defeat in court. The capacity of the legal doctrine to limit the censors at this level depends on the relative merits of the censorship order, and on the willingness of the distributor to seek a possible remedy in court. The effective check on the censors here is bureaucratic. Where a film proprietor shows signs of resisting a censorship order, an assistant attorney general or an assistant corporation counsel usually has, in effect, a veto over the licensing decision. This power is not infrequently exercised. The legal doctrine today is likely to induce caution in government counsel even where it has failed to do so in the censors. In effect, then, the legal department is both an ally and an adversary of the distributor. The relationship between the two can be characterized as a war of nerves. There is much probing by both sides, but in the great majority of cases the conflict is settled through compromise.

The bargaining usually takes place at a rescreening, with the distributor or his counsel or both present, along with the censors and government counsel. In New York, government counsel usually took part only in an appeal to the Board of Regents, which was the next step for a distributor not satisfied by negotiations at the rescreening. In Chicago, a distributor taking an appeal to the Motion Picture Appeal Board is formally invited to "present evidence" in support of his film to the board, the members of which have already viewed the film. In fact, this meeting functions less as an opportunity for the distributor to persuade the members of the board of the merits of the film, than as a chance for the board and its counsel to find out how far the distributor intends to go and what he will settle for. With some boards, the bargaining may often take place entirely on the telephone. And the Kansas board was known to have withdrawn censorship orders at least twice in three years, largely on the basis of letters written by a leading censorship attorney on behalf of his distributor-client.

For most boards the government counsel is technically only an advisor. Yet it is unlikely that any censor board today would ignore counsel's advice. In Detroit, the assistant corporation counsel has apparently taken complete charge at the rescreening. At that point "the matter is out of our hands," according to a member of the Licensing Bureau, and all later complaints that may be received from the public about the film are referred by the bureau to the corporation counsel's office.

Though the weight of a legal department's caution on censorship appears to be great, information on this influence is not easy to obtain, particularly since government counsel are not anxious to acknowledge their restraining role. In most instances their influence has probably been limited to particular deletions and censorship orders. Yet occasionally, their "advice" has been more sweeping and clearly of a policy-making nature, as in the case of reluctant censors persuaded to approve nudity in documentary films. In Chicago, the assistant corporation counsel who has advised the Motion Picture Appeal Board is said to have "talked with" the members of the Film

Review Section about the new doctrinal developments relating to nudity and obscenity. As a result of this meeting, the Review Section stopped rejecting run-of-the-mill nudist camp films.

Though government counsel can be expected to be formidable negotiators, they have, in recent years at least, been highly particular about letting matters go to the courts. According to a member of another board, any distributor who actually went so far as to file a suit against the Kansas board got "an automatic reversal because they're afraid to go to court." Indeed, in the view of Dr. Henry Rago of the Chicago Appeal Board, "We must ask ourselves repeatedly, 'is this really the film we want to argue about with Justice Brennan?' " On each of the relatively few films denied license since its creation in 1962, the Appeal Board appeared either to be intelligently preparing for this sort of eventuality or else trying hard to impress the distributor with its own determination—or perhaps both. In these cases the board issued "Final Rulings," ranging between ten and fifteen pages. These are probably the most elaborate and legally sophisticated movie censorship orders ever written; in fact, except for the absence of cited authority, they are barely distinguishable from court pleadings. Such concern for the law and for building a legal position would have been unimaginable even as recently as the early 1960's. The plight of the censors today, in the face of a determined distributor, is summed up in the words of one censor who, on this point at least, preferred to remain anonymous: "They [the distributors] have taken nearly all our law away, and if they wanted to, they could probably force us into a corner completely."

Incidence of Resistance

Under these circumstances, a study of free speech in the film medium must turn to questions of how often and under what conditions distributors do resist censorship orders. Except in the case of Chicago, where the administrative appeal process is relatively formal, reliable data are not available. Estimates made by the censors themselves, however, provide some idea of the incidence of the negotiation and bargaining which limits censorship today.

In Maryland before the *Freedman* decision there were between five and ten rescreenings a year, and the board was taken to court on the average of slightly less than once a year. In Virginia, a member of the state attorney general's office sat in on about twelve rescreenings a year. In 1964 the board was taken to court for the first time in several years. During the last few years that the New York Motion Picture Division was functioning, distributors asked for rescreening on nearly every censorship order—the earlier rate had been about 50 per cent. In 1964, four appeals were taken to the Board of Regents, and in two of them the division's order was overturned. Over the years, the Regents upheld the division in approximately 90 per cent of the appeals. The Regents themselves were taken into court on censorship orders on the average of once a year in the 1960's. In Kansas, where the first rescreening was merely a matter of the board alone viewing the film a second time, the board was asked to rescreen on almost every censorship order. On the other hand, second rescreenings, which resulted from the distributor routinely threatening to sue the board, occurred about six times a year. The distributor's next step, the actual filing of a suit, occurred on the average of twice a year, but there had been no trial on a censorship order since the *Holmby Productions* v. *Vaughn* in 1955.

The Detroit Licensing Bureau has been involved in about ten rescreenings a year, and reversed by the corporation counsel's office about 20 per cent of the time. Only once in the last twelve years has a film proprietor gone to court. The Milwaukee Motion Picture Commission has held a rescreening whenever it has been asked to do so, but the commission's executive secretary was not able to recall a single instance in which the commission reversed itself completely, though it has apparently compromised from time to time. How often local exhibitors ignore a commission recommendation is not known, though the executive secretary has maintained that this "almost never happens." When it has, however, each side, for reasons of its own, has been anxious not to have it publicized. An *ad hoc* "liaison committee" of film proprietors and commission members has been set up several times to settle differences. In 1963 an obscenity complaint was actually filed against an exhibitor who showed the "hot" version of *Not Tonight, Henry,* after the commission had approved the "cool" one. The matter was eventually settled informally.

In the three years 1964–1966, distributors went to the Chicago Motion Picture Appeal Board in about 40 per cent of the cases in which a film had been rejected or ordered cut by the Film Review Section. A few of these appeals were eventually dropped by the distributors, but in the vast majority of the others the board issued a more liberal ruling than the Review Section, and reversed that body completely in about 50 per cent.

Based on the foregoing data, the rough ratios of distributor resistance to censorship orders at the administrative level were as follows: Kansas, one to one (first rescreening), and one to three (second rescreening); Maryland, one to five; New York, one to one (rescreening) and one to seven (appeal to the Regents); Virginia, one to three; Chicago, two to five. The ratios, of course, do not reflect distributor resistance limited to telephone calls or letters, and use of the telephone is relatively common. The incidence of administrative appeal—that is, formal or informal negotiation—was in marked contrast to that of judicial review. In the five-year 1960–1964 pre-*Freedman* period, state censor boards appear to have been taken to court and trial had in eight instances on the merits of censorship orders: Maryland, four; New York, three; and Virginia, one. In all, 535 censorship orders were issued by the four boards during that period.

Factors in Resistance

Factors affecting a distributor's decision whether or not to resist or appeal a censorship order are diverse. Some involve matters entirely under the distributor's control, while others do not. It comes as no surprise that neither the artistic integrity of the film itself, nor the principle of freedom of speech, is normally decisive. Though resistance to censorship is frequently rationalized in terms of a concern for free speech, it is seldom motivated by it. No doubt some distributors are moved philosophically, and others, as one experienced litigant put it, just plainly object to being "put upon." Nevertheless, it is not unfair to say that the average distributor has little interest in the civil liberties dimension of his situation, except to the extent that he can use the law to protect and enlarge his own enterprise. This attitude has marked many members of the film industry over the years, and today, as in years past, it is a major ally of censorship.

Though a favorable position on the merits of a censorship order is seldom overlooked, the main factors influencing resistance appear to be economic. Sometimes these may overlap with the preservation of artistic integrity. This is likely to be the case with a small group of movies known as art films, whose fortunes depend upon reception by a relatively discriminating and intelligent audience. With such films, distributor resistance may be vigorous if censorship threatens to ruin a scene or a major point in the film. It is also censorship of this sort of film—*The Virgin Spring, The Lovers, The Sky Above and the Mud Below, The Silence, Lady Chatterley's Lover, Woman in the Dunes,* for example—that has given the censors some of their worst publicity in recent years.

Another type of film in which deletions are likely to affect economic prospects in a major way is the so-called exploitation feature. Here the very excesses of nudity or eroticism ordered cut may be the film's only box office strengths. In such cases, distributor resistance is likely if it appears that the film will have better-than-average commercial possibilities were the deletions to be restored.

Yet, all things considered, preserving the inviolability of a film does not rank high in motivating a distributor to resist censorship. Perhaps this is nowhere better illustrated than in those instances where a film is submitted in two versions, a "hot" one—with greater nudity, eroticism, or violence—which has been made for European distribution and for the American market wherever the distributor can get away with it, and a "cool" one for use where objections are made to the former. Though the practice is largely confined to exploitation films, similar tactics have been used on occasion by major American companies. For example, the distributor of *Irma la Douce,* a film aimed at general distribution in the United States, is said to have submitted an alternate ending of 500 feet (about five and a half minutes) to one city censor board. The company apparently feared that the prostitute-heroine's parturition in the sacristy of a Roman Catholic Church, right after her marriage ceremony, might prevent this comedy from receiving a "general audience" permit.

The *Irma la Douce* incident also reflects the willingness of most major American distributing companies to suffer censorship if it is the only way to escape an "adults only" rating. It is true that major American productions are not often involved in censorship, but where they are, their distributors —who are those usually having the greatest resources with which to fight censorship—have a well-deserved reputation among the censors for "cooperation." For these companies, classification works a far greater economic burden than censorship. An "adults only" permit may prevent a film from moving into neighborhood theatres following a successful downtown run, and may decrease its chances of playing at some later date as one half of a double bill.

A major factor in determining resistance is the nature of the film market at stake. All large markets are necessarily important, but the one represented by New York is crucial, and while that state's Motion Picture Division was active, this fact made it the most powerful licensing body in the country. New York City exhibition is vital not only for the receipts it represents, but also for the national trade advertisement it carries. Foreign or art films, particularly, depend on favorable New York reviews for any chance of wide national distribution. Probably only distributors of cheap "nudie" films, which do not depend so heavily on intra-industry advertisement and the New York "showcase" effect, can afford to lose out on New York exhibition.

Where censorship was involved, New York could be "won" by going along with a censorship order, however, as well as by resisting it. Both alternatives had their risks. In the first, the required changes might ultimately damage the film at the box office. In the second, there were the costs and the delay of administrative or judicial appeal, as well as the less-than-100 per cent chance of prevailing (discounted somewhat, perhaps, by the advertising effect of the publicity that usually accompanied any censorship appeal to the Board of Regents or to the courts). The New York marketing imperatives were probably a major reason why the Motion Picture Division rejected so few films outright. (See Table 4, p. 106.) Except in the case of exploitation films, an outright rejection by the division—which had its own reasons for wanting to stay out of court—in effect forced the distributor to take a major loss or to make an appeal.

Similar marketing imperatives hold to a lesser degree for cities like Chicago and Milwaukee which are gateways to regional and subregional markets. How much a small midwestern exhibitor will bid for a film, and, in fact, whether he will bid at all, depend in large measure on how well the film ran in the nearby big city. A distributor's chances of obtaining small-town or suburban rentals in a regional market are all but wiped out if a film does not play in the regional center. Away from the regional centers, however, the advertising effect of exhibition is less important, and a distributor can base his prospective gain or loss entirely on the basis of anticipated receipts from the area over which the licensing board has jurisdiction. For example, a highly successful distributor of foreign and art films maintained that in the case of Kansas, which lacks any important "showcase" center, the farthest he would probably go in resisting a censorship order would be to "have Ephraim London [the censorship attorney] write them a letter."

A distributor who decides to resist a censorship order knows that he will have to bear two costs: the immediate expense of representation during an appeal, and the expense of delay—that is, of having capital in the film tied up for weeks, months, or perhaps even years. These two potential costs afford much of whatever leverage the censors have in bargaining with distributors today. Litigation costs, which are likely to run to several thousand dollars in carrying a case to the appellate level, may be prohibitive for the small distributor. For example, in foreign or art film distribution, where small distributors abound, fully 80 to 90 per cent of all foreign films have receipts of less than $50,000. At the same time, the cost of "launching" such films—the cost of prints and promotion—normally ranges between $30,000 and $40,000. These economics leave little room for added expenses. On the other hand, the larger distributor, who deals with films made on large budgets, has a different problem. He has had to invest heavily in purchasing the rights to the film and in undertaking the kind of large-scale promotion campaign usually necessary to realize a profit. In his case the delay involved in appeal ties up a large amount of capital which could be used productively elsewhere, and on which the interest alone would often exceed the litigation costs of most censorship appeals. It is hardly surprising, then, that most censorship litigation has been carried on by middle-sized distributors (often fresh from a box office success with another film), handling a relatively inexpensive film.

Censor Leverage and the Freedman *Doctrine*

Given the economics of distribution, the censors have been accused of applying a kind of double standard against the small distributor, who is usually without great resources, and of intentionally dragging out the licensing process in the case of the larger distributor. There is little doubt that the censors have from time to time been guilty of both practices. One of the members of the Virginia board admitted to me that the board could and did "get away with much more against 'fly-by-nights,' " who often can't afford a lawyer or involvement in litigation. Likewise, the Maryland board, according to its executive secretary, has been more likely to "stick to its guns" when it knew the distributor was without resources. The fact that many, if not most, of the distributors in this category handle "nudies" and other exploitation films, turned out for what the trade sometimes calls "hit and run" profit, has convinced many censors that all is fair against these proprietors.

It is impossible to know how often or to what extent the censors have deliberately procrastinated on films they found objectionable. Every board has been accused of the practice by disgruntled distributors. At the time I interviewed members of the Virginia board, they were concerned with "bed scenes" in *The Christine Keeler Story* and had resolved to "do something about the film." At that point, they had had the movie in their offices for three weeks. One of the members admitted that they "could use the excuse that a board member was ill." This was, in fact, the case, though it had not always been the practice for all three members of the board to view every film.

Delay can be a formidable censorial weapon at any time, but it has provided especially critical leverage when a film was scheduled for an immediate or "rush" booking and the censors knew this. Likewise, delay that prevents a film from opening during the last two weeks of December or during the Easter week, by far the most profitable periods of the year in movie exhibition, can be especially costly, particularly in the case of a large-budget film. In fairness to the censors it should be noted that deliberate delay, where practiced, has probably been highly selective and limited to those cases in which it was believed a distributor would be otherwise uncompromising.

Delay where no censorship is involved at all has been exceptional. In fact most boards have made a point of going about their routine tasks with dispatch. Some boards have been known to make after-hours examination in the case of a late-arriving film scheduled for an immediate booking. In a few instances, boards have even been willing to allow a film to open without prior examination when an immediate engagement was pending and the board could not view the film in time.

Before the *Freedman* decision required a reforming of licensing procedures, a distributor's remedy against the double standard, like that against the censorship order itself, was to convince the censors of his determination to carry the matter to the courts. However, government counsel have been alert to mere bluff, and a distributor who had no history of litigating might have found it necessary to undertake all the preparations for trial in order to be convincing. Distributors who had actually gone into court previously, of course, have been the most respected of all. For instance, I was told by one censor that his board had to "watch out" whenever one of the Times Film Company's pictures came through. The appearance of Ephraim London, an attorney who has never lost a censorship case, at a rescreening has also been impressive. In fact, in the case of the Kansas board, a mere letter from London was apparently persuasive, even when the distributor had never taken that particular board to court and had no intention of ever doing so!

Even so, willingness to go to court if necessary, so effective against the double standard, was no remedy for delay imposed by the censors. Indeed, it was against the determined distributor that deliberate delay may have been the only bargaining lever available to the censors. In such a contest, however, the decision in *Freedman* is likely to make a major difference in the future. That decision requires that any prior restraint imposed be brief. The censors must either promptly license a film, or promptly take the matter into court themselves. In theory this should end the kind of deliberate delay noted above. For example, the new Maryland licensing law enacted after the *Freedman* decision provides that the Maryland board must view a film within five days of its submission, and if it is not then licensed, the board must file a complaint in Baltimore City Court within three days. On the other hand, the Chicago licensing ordinance, which was also amended after the *Freedman* decision, still allowed a maximum of fifty-five days between submission of a film and the application by the city for an injunction to prevent its exhibition. The fifty-five days, however, were broken up into several deadlines which may have made deliberate delay difficult.

In requiring prompt judicial determination, the *Freedman* rules should also work to reduce the costs of delay imposed by litigation. The new Maryland law, for example, requires the Circuit Court for Baltimore to set a hearing within five days after the Board of Censors files a complaint, and to hand down a ruling within two days.

By also shifting the burden of proof to the censors, the *Freedman* doctrine should have an effect on the double standard, since it eliminates the necessity for the distributor taking the censors to court. Yet it is doubtful that the *Freedman* doctrine will erase the double standard entirely, since even an uninitiated court appearance may be expensive, and perhaps all the more so because of the speed with which it must be made under the new rules. Also, since local trial courts in the past have been more favorably disposed toward movie censors than have appellate courts, a distributor may still be faced in most cases with the necessity of carrying an appeal. But the *Freedman* doctrine will, under any circumstances, make it harder for the censors and government counsel to take the measure of a distributor's intentions to resist.

The Boons of Censorship

Paradoxically, there are circumstances in which the film proprietor may actually favor censorship of his film, or where he may find advantages in the licensing requirement itself. These are roughly of three kinds: those involving the element of publicity, those involving certain kinds of intra-industry bargaining, and those involving the possibility of extralegal action or the exercise of other controls against movies.

At the option of the distributor, a censorship controversy is an occasion for publicity. And as is well known, publicity of this nature, indeed of almost any nature, is a form of advertisement in the motion picture business. This being so, a distributor may be tempted to use the censors and the licensing process as pawns in what he may see as a far larger game than the one of getting the film licensed intact. Some film proprietors, in fact, have even been suspected of inserting material in their films that they were certain the censors would find objectionable. In these cases, most though not all of which involve exploitation films, the entire censorship institution may be thrown into reverse gear. The Detroit Licensing Bureau, for example, has actually refrained from ordering "borderline" deletions when it appears that the film "has nothing to recommend it except trouble with the authorities."

The publicity game is not limited to "fly-by-night" distributors. According to a leading film critic, himself an anticensorship stalwart, one major distributor who had taken an appeal to the New York Board of Regents was "very unhappy when the Regents reversed the Motion Picture Division and gave him a license." The workings of the publicity game can also be seen in the interaction of Embassy Pictures and the Maryland board over the board's handling of three films in 1963. Apparently under threat of litigation, the board reversed original censorship orders and licensed the three films—*Seven Capital Sins, Night Is My Future,* and *Landru.* The distributor then advertised them as having been initially refused licenses by the board.[1] In another but unrelated instance in the same state, *Tom Jones,* which was licensed without incident, could only be advertised as "the uncut version."

Sometimes the censors can be used as instruments in intra-industry bargaining. According to one trade journalist, an American distributor in negotiating for the American rights to European productions often obtains better terms if he can show that some censorship authority will require deletions. At one time the New York Motion Picture Division gave an advisory ruling—that is, an opinion before the film was actually submitted formally—whenever a distributor asked for one. According to Louis Pesce, director of the division, "we found that these opinions were factors in the price of the film purchase. In one case it dropped from $100,000 to $75,000 because of an adverse report. Some distributors would come in and practically beg for a cut, even a little one somewhere in a film that didn't warrant any. So we stopped giving unofficial opinions."

Finally, the licensing of a film can be a form of insurance against an obscenity prosecution, or against harassment by local groups or by local officials acting extralegally. As such, the insurance tends to benefit exhibitors, who are likely to be local residents, more than it does distributors. The insurance phenomenon—one of the most significant and least appreciated aspects of present-day prior censorship—is examined in greater detail in Chapter Seven.

The Costs of Licensing

Distributors face two kinds of expense in obtaining a license for a film, neither one having anything to do with actual censorship of the film. One set of costs is the examination fees charged by the licensing board itself, or, where the board has no projection facilities of its own, the expense of arranging a screening for the censors. The other set of costs, which is the harder to calculate and which may far exceed the licensing fees, is that incurred by the logistics of getting a film to the licensing board. Both kinds have been a source of much irritation in the film industry.

From time to time, elements in the industry have contended that prior censorship is maintained for the revenue it can bring into the state treasuries and that censor boards are "multi-million dollar a year" enterprises. Though licensing fees can sometimes be burdensome and apparently excessive, the size of the licensing operation and the profits available from it are vastly exaggerated by the complainants.

Of the seven censorship systems studied here, five—those of the four states and of Chicago—have charged fees. In Detroit and Milwaukee, however, the distributor has had to bear the expense of arranging a screening for the censors. This obligation may require the renting of a projection room and the hiring of a projectionist, though in many cases the censors view the film at a screening the distributor has previously arranged for local exhibitors. The cost to a distributor of arranging a special screening for censors alone may range between $50 and $150. In the case of Milwaukee, however, fewer than 20 per cent of the films rated have actually been examined before exhibition.

Fees, which are based on 1,000 feet of film, ranged from $2.00 in Virginia to $3.50 in New York for the original print, and from $1.00 in Virginia and Chicago to $1.50 in Maryland for duplicate prints. Thus the cost of licensing an average feature film (about 10,000 feet) in its original print ranged from about $20 in Virginia to about $35 in New York. The range for duplicate prints is correspondingly lower. In 1965 the Maryland legislature ended fees for duplicate prints; previously about 85 per cent of the board's receipts had come from such charges.

In the past, licensing was unquestionably a money-making operation, at least for the state boards. Compilations for the Maryland and Virginia boards indicate sizable accumulated surpluses over the years (see Table 8). These were turned over to the state treasuries. According to its president, the Kansas board accumulated about $100,000 in surplus over several years, which was transferred to the state treasury. Yet most of these surpluses were realized in the 1930's and 1940's, when many more films and prints were examined. Some boards and legislatures now reduce fees when receipts outstrip licensing expenses.

TABLE 8   *Receipts and Expenditures for the Maryland Board of Censors and the Virginia Division of Motion Picture Censorship*

	Receipts	Expenditures	Surplus
Maryland (1916–1966)[a]	$2,430,945	$1,919,044	$511.901
Virginia (1922–1965)[b]	1,816,567	1,303,144	513,423

[a] Maryland, Motion Picture Censor Board, *Fiftieth Annual Report, Fiscal Year, 1966.*
[b] Virginia, Division of Motion Picture Censorship, *Report for the Fiscal Year Ended June 30, 1965.*

In recent years two of the state boards, Maryland and Virginia, were unreliable money-makers (see Table 9). The Virginia board, in fact, operated at a deficit in each of its last six years. The situation was different, however, in New York and Kansas. In the 1963–1964 two-year period, the Kansas board had receipts of $75,357 and expenses of $49,558. Even larger current annual surpluses were accumulated by the New York Motion Picture Division. Its director estimated that annual receipts were approximately $260,000 and annual expenses approximately $150,000. Thus the ratio of receipts to expenses in recent years has varied considerably from board to board and from surplus to deficit (see Table 10). Taking the figures for the fiscal year ending June 30, 1965, the last in which all the four boards were fully operational, rounded combined totals are as follows: receipts $419,000; expenses, $288,000; and surplus, $132,000. Though these figures are sizable, they do not indicate that licensing is a multi-million dollar a year operation. And though the surplus total appears high, and in terms of percentage of receipts probably unnecessarily high, most of it was accounted for by a single board, New York's. It should also be noted that in the accounting of their expenditures, none of the boards included office rent or other "hidden" expenses, such as the costs of litigation.

TABLE 9 *Annual Receipts and Expenditures of the Maryland Board of Censors and the Virginia Division of Motion Picture Censorship, 1960–1966*

Year	Receipts	Expenditures	Surplus	Deficit
		Maryland		
1960	$69,775	$62,430	$ 7,345	—
1961	66,115	64,813	1,302	—
1962	63,686	64,146	—	$ 406
1963	66,767	66,269	498	—
1964	69,179	64,571	4,608	—
1965	51,137[a]	67,311	—	16,174
1966	11,197[b]	66,115	—	54,918
		Virginia		
1960	$41,970	$42,959	—	989
1961	43,621	48,349	—	4,728
1962	45,334	47,954	—	2,621
1963	46,274	48,329	—	2,055
1964	44,927	51,316	—	6,389
1965	41,926	52,774	—	10,848

Figures in table are taken from the annual reports of the boards for the fiscal years ending June 30. The Virginia board was discontinued in 1966.

[a] During fiscal 1965 the state legislature eliminated fees for duplicate prints.

[b] Fees from original prints only.

Expenses for the censor boards appear to be modest, with salaries accounting for 80 to 90 per cent of the listed expenditures. On state boards in 1965, the salary ranged from $2,100 for a member of the Kansas board to $14,590 for the director of New York's Motion Picture Division (see Table 11). The visitor to board offices is likely to be impressed by the leisurely pace of activity, and there is some basis for believing that the boards are

TABLE 10 *Receipts as a Percentage of Expenditures for Four State Boards of Censors*

Board	Percentage
New York ("recent years")	175
Kansas (1963–1965)	152
Virginia (1960–1965)	91
Maryland (1960–1966)	87

Sources: Percentages for the Maryland and Virginia boards are based on receipt and expenditure figures in their annual reports; those for New York and Kansas are based on receipt and expenditure estimates of the director of the Motion Picture Division and the president of the Board of Review, respectively.

TABLE 11 *Salary and Basis of Appointment of Censors, 1964*

Position	Salary	Basis of appointment
New York, director	$14,590	merit
New York, assistant director	11,385	merit
New York, reviewer	8,212	merit
Maryland, executive secretary	7,000	merit
Chicago, Review Section head	7,000[a]	merit[b]
Detroit, member	7,000[a]	merit[b]
Virginia, member	6,608	political
Chicago, Review Section member	5,000[a]	political
Maryland, chairman	4,500	political[c]
Maryland, member	3,600	political[c]
Maryland, reviewer	3,600	merit
Kansas, president	2,400	political[c]
Kansas, member	2,100	political[c]
Milwaukee, executive secretary	1,200	political
Chicago, Appeal Board member	50[d]	political
Milwaukee, member	none	political

Information was obtained from interviews of censors.
[a] Approximate.
[b] Under police department.
[c] Three-year term.
[d] Fee, per meeting.

somewhat overstaffed and underworked. In fact, a Maryland exhibitor once publicly charged that the state Board of Censors needed to work on the average only two hours a day to complete its examinations.[2] Board offices themselves are generally unimpressive: the Maryland office is located in the basement of the state office building, and the Kansas office was over a firehouse in Kansas City. In Milwaukee, the "advisory" Motion Picture Commission has received modest financial support from the city. According to its executive secretary, its budget is under $5,000, and includes pay for a part-time civil service stenographer. The executive secretary, who receives a salary of $1,200 a year, is the only paid commission member. Most of the commission's work is done from his home.

It is hard to gauge the impact of licensing fees on the film industry generally, or on the circulation of movies in particular. Large distributors, who have the most films and by far the most duplicate prints, and who thus pay the biggest share of fees, are probably affected the least. Except in the rare instance of an extremely heavy "saturation" booking when a film runs simultaneously at many theatres, perhaps as many as a hundred or more in a metropolitan area, licensing fees are likely to be, in the words of one distributor, "a negligible burden." If licensing fees alone have a restrictive effect on the circulation of movies, it is probably only where the rental returns from an engagement in a licensing jurisdiction are likely to be so small as to make it unprofitable for a distributor to ship the film in at all. This situation would arise when the number of prospective engagements was small, or the engagements were low-rental ones. For example, for many small theatres, usually located in small towns, rental prices for second, third, or even later runs may range below $100 for an engagement. According to one Maryland exhibitor, distributors of foreign films have often been reluctant to ship in Polish-language films, whose limited market is among Baltimore's Polish-American population, because licensing fees cut into much of the modest rental price.[3]

The cost of furnishing a special screening for censors, as is occasionally done in Milwaukee, can also have a restrictive effect on the circulation of films. In some instances this cost may approach the rental prices themselves, for those foreign or small independently produced American films which do not play to a large audience in the city.

The costs imposed by licensing, other than those for fees or special screenings, vary with the particular booking situation. I know of no statistics here, but the costs in some cases are probably far greater than the licensing fees. Shipping is one such cost, though a minor one. A greater one is that resulting from a print's being out of circulation, and therefore out of productive use, while it goes through the licensing process. Most boards manage to examine films within one to three days, but even this relatively short period is an interruption in the productive life of the film or print. Where a board requires that its seal be affixed to every duplicate print for purposes of later inspection, the routing of prints into the censor board offices can be a formidable logistical problem, particularly in the case of a film scheduled to open in a large number of theatres in the area at the same time. Another costly situation can arise when a film, licensed and affixed with a seal, is shipped out of the licensing jurisdiction and is then later shipped back in for another engagement. Exhibitors or their projectionists in the state or city outside the licensing jurisdiction usually cut off and discard the licensing seal to prevent it from flashing on their screens. When the print reenters the licensing jurisdiction, it must then have another seal affixed, which usually means being routed again to the censor board offices.

It is clear that licensing is expensive and even burdensome. The greatest absolute costs are borne by large distributors, who as a group are the least involved in censorship. But the greatest relative costs are probably borne by smaller distributors. In only a few instances do these costs appear prohibitive, and therefore a bar to the circulation of films. In every case, however, they add to the cost of doing business. These facts considered, there seems to be no reason why licensing fees should exceed the costs of operating the licensing system; that is, there is no reason why a state should make a profit from movie censorship. A surplus might be defended if it were in some way reinvested with the aim of easing the strains of licensing on the film proprietor and on the freedom of speech. Hiring better censors or speeding up the licensing process where this is yet possible might be two such reinvestments. But short of this sort of use of surpluses, state profit from censorship is not easily defended.

Fees are now based mainly on the length of the film and secondarily on the number of prints. Yet, to the extent that the fee for the original print is higher than that for each of the duplicates, the fee schedule is regressive. The current system also penalizes the large distributor who never has a censorship problem—for example, Buena Vista Films, the Disney Company, which spends thousands of dollars a year on licensing without ever having a deletion. Yet to base the fee arrangement on either the ability to pay (that is, on the number of prints), or on the amount of censorship would only raise several other inequities. Under these circumstances and in light of the always-present logistical costs of licensing and the occasional prohibitive effect of licensing fees, there are good reasons for eliminating licensing fees entirely, and for having all licensing board expenses assumed by the respective states and cities.

The Constituents

Some members of the movie industry, especially some of those who have sparred with the censors in the courts, have not only argued that the boards of censors exist today only to raise revenue and to provide political jobs, but also that they have little or no public support. In fact, the contrary seems to be the case.

There is unquestionably a large public that favors greater restrictions on motion pictures. Not all of this public appears to favor governmental action though, as the Motion Picture Association of America itself has pointed out, an increasing number of measures aimed at curbing the content of movies have been introduced in state legislatures.[4] And not all of the public appearing to prefer governmental restriction supports general licensing, though it seems likely that more proposals for general licensing would be advanced if the legal future of that institution seemed more promising. On the other hand, classification was established in Dallas in 1965, and bills proposing such regulation were introduced in six state legislatures in 1964. And though licensing lapsed in New York, Virginia, and Memphis in 1965, and in Kansas in 1966, following adverse court decisions based on the *Freedman* requirements, I know of no state or major city with licensing to have abandoned it voluntarily. In fact, in most former licensing jurisdictions there have been annual, though thus far unsuccessful, attempts to reinstate prior censorship in amended form. And in Maryland, the legislature, faced with an opportunity to drop licensing completely after the *Freedman* decision, amended the licensing law within three weeks of the decision. Under these circumstances, a conclusion that there is no public that supports prior censorship seems unwarranted.

The exact nature of this public and its influence on censorship is another matter. Generally speaking, concentrated pressure from a particular group on a board appears to be unusual, though there are some exceptions to this rule, such as the situation in Chicago which will be described. Indeed, with licensing boards having so little room in which to exercise discretion today and with their constitutional status so uncertain, the effectiveness of concentrated pressure on them is questionable. This is apparently understood by many, if not most, groups interested in greater restrictions on motion picture content. Concentrated pressure from these groups is more likely to be felt today by legislators.

Though the boards "listen to" and "talk with" groups concerned with morality questions, and tend to respond to these groups in a general way, the censors typically are eager to point out that they do not respond to special group interests. Indeed, even many of their adversaries in the film industry concede that the censors are largely independent. If they are in fact, it is probably due in large measure to their confinement by the laws, and particularly to the impact of the *Miracle* case, which itself grew out of a response to a special group interest. If there is one lesson in constitutional law that the censors have learned, it is that censorship orders cannot appear to be associated with religious interests. For example, it is said that at one time the Providence, Rhode Island, police censor would not approve a film "condemned" by the Legion of Decency.[5] Today this orientation would be in the "unthinkable" realm on any major licensing board. In fact, for the major boards, the National Catholic Office for Motion Pictures (Legion of Decency) ratings for many films come out too late to be considered, at least at the time of initial examination. In Chicago, where overt Catholic pressure on the censors is present, Sgt. Robert Murphy, head of the Film Review Section, has maintained that about 50 per cent of the films given the Catholic Office's "B" rating ("morally objectionable in part for all") receive a "general audience" permit, while some films with "A-3" rating ("morally unobjectionable for adults") are given an "adults only" permit.

Though none of the boards appear to consult regularly or formally with particular groups, all of them have occasional communication with a variety of community organizations. In many instances this is by telephone, letter, or petition, though it is also often through face-to-face contact. Many censors address civic groups and attend their meetings. The Detroit police censors, who do not keep a record of the number of films censored, carefully tally their public appearances. In 1964, for example, members of the Licensing Bureau made 28 speeches and attended 152 meetings of various groups. Most censors see this sort of contact as allowing them to "keep up with community thinking." And, indeed, in an era when censors may be summoned to the witness stand and cross-examined on their deepest censorial thoughts, group contact may allow them to speak more authoritatively about "community standards." The strong morality interest of most of the groups with whom they have contact may also rally an often badly flagging censorial self-confidence.

At the same time, the group contact is a two-way street. In it the censors have a chance to engage in a form of politicking. From time to time film interests in almost every licensing jurisdiction have sponsored legislation to eliminate prior censorship; and since this is true, the opportunity presented by group contact for converting general concern over movie content into active support for their work is seldom lost on the censors. Though the groups with which the censors have contact may range from the Ethical Culture Society to the American Legion, most of their interaction is with church-affiliated lay groups, clergy associations, women's clubs, and the Parent-Teacher Association and other school groups.

In addition to group contact, censor boards receive a number of complaints about films from individuals. Most of these are made by letter or by telephone. The New York Motion Picture Division received approximately one hundred of these a year. According to the censors on all boards, almost all of the complaints charge the board involved with being too permissive. Many of the complaints are stimulated by the exhibition of a particular film. In many instances, the persons complaining have not seen the film, but have based their charges on advertisements or "coming attractions" which they have seen. A few of the complaints are termed "crackpot."

The subject of most of the complaints, and of the group interest in movie content as well, is excessive nudity and eroticism. There is much less concern with extremes of violence or brutality. The director of the New York Motion Picture Division found that most of the concern made known to his office was addressed to the apparent need for the protection of children. A few complaints relate to group image, usually involving the portrayal of Negroes.

Except for the restraining influence of the legal departments, the boards of censors are apparently subject to little pressure from other governmental sources. No censor whom I interviewed acknowledged any policy directives or pressures from any other executive, or any legislative, source. In Kansas, legislative delegations occasionally toured the board's office, apparently in

connection with proposals to eliminate the board. In one instance, a delegation came to view *Les Liaisons Dangereuses* after the distributor had filed a
suit following the board's denial of a license. At that time, according to the
president of the board, the legislators congratulated the members on their
action. Indeed, if there are few governmental pressures on the censor
boards to be more restrictive, it is probably a case of enlightened self-denial. A policy of greater restrictiveness would very likely be self-defeating,
since it would almost surely result in suits which would, in turn, endanger
whatever remaining authority the censors may have.

The situation in Chicago is an interesting example of this self-denial, reflecting an attempt to maintain prior censorship *in spite of* pro-censorship
pressures. Before the creation of the Motion Picture Appeal Board in 1962,
censorship was entirely in the hands of the police department, with right of
an appeal to the mayor. The censors were known to be highly responsive to
Roman Catholic pressure, which has always been strong and well organized
in the city on morality issues. Though its members are appointed by the
mayor, the Appeal Board was designed to be independent, or at least to
appear to be independent, of other administrative units, including the may-
or's office. The city censorship ordinance provides that the board's actions
"shall be final and shall be subject to judicial review as provided by law."[6]
Inevitably this appellate arrangement had a frustrating effect on the city's
strong pro-censorship groups. Two of the board's decisions in 1964—the
licensing of *Promises! Promises!* with several nudity scenes, and the granting of a "general audience" permit to *Tom Jones*—resulted in an intensive
but unsuccessful campaign to have the rulings reversed. In both instances
the mayor's office was reported to have been "deluged" with letters of
complaint.[7] The letters, most of which were similar in wording, appeared to
come mainly from certain Roman Catholic parishes. In the *Promises!
Promises!* situation, a Catholic editor telephoned each member of the Appeal Board, and questioned him at length on how he had voted on the film.
Two members of the board later termed the calls "badgering." In the cases
of both films, Mayor Richard Daley issued a form letter to those who had
complained. The letter cited the Appeal Board's statutory status, noting
that no city office, including that of the mayor, had authority to interfere
with the board's action.[8] The Appeal Board is, in fact, independent of the
mayor's office probably only so long as the mayor wishes it to be so, since
he has power to dismiss its members at will. But the board's real or apparent independent status has had the effect, no doubt by design, of diverting
resentment at censorship or the lack of it from the mayor's office.

The Chicago situation suggests an interesting transformation of prior
censorship. If the Appeal Board maintains its liberal approach, and if a license for a film is a kind of insurance against other forms of control, then

the real constituents of the Appeal Board may not be procensorship groups at all, but those who are interested in enlarging and securing freedom of speech in motion pictures.

The Censors

Perhaps the most stigmatized aspect of censorship over the years has been the qualifications and the personalities of those who have done the censoring. In his protest of English licensing laws in 1643, John Milton provided the classic libertarian description of the censor's job and a pessimistic prediction about those who would be likely to fill it: "Seeing those who now possess the employment by all evident signs wish themselves well rid of it, and that no man of worth, none that is not a plain unthrift of his own hours, is ever likely to succeed them, except he mean to put himself to the salary of a press corrector, we may easily forsee what kind of licensers we are to expect hereafter, either ignorant, imperious, and remiss, or basely pecuniary."[9]

Attacks on movie censors in both popular and scholarly works are legion.[10] Alleged faults range from a lack of aesthetic sensibility, to deep psychological traumas giving rise to a morbid interest in seeking out matter to be kept from the sight of fellow citizens. According to one modern libertarian critic, "Common experience is sufficient to show that their attitudes, drives, emotions, and impulses all tend to carry them to excesses. This is particularly true in the realm of obscenity, but it occurs in all areas where officials are driven by fear or other emotion to suppress communication."[11] This indictment conforms to the popular image of the censor, and, indeed, evidence may be found in the history of movie censorship that would seem to support it.

Nonetheless, it does not characterize today's movie censor. Recent developments in the legal doctrines of prior censorship and obscenity have removed much of the discretion the censors once enjoyed, and at the same time have drawn considerable public attention to prior censorship. Under these circumstances, government projection rooms cannot hide a morbid personality, and censor boards, struggling merely to stay in business, can ill afford idiosyncratic behavior. In short, the Anthony Comstock type would be hard to find among today's censors. In fact, the censors as a group would seem no less well-balanced as personalities than those who exercise much more power over movie content, namely, the producers, distributors, and exhibitors.

However, the skill and training censors bring to their work presents a more fertile field for criticism. To begin with, more than half of the censorial positions on the seven major licensing boards examined here are political appointments, and most of these are filled through patronage. As indicated in Table 11, these jobs, as well as most of those on merit, are low paying. With the exception of New York, little attention has been given to establishing any requirements for the censorship positions. Few standards for selection have been set out either in law or in practice. In Maryland, the licensing law requires that board members be citizens of the state and that they "be well-qualified by education and experience to act as censors."[12] Similar provisions were in the Virginia law. This requirement, however, apparently was interpreted to mean only that the appointee have had some partisan connection with the party in power. The only licensing law setting out specific requirements for censorship positions is Chicago's ordinance creating the Motion Picture Appeal Board. It requires that members be "experienced or educated in one or more of the following fields: art, drama, literature, philosophy, sociology, psychology, history, music, science or other related fields."[13]

When jobs are under civil service, examination is usually required for appointment. In Detroit, the police department has evaluated a candidate's past record on the force as well. In Maryland, the examination for the job of reviewer apparently includes testing for some knowledge of the law relating to movie censorship. The New York state examination for reviewer went further than any other in setting out requirements. Applicants were required to have a baccalaureate degree and some experience in education or social work, part of which could be satisfied by graduate work in such fields as education, sociology, journalism, or Romance languages, or by foreign travel or foreign residence. Applicants were also tested on their knowledge of history, literature, one or more foreign languages, and the law of movie censorship.

In light of these requirements it is not surprising that the educational and occupational biographies of the employees of the state's Motion Picture Division should have been more weighty than those of most censors on other boards. The division's director held a B.A. degree in sociology and had done graduate study in psychiatric social work. He was also fluent in Spanish and Italian. Before joining the division he had been a children's court social worker. The assistant director had an M.A. degree in education and a certificate from the Sorbonne for teaching French. He had formerly been a social worker for a federal agency. Of the reviewers, one of whom was a woman, two had master's degrees, one in French and the Romance languages, the other in education. Three of the reviewers, however, held second jobs, two teaching in adult education at night.

In Maryland, in 1966, one of the board members had a college degree, two were high school graduates. The chairman had a hardware business and was chairman of his county's Democratic Central Committee. One of the associate board members, the wife of an advertising executive, was a sculptress. The other associate board member was a bondswoman. All were in their late forties or early fifties and all were parents. They worked two to four days a week at their board duties. Although a religious "balance" in their appointment is denied, it happens that the three members were Protestant, Jewish, and Catholic respectively. The board's executive secretary, a bachelor in his early fifties, had a degree in accounting and had been attached to the board for seven years. The two reviewers, a man and a widowed woman, were high school graduates. The woman, who was chief reviewer, had formerly been a board member. The executive secretary and reviewers were under civil service.

The three members of the Virginia board were women, all widowed. Two were in their early eighties and one in her late seventies. Two had been on the board for fifteen years, one for ten years. Two were college graduates, one holding a degree from the Conservatory of Music in Amsterdam. Two members had served on the Democratic State Central Committee. One had also directed the Virginia Arts Project during the New Deal. Another member had taught voice in two colleges. The husbands of all three women (one of whom had been a lawyer and another a judge) had been active in the Byrd machine. The board members, who appeared alert and active, had apparently become something of an institution in themselves, partly because of their age and sex. A special act of the state legislature had allowed them to continue past the mandatory retirement age of seventy.

The three board members in Kansas were also women, but unlike their Virginia counterparts, they were all Republicans and all in their middle or late forties. None was a college graduate, though two had attended college. All were housewives and mothers, and all had been "active in civic affairs." It is to this that they attributed their appointments. One of the members had not realized that the state had movie censorship until just before her appointment. Though the jobs were supposedly full-time, salaries for the positions had not been increased since 1925.

The Detroit Licensing Bureau has been the only one of the seven major licensing agencies in which policemen actually examine films. The bureau members appear to range in age from the middle-thirties to middle-fifties. All have "worked their way up from the force," which is to say that one must have had previous experience as a policeman before he can enter the bureau. Apparently a bureau assignment is looked upon as a desirable post, since there is always a large surplus of applications. The bureau prefers that members have at least two years of college. In choosing among applicants, "intelligence," "general knowledge," and past record on the force are weighed heavily.

Members of the Milwaukee Motion Picture Commission have been chosen by the mayor, with the apparent aim of making the commission, in the words of its executive secretary, "widely representative of the community." In 1967 the commission had among its nine members a union official, a corporation executive, a doctor, a barber, a used-car dealer, a public relations director, and lay representatives of the three major faiths. The commission has also been the only censorship body to have the film industry represented on it, in this case by the president of an exhibitor's trade association. The commission appeared to be dominated by its executive secretary, chosen by the members from their own ranks. The secretary, a retired postal supervisor, has held the job since 1954, and has been on the commission since 1940.

In Chicago, the makeup of the Film Review Section and the Motion Picture Appeal Board have been in contrast. The former group has consisted of six women, ranging in age from the middle-fifties to middle-seventies, appointed by the police commissioner. They are the famed "policemen's widows," a high-spirited group whose decisions and opinions in the past often supplied censorial comic relief in Sunday supplement stories and occasionally, as when two of them engaged in a book-throwing fight, in the headlines as well.[14] Though all are widows, actually only one is the widow of a policeman. The husbands of the others were aldermen, precinct workers, and one was a member of the city library board. The group is marked by a religious balance that is no doubt intentional. Two members are Protestant; two, Roman Catholic; one, Jewish; and one, Greek Orthodox Catholic. One long-time member is a Negro and considers herself to be "the Negro representative on the board."[15] Technically the jobs are under civil service, but apparently no examination has been given for more than twenty-five years. The head of the Review Section is a police sergeant in his early forties who formerly served with the department's youth division. Formally, he handles the office work of the Review Section and votes to break ties. He is also charged with maintaining harmony among the members and with allaying the many pressures that are brought to bear on the section. The job, which had had four occupants between 1959 and 1967, apparently is not an easy one.

The five members who have made up the Appeal Board, four of them men, are in their forties and fifties. The members include a psychiatrist at the University of Chicago's School of Social Service, the dean of the Loyola University School of Social Work, the editor of *Poetry,* a psychiatrist with the Chicago Board of Education, and an attorney once active in amateur theatricals. The board, as stated before, has a reputation for permissiveness. One of its members, Dr. Ner Littner, a psychiatrist, admits accepting appointment to the board "in the belief that there were films of artistic merit that were not allowed to be shown because they were not understood. It was a challenge of using my psychiatric background to rescue such movies that brought me to the board."[16] Perhaps its most permissive member is Dr. Henry Rago, who has edited the monthly *Poetry* since 1955. He probably ranks as the country's most unusual censor, since he is against censorship. He is, instead, a strong advocate of classification, favoring, in fact, a rather high age limit of nineteen or twenty years. He has been in a minority on a number of occasions when the Appeal Board has rejected a film entirely, and has written "dissenting opinions" in some of these instances. He conceives of the board as a kind of "arbitration" body, with its members acting as "judges" rather than censors. Dr. Rago wrote his Ph.D. dissertation on "The Philosophy of Aesthetic Individualism," in moral philosophy at the University of Chicago, and has what may be described as a Jeffersonian view of free speech. Though his views do not reflect those of all the Appeal Board members, his appointment as a censor is probably the most striking indication of how far movie censorship has retreated since the day in 1951 when the New York Board of Regents rescinded a license for *The Miracle*.

What a "good" censor is depends, of course, on how the evaluator balances several diverse considerations, among them his conceptions of free speech, the harmfulness of "obscenity," and respect for entrepreneurial interest. For those concerned with only, or even primarily, the harm of alleged obscenity, most of today's censors may seem well chosen, since they appear to be conscientiously responsive to such concerns. In addition, many of the political appointees reflect, by accident or design, the pluralistic character of their communities.

On the other hand, for libertarians with an absolutist view there can be no such thing as a good censor, since any and all censorship is bad. For other libertarians, however, the question may be more complex. If it is assumed that the content of films is likely to come under some form of control or other, or that censorship energies will at least attempt to control the content of films by one means or another, then there can be good censors. From the standpoint of free speech, such censors would have to do more than merely reflect the concerns of their traditional constituencies. They would have to be capable of making balanced judgments in which these concerns were merely one of several elements in the censorship equation. By this measure, the recruiting processes examined here, with the possible exception of New York's, are poor ones, since they are not designed to draw individuals with talent for making careful judgments (though many of the present censors, to be sure, are not lacking in these talents). The selection of censors probably could be improved, first, by making the recruitment process more discriminating, that is, by taking it out of the realm of patronage appointment and by requiring examination; and second, by making the positions more attractive, that is, by increasing the pay.

Greater discrimination in the selection of censors should probably aim at uncovering two qualities: a sense of aesthetic appreciation, particularly an awareness of the ways in which an artist can and does communicate ideas; and a degree of sophistication concerning the place of censorship in the law and in a democratic society. The former skill might eliminate the rejection or cutting of award-winning films that has so often, at least in the past, put censors and film critics on opposite sides of the fence. The latter skill should insure a minimum understanding of the concept of obscenity as it appears to be developing in the law, an appreciation of the heavy burden that a licensing system can place upon the property of a film proprietor, and, particularly, an awareness of the fundamental contradiction of censorship and a free speech society. These qualities will not be easy to unearth, since they are essentially matters of judgment and sensitivity rather than of knowledge and experience. Certain requirements, such as an appropriate degree of formal education, for instance, though not guaranteeing these qualities, might increase the chances of obtaining them.

As we have seen, the limits of censorship do not depend entirely or even mainly on the censors' self-restraint. Because institutional checks on the censors are so well established today, freedom of speech can be safeguarded even against bad censors. The emerging legal doctrine of prior censorship and obscenity is unfriendly to the censors, while at the same time the courts, particularly under the *Freedman* rule, are more accessible to a film proprietor than at any time in the past. At a more informal level, a tendency toward censorial excess is likely to be further checked by government legal departments. Even so, the quest for censorial self-restraint should not be abandoned. Internalized restraint is probably the most effective protec- tion free speech can have; there is already evidence of the development of an "unthinkable" area of censorship. In a society that places a high value on the rule of law, the habit of restraints imposed from without, by court order, may become the habit of restraints self-imposed. These, in turn, may eventually take their place in the socialization process itself.

It is perhaps with this in mind that the drama critic and playwright Walter Kerr has conceived of the ideal censor, who partakes of those qualities that ought perhaps to mark all men who make decisions for other men. Described in markedly unMiltonian terms, Kerr's censor is:

a man who has given an unattractive and unrewarding job to do, who does it only because the specific responsibility has been thrust upon him, who knows that his political responsibility may be at odds with the interests of art, who is prepared to override the interest of art only in the most extreme urgencies, who goes about his business with little confidence in his own rectitude and after an anguished examination of his own motives, who comes to his rare proscriptions in genuine pain, and who thereafter hopefully and steadily reviews his work toward possible revision. The good censor would be, I think, something close to a tragic hero. He would not, if he had any awareness of the complexities with which he was dealing, ever be a happy zealot.[17]

The Bureau of Customs

The Bureau of Customs has examined imported films for more than thirty years under the Tariff Act of 1930. Even so, it was only with the explosion of the foreign film market in this country in the last fifteen years that the bureau's examination process has come to resemble that of a licensing board's. Today, the similarities between Customs censorship and that of major state or city licensing boards are far greater than the differences. Customs censorship is both more and less restrictive than state and municipal censorship. On the one hand, the bureau is generally thought to be more permissive on the obscenity question. Indeed, those state and locally censored foreign films that have been involved in the Supreme Court's leading censorship decisions—*La Ronde, Game of Love,* and *Lady Chatterley's Lover*—were all approved by the bureau. In the opinion of one film critic whom I interviewed, "The Bureau doesn't do much more than stop the more flagrant nudity films and act as a kind of DEW line for state and local boards." On the other hand, the consequences of Customs censorship are far greater than those of state or local licensing. The latter censorship means, at worst, the loss of a local or perhaps a regional market (except in New York, where it may also have meant the loss of national advertisement). Censorship by Customs, however, means loss of the entire American market.

An imported film may be examined at any port of entry. But about 90 per cent enter the country through New York. The bureau keeps records only of the number of feet of film examined, on the theory that the calculation of duty—which, of course, is no longer the primary reason for examination—is based on length rather than on unit. (In fact, mere length can be determined without screening.) In the four years 1963–1966 in New York, the bureau examined an average of eight to ten million feet of film a year, all but about 5 or 6 per cent of which was intended for commercial exhibition. With 9,000 feet the approximate average length of imported features, the bureau examined footage roughly equivalent to 900–1,100 features a year. However, not all of the imported film is in the form of finished features when brought in.

Each film or part of a film-to-be entering through New York is examined by one of two Customs reviewers in the Prohibited Imports Section, Division of Imports Compliance, Office of Rules and Regulations, at the customshouse. Some films are viewed completely, while others are merely spot-checked. When a questionable part is found by a spot-check, the entire film is examined. For every film examined, the reviewer writes a report consisting of a brief synopsis and a record of any questionable footage. Unless the reviewer recommends that the film be detained it is then admitted. Films that present no censorship question usually move through the examination process in two working days.

When the reviewer believes that the film presents a question of obscenity, it is viewed by a supervisory administrative aide in the Prohibited Imports Section. If the aide also believes there is a question of obscenity, the film is referred to Irving Fishman, Director of the Division of Imports Compliance in New York. Upon viewing the film, Fishman may consult with Huntington Cairns, the bureau's advisor on obscenity matters, in Washington, as well as with Department of Justice lawyers and perhaps even the local United States attorney. Cairns, himself a lawyer and social scientist, was hired by the bureau as a consultant after the calamitous *Ulysses* case[18] in the 1930's. Since then, his advice has usually determined the bureau's action when a question of artistic or literary merit or social value seems intermixed with one of obscenity. In movie cases, Cairns has ordinarily sustained Fishman's judgment without actually viewing the films himself. Fishman, who has worked closely with Cairns for twenty-five years, explains this by saying he knows "the way Cairns thinks" on these matters. If the film is found objectionable by Fishman, alone or in consultation, it is then officially seized and the matter is referred to the United States attorney at the port of entry, for forfeiture proceedings. (In 1965–1966, when Fishman was Assistant Deputy Commissioner of Customs in charge of the Restricted Merchandise Section of the bureau in Washington, films detained on review by the supervisory administrative aide were sent to Fishman in Washington.)

At ports other than New York, films are usually examined first by a deputy collector. If found objectionable, they are sent to Fishman for review in New York. Thus, over the years, in occasional consultation with Cairns, Fishman has been the chief censor of films for the bureau. However, examination of motion pictures is only a minor part of his total work.

The bureau's authority is not limited to seizing obscene materials, but extends to those which urge treason, insurrection, forcible violation of the law, or which threaten to take life or inflict bodily injury. But, as in the case of state and local boards of censors, the movie censorship work of the bureau today is, for practical purposes, a matter of barring obscenity. Here, the bureau's censorship is limited largely to the same major subjects that concern state and local boards: nudity in an erotic context and, to a lesser extent, certain eroticism without nudity—usually physical familiarities and dances. The bureau objects also to the showing of genitals or pubic hair in nudist films. Unlike several of the state and local boards, the bureau appears to have little or no concern with profanity or "indelicate" words, sex education, use of narcotics, extreme violence or brutality, or derision of race or religion. An illustration of the bureau's censorship of a feature film is the following New York reviewer's report on *The Eavesdropper:*

Description. Story of flaming youth—an "angry" young man and apathetic girl get together for the sheer boredom of it all. Martin is somewhat an over-suspicious fellow, who is strongly dedicated to the proper running of the government. One of the episodes that he indulges in with his "beatnik" companions is to incite a riot by tossing a few incendiaries at the local constabulary. He and Lola spend a few days together in a hotel and let nature take its course. His eavesdropping causes quite a few people embarrassment and disgrace when he accuses a troupe of itinerant actors of attempting to assassinate the president during one of his public appearances.

Objections. Reel 5: Very suggestive lovemaking scene. Boy unzips girl's skirt, takes off his shirt, and then removes girl's blouse at the same time stroking her breast—almost ¾ view of bare breast.

Reel 6: Continuing into reel 6 this lovemaking scene goes into bed where the contortions and actions suggest possible sexual relations. Total, 34 feet.

In many cases imported movie footage is in the form of "rushes"—that is, unedited film which is to be put into feature form and in some cases added to after entry. The reviewer's report below is on such rushes of a British documentary, *Teenagers.* Totaling about 26,000 feet, they were shot in Great Britain, France, and Italy, and imported in three shipments. The recommended deletions probably come close to ranging over the entire spectrum of Customs censorship, except for genital exposure.

Description. Documentary on teenager behavior. Boys on motorcycles bringing girls to a cafe. Teenage band entertains them. They dance, drink cognac from a bottle and kiss. Then other boys bring girls to the cars where there is more kissing and petting.

Objections. Reel 3: Several strip scenes occur in a movie watched by teenagers. In one short sequence breasts are briefly exposed. (19.5 feet)

Reel 5: Young woman disrobes in front of several young men. When she is nude down to her waist, they touch and fondle her breasts. Then she sits on one man's lap and he caresses her nude breast. (232 feet)

Reel 8: In a very heavy petting scene, a boy lifts up girl's skirt, rubs her posterior as she attempts to pull skirt down. (59 feet)

Reel 11: A stripper removes her brassiere and is shown naked from the waist up.

Reel 19: A prostitute picks up a customer and takes him to her flat. She is seen disrobing through the skylight, and reclines on a bed, naked from the waist up. (note: there are several retakes of this same scene.) (186 feet)

Informal negotiations with the importer (usually the film's American distributor) may take place any time after a film has been detained for administrative review. The supervisory adminstrative aide notifies the importer of detention by letter, though neither a description of the objectionable parts of the film nor the specific reasons for detention are given. This information may be obtained by the importer informally, usually by telephone. In cases where the importer has not viewed the film previously abroad, it may be sent to him under Customs seal for his own examination.

When the importer is unable to persuade Customs officials that the film is admissible, he has several choices open to him. He can agree to forfeit the film, thus saving the Government the time and expense of a formal proceeding that is otherwise required by statute. Though such an assent is quite common in the seizure of articles and printed matter, it would be unusual for an importer to give up commercial property as potentially valuable as a feature film, particularly where alternatives are available. One of these alternatives is to request permission to reexport, thereby usually avoiding a major loss on the film. This permission is nearly always granted. Another possibility is bringing the film "into conformance with Customs statutes"—a bureau euphemism for the forbidden term "censorship"—by agreeing to the cutting and forfeiting of objectionable parts. The film, minus the objectionable parts, is then admitted. Still another alternative, and apparently the one Congress had in mind when it passed the Tariff Act of 1930, is to allow the matter to go to trial in the forfeiture proceeding. Here trial is *de novo,* but in the case of articles and printed materials, at least, the proceeding is seldom contested.

In the three years 1963–1965, an average of forty-five films a year were detained by the bureau in New York. However, in 1966 the number of detentions had dropped to twelve, a decrease Fishman attributed to greater difficulty in meeting the constitutional tests of obscenity. Normally, about half of the films detained are "brought into conformance" and about a sixth are reexported. The remaining films—about a third of those originally detained—are eventually released and admitted without changes.

As with state and local licensing, censorship totals do not reveal the character of censorship and may give an inflated picture of restrictiveness. It is true that reexportation, for example, may be the equivalent of a licensing board's outright rejection of a film, and thereby signal a complete bureau victory. On the other hand, where the distributor had not previously seen the film himself, reexportation may be resorted to for purely commercial reasons. That is to say, the distributor may have decided the film was not worth marketing anyway, quite apart from Customs examination. If importation has been under bond, the importer may have several months in which to reexport without being liable for payment of duty. Also, if the eventual release of one-third of the films detained is any indication, the bringing of others "into conformance," no doubt, includes instances of compromise by the bureau.

Fishman estimates that about three films a year, for all ports of entry, are taken beyond administrative review in the bureau—that is, to the stage where a United States attorney prepares forfeiture proceedings. But almost no cases go to trial. In fact, before the *491* action in 1965,[19] the last trial on the merits of a bureau seizure of a movie was the celebrated *Ecstasy* case,[20] thirty years earlier. Usually when a distributor goes beyond the administrative review it merely means, according to Fishman, that he negotiates with the federal attorney "just as he would with us."

Customs censorship, then, appears to be marked by much less distributor resistance than that of state or local licensing. There are several reasons why this should be the case. The most important, no doubt, is the greater permissiveness of the bureau's rulings. Assimilation of the changing legal doctrine of prior censorship and obscenity has been greater in the bureau than on most of the state and local boards. Administrative review in the bureau has been in the hands of men like Cairns and Fishman, whose intelligence, education, and interests largely insure against censorial excesses. The hiring of Cairns in the first place was aimed at preventing censorship decisions that would result in courtroom defeats or that would give the bureau an image of cultural illiteracy—the sort suggested by the *Ulysses* case. For both Cairns and Fishman, censorship is a very small part of their work, and their careers are not dominated by it.

For those few appeals taken beyond administrative review, the familiar check of the legal department, so evident in state and local censorship, appears to be only slightly less important than it is at those levels of control. According to Fishman, "It is difficult to get federal attorneys to take obscenity issues into court. They would much rather have a narcotics case."

Finally, as with state and local censorship, there are reasons of the distributor's own for not resisting a censorship order. Among these are the costs of litigating, even when he does not have to carry the burden of proof, and the costs resulting from delay, which may be considerable even in the administrative appeal alone. The bureau maintains that a film can be reviewed administratively in two weeks.* Yet according to one industry figure, two weeks is merely a minimum, with review sometimes taking as long as two months. Carrying resistance to the point where forfeiture pro-

---

* In a twenty-one month period, January, 1964, to September, 1965, twenty-four feature films received administrative review. The time lapse in the reviews ranged from three to twenty-eight days, with an average of thirteen. *United States* v. *One Carton Positive Motion Picture Film Entitled "491,"* 367 F. 2d 889, 901, n. 14 (2d Cir. 1966).

ceedings are filed, or to actual trial, of course, requires considerably more time. In the *491* case, five and one-half months elapsed between the film's arrival at the port of entry and its delivery to a United States attorney for forfeiture proceedings. The resulting litigation required another seven months. However, the trial record indicated that much of the delay was of the importer's making. Perhaps the factor most discouraging to resistance is the DEW-line function of Customs censorship. A film meeting objections from the bureau very likely would meet them from state and local boards of censors.

As with the state and local licensing, real resistance could be much rarer than appears on the surface. The publicity game may encourage a pseudo-resistance, and intra-industry bargaining may result in an actual invitation to censorship. According to Fishman, who is perhaps exaggerating here because of impatience with the practice, in 90 per cent of the instances in which an importer has gone beyond the administrative review he was seeking publicity rather than a test of the law. Even at the stages of administrative review, Fishman maintains, "importers constantly request that a film be held up." One importer once asked that a decision be delayed until word of its original detention got into the newspapers.

There appears to be much less group contact for the bureau or for its deputy collectors than for the average state or local board of censors. This may be another reason for the greater permissiveness associated with Customs examination; that is, the bureau is further removed from the censorship constituency than are state and local boards. The New York office, for example, receives only about ten letters of complaint a year, and only rarely a telephone call of this nature. Occasionally after a "bad" film, the entire bureau may receive as many as fifty letters. An epistolary outpouring of this kind may be noted by the bureau, but the protests it is more likely to respond to are those expressed more generally, and not necessarily directed to the bureau. For example, complaints to Congress, in one form or another, or attacks in the press on particular kinds of films or on the content of films generally may be taken into account in forming a concept of national standards.

Customs examination puts far fewer economic strains on the film proprietor than does state or local licensing. First, there is no examination fee; duty, of course, is paid independently of censorship review. Second, the logistical cost of Customs examination is minimal. Even without censorship an imported film would have to be sent to Customs, in any case, for the calculation of duty. The examination process itself probably does not keep a film out of circulation much longer than would the mere calculation of duty without a screening. Serious delay of a film raising no question of obscenity or other proscribed content is likely only when it is brought in through a port which does not receive many motion pictures. In such cases the local Customs officials might have to make special screening arrangements, or send the film to another, better equipped port office for examination.

The qualifications of Cairns and Fishman as censors are apparent, yet the initial screening of movies in the various ports falls to diverse personnel. These employees have not been hired nor retained in their positions with the censorship of movies in mind. Over a period of time they may have received considerable instruction in movie examination by occasionally having films forwarded to Washington, yet the bureau's decisions on movies do not circulate among the various ports. The situation is different in New York, and needs to be, since the great majority of imported films enter through that port. There the bureau has two full-time reviewers, apparently making New York the only port with personnel whose main task is screening movies. At one time these reviewers were recruited from the ranks of the Customs service, but this source is said to have been exhausted and examiners are now selected through civil service. Apparently the only requirement for the job, beyond that of the civil service examination, is an understanding of at least two foreign languages. A college education is not required, though the two men who held the positions in 1965 did have college degrees. The jobs are of the GS-7 rank. The supervisory administrative aide who now reviews the reviewers' recommendations is a woman who, though not holding a degree, has worked closely with Fishman for several years. Her job is at the GS-9 level.

IV

THE WIDER MILIEU
OF CENSORSHIP

7

Informal Censorship and Control by the Criminal Process

Prior censorship, with its high visibility and special disfavor with libertarians, has clearly been the most debated and stigmatized control on motion pictures. Yet even without prior censorship the movies would not be "free" in any meaningful sense of that term. Freedom in the medium is actually subject to a number of controls or censorships, many of which are far more restrictive and effective than prior censorship, and some of which may be increasingly exercised for the very reason that prior censorship itself has become less effective. Against a background of several censorships, rather than one, the task of securing freedom of speech in motion pictures in a mass democratic society becomes a far more complicated enterprise than it would seem to be in the somewhat insulated and abstract courtroom contest over a censor board's order.

Control through obscenity prosecution and by informal censorship—extralegal action by public officials, their censorial use of powers not directly related to the content of films, and the pressure of private groups—are examined below. (More circumspect private action in the form of advisory film ratings, as well as voluntary restraints imposed by the film industry upon itself and those self-imposed by film-makers individually, will be considered in Chapter 8.)

A Preferred Method of Control

For many libertarians opposed to prior restraint in any form, a criminal prosecution for possession or exhibition of an obscene film is a preferred means for controlling the content of movies. Yet reliance on the criminal law is often accepted uncritically as though it were in itself a solution to the problem of reconciling freedom and control.

Traditional preference for the criminal law over prior censorship rests on several supposed advantages of the criminal process.[1] For example, the criminal trial is said to provide several important procedural safeguards for the film proprietor: presumption of innocence, the heavier burden of proof borne by the government, availability of a jury, etc. Theoretically, the criminal process also allows the film itself to have entered the "free market-place of ideas" before any restraint can take place, thereby allowing opportunity for greater public notice and criticism. Moreover, when the film in question has not been confiscated, or exhibition of it enjoined, the exhibitor is at least at liberty to show the film until the obscenity issue is adjudicated. And, finally, countless innocent films need not be examined in order to bar a relatively few objectionable ones from exhibition. Thus, when compared with prior censorship, the criminal process is felt not only to afford greater fairness to the film proprietor but also to place a lesser burden on free speech. Yet this preference is open to question on both counts.

First, with recent reforms of the licensing process, the differences between a criminal prosecution and prior censorship as methods of control have become fewer and less striking. In particular, the decision in *Freedman* v. *Maryland* has met many of the procedural objections once raised against licensing. Now, for example, delay in the issuance of a license is limited, the government must carry the burden of proof on the obscenity question, and final determination of the obscenity issue must be prompt and must be made by a court. The great contrast between the criminal process and licensing in large measure disappears as the procedural gap between these two methods of control is narrowed.

Second, the traditional preference for the criminal process tends to overlook, or at least to minimize, some very serious burdens that that process may place upon a film proprietor and, therefore, upon free speech. With the present doctrinal uncertainty surrounding obscenity, reliance on the criminal process forces an exhibitor into an unenviable and necessarily inhibitive "guessing game" with authorities on whether a film is proscribable and, consequently, whether he is committing a crime by showing it. In addition to the always-present possibility of conviction and large fine or imprisonment, there is the probability of delay. To take an extreme example, in *Jacobellis* v. *Ohio,* in which the United States Supreme Court reversed the conviction of a theatre manager for possessing and exhibiting an obscene film, the litigation consumed four and one-half years. Nor was the film shown during that time. Moreover, the indictment was no guarantee of the presumption of innocence outside the courtroom. In the *Jacobellis* situation the six-month period between arrest and conviction saw the theatre manager become the object of assorted indignities apparently inspired in large measure by a group of local authorities and church leaders. (See pages 163–66.)

Heavy costs may be another burden of the criminal process. One distributor and veteran litigant whom I interviewed estimated that with experienced counsel the average trial costs in an obscenity case range between $5,000 and $6,000. Furthermore, even if the film in question is vindicated, few local runs would ever recoup such an outlay for an exhibitor-defendant. More importantly, because local trial judges and juries often find obscenity defendants guilty, vindication frequently requires an appeal. The costs of carrying a film all the way to the Supreme Court, for example, may range between $25,000 and $60,000.

In addition, the criminal process attacks the exhibitor, the very person in the motion picture business who has the fewest resources—material or psychological—with which to defend himself on a criminal charge. Whether the theatre owner himself or merely a hired manager, the average exhibitor is not a wealthy person. He is also likely to be a local resident, and thus someone who depends in large measure on personal goodwill for his economic and social well-being in the community. On the other hand, the distributor, who is likely to have greater material resources and who is seldom a local person, is rarely involved in the use of the criminal process to control obscenity in films.

Perhaps the most serious objection to "solving" the problem of controlling movies by reliance on the criminal process is that often public officials themselves do not rely upon it. That is to say, expectation that the criminal process will be the method of control preferred by officials tends to ignore both the economics and the politics of law enforcement in obscenity controversies. It is true that some exhibitors have actually been tried for showing or possessing allegedly obscene films, that convictions and acquittals have been obtained, and that appeals have been taken, etc. But such invocation and completion of the criminal process is exceptional. Prosecutions are relatively uncommon for two understandable reasons: they are expensive, and convictions, which may or may not be hard to obtain at trial, are hard to have upheld on appeal. As already noted, recent doctrinal developments which have allowed an increasing permissiveness in the communication of erotica have considerably narrowed obscenity as a legal concept. As these developments have made counsel for boards of censors reluctant to take censorship rulings into court, they have also made prosecuting officials hesitant to go to trial on an obscenity issue. Yet these developments have not prevented the same officials from threatening to prosecute, nor from actually using parts of the criminal process—arrest, confiscation, and the attendant publicity—as devices with which to influence local exhibition policies. "Reliance" on the criminal law as the chief means for controlling erotica in the movies would appear less likely to result in criminal trials and adjudication of the obscenity issue than in law enforcement officials using the criminal process as a means of intimidating local exhibitors.

Finally, public officials may choose not to use any part of the criminal process at all, preferring a flank attack to the frontal assault on objectionable films. Leverage of the authorities on the exhibitor here may be based on proceedings or the threat of proceedings—such as theatre license revocation—not directly connected with the obscenity issue, nor, in fact, having any reasonable relation to the content of films at all.

Official Control by Methods Other Than Obscenity Prosecution

An exhibitor may be hurt by official action in a variety of ways. He is an entrepreneur who is vulnerable to threats of, or actual attempts at, interference with his property, reputation, the convenience of his customers and employees, and even his personal liberty. The ways in which the exhibition of particular films or exhibition policies generally can be the object of restrictive action by agents of government are inventoried below. This catalog of informal censorship is based on a survey of motion picture trade journals, including some published primarily for exhibitors, during a two and one-half to five year period.[2] This data, along with reports of private action against exhibitors, is summarized in Tables 13 and 14.

In most, if not all, of the situations described below, officials appeared to be responding to pressures within their communities. In a few instances, they seemed to be acting with considerable hesitation and only after they had tried to blunt the censorial energies. The ambitious local official who undertakes a one-man "cleanup" campaign in Comstock fashion—that is, the sort who occupies the first rank in the classic libertarian demonology—is not a familiar figure in these cases. This finding is at odds with the contentions of many libertarians who believe that official action or threats against exhibitors are to be understood more in terms of the persuasions and ambitions of the local officials themselves than in their response to community pressures. Though public officials may actually be at the bottom of an occasional censorship controversy, the reports repeatedly indicate the presence of community pressures. The libertarian view of the official as prime mover may also reflect a reluctance to recognize that there may be widespread public dissatisfaction with motion picture content, as well as a hesitancy to indict what may actually be the community majority.

In many of the trade press reports of informal censorship, the local authorities often went out of their way to deny that what they were doing was censorship. The felt need to make such unComstockian disclaimers hardly indicates that these authorities see themselves functioning as single-minded crusaders against evil. A more likely description of the role of these officials is that of temporary agents of restrictive community forces, the interests of which must be given high priority because of the political power they may represent.

Incipient Use of the Criminal Process

Where public officials invoke the criminal process against an exhibitor, they may intend to have the issue of obscenity ultimately adjudicated. However, quite apart from such considerations, arrests and confiscations can also serve as harassing devices against recalcitrant exhibitors when other methods of persuasion have failed.

Whatever the intent, the common pattern of action here is arrest of the theatre manager and confiscation of the offending film. This usually occurs after a regular performance witnessed by a prosecuting official, though in many cases the arrest and seizure are made by policemen or detectives acting alone. Often action is taken during a performance, with the law officers dramatically entering the projection booth, ordering the house lights turned up, and allowing a nervous manager to appear on stage to promise the surprised members of the audience that their admission will be refunded.

There are variations on this pattern in terms of both the subjects arrested and the objects of confiscation. In some areas, projectionists have been arrested with theatre managers. In Kansas City, Missouri, a cashier, doorman, and concession-stand operator, as well as the manager and projectionist, were subpoenaed to appear before a grand jury as a result of one police "raid."[3] Police have been known to seize projection equipment along with the film, and in a number of cases seizure of a film has taken place without a search warrant. In one Pennsylvania town, police took the print of a newly arrived film even though they had apparently staged their raid on the basis of complaints about a *previous* film which had completed its run. In this raid, police also confiscated the box office and concession receipts.

Where a drive-in is involved, police action may be on a larger scale and in many ways resemble a vice raid. In Pittston, Pennsylvania, eight state troopers and six city policemen, all of whom entered a local drive-in in unmarked cars, not only seized the film and arrested the manager but also checked the patrons' cars as they departed, making a count of "juveniles" and taking their names and addresses.[4]

Revocation of Theatre Licenses

An official action reported with increasing frequency is the revocation of, or the refusal to renew, an exhibitor's business or occupational license. In many cases this type of action has lacked specific authorization; that is the local officials were without statutory authority to revoke or to refuse to renew a theatre license on the basis of their disapproval of films shown at the theatres in question. However, in other instances officials have been given specific censorial authority, as in the case of Miami, Florida, where the city council authorized the local executive authority to withhold licenses from exhibitors who showed or planned to show "obscene, lewd, lascivious, indecent or filthy" films.[5]

In addition to revocation or attempted revocation, many exhibitors have been licensed with either formal conditions or informal understandings on exhibition policy attaching to their permits. In Bridgeport, Connecticut, an exhibitor whose license had been revoked for screening of what was said to be indecent entertainment was given another license two months later, subject to the written condition "that exhibitions would come under the strict surveillance of the Superintendent of Police and shall conform to the accepted standards of good taste."[6] Authorities in a Massachusetts town renewed a local exhibitor's license on a biweekly basis, and only then on condition that he planned to show "refined" movies. He was required to present titles of the scheduled films to the mayor every two weeks.[7] In Miami, Florida, an exhibitor who had obtained a temporary injunction against the city for refusing to renew his license was given a new license after he agreed to drop his suit *and* discontinue exhibition of "nudies," substituting, instead, "family-type" films.[8] In some Rhode Island towns, local authorities have issued theatre licenses only after exhibitors have promised not to show films condemned by the National Catholic Office for Motion Pictures (formerly the Legion of Decency).

Exhibition without a license may bring other official action. A drive-in operator in Grand Rapids, Michigan, whose license had not been renewed because he had shown allegedly obscene films, was raided when he continued to operate. The general-audience film being screened at the time was seized, as were the night's box office receipts.[9]

Whether in the form of revocation, refusal to renew, or attached conditions, the use of theatre-licensing power against the content of films is clearly of dubious constitutionality. Yet this form of official censorship appears to be effective particularly where it is timed to work the greatest economic hardship on the exhibitor. Even if an exhibitor is willing to resist, his effective remedy—an injunction against the local officials—requires the hiring of counsel and possibly a temporary suspension of operations.

New Legislation Aimed at the Content of Films

Attempts by state and municipal legislative bodies to set up controls on motion pictures other than through prior censorship appear to be on the increase. Many of these measures are highly restrictive; and, though their constitutionality is clearly in doubt in some cases, they all would provide police and prosecuting officials not only with additional formal powers against the content of films, but new means of intimidating the film proprietors.

A large number of these proposals are efforts to redraft obscenity statutes, often to increase the penalties for second, third, etc. offenses. Some proposals go beyond the proscription of obscenity. A bill introduced in the North Carolina legislature in 1965 would have made it a criminal offense to show movies portraying drug addiction or acts of mayhem "in an attractive manner," while an ordinance in High Point, North Carolina, barred "any picture of a female person over the age of twelve whose breast or breasts are nude."[10]

A 1963 Texas measure would have required films to carry the Motion Picture Code's Seal of Approval before they could be shown.[11] In effect, such a law would have virtually eliminated the showing of foreign films; that is, unless the distributors of those films were to change their prevailing policy of refusing to submit them to the Motion Picture Production Code Administration (which charges a fee for the examination service). Officials in at least one municipality—Lee's Summit, Missouri—actually did enact such a law in 1964.[12]

Probably the type of control most frequently proposed in recent years has been one that would make it a crime to show certain types of films to juveniles, usually persons under eighteen. In most cases these proposals would establish a less rigorous test for obscenity than the now prevailing *Roth-Alberts* standard. For example, a measure in the 1965 California legislature would have barred exhibition of "morally corruptive" films to anyone under eighteen. "Morally corruptive" was defined in the bill as

. . . that which an average person, applying contemporary community standards, would conclude is improper for distribution to minors under 18 years of age because the predominant appeal of the matter, taken as a whole, is to the prurient interest of such minors; that is to say, a shameful or morbid interest in nudity, sex, or excretion, which goes substantially beyond customary limits of candor in describing or representing such matter to a minor under 18 years of age.[13]

Ten obscenity control bills, each designed to bar the dissemination of offensive material to minors, were introduced in the 1965 session of the New York legislature alone. One of the bills that included movies within its provisions was enacted.[14] During 1965, similar bills were introduced in the California, Florida, Massachusetts, Missouri, Montana, Nebraska, New Jersey, Oregon, South Carolina, Tennessee and Wisconsin legislatures.[15]

In several communities, drive-ins whose screens are visible from neighborhood homes and streets have become the target of special legislation. Such "public" exhibition has been frequently proscribed with standards more restrictive than that of obscenity. In 1966 a federal court of appeals upheld a Texas city's ordinance forbidding exhibition of any film visible from any public street in which "the bare buttocks or the bare female breasts of the human body are shown or in which striptease, burlesque or nudist-type scenes constitute the main or primary material . . ."[16] Elsewhere, drive-in "visibility" ordinances have been combined with zoning regulations to put a double pressure on the theatre. In one North Carolina community, a drive-in operator, charged with violating an ordinance forbidding any "nude or seminude" picture to be visible to the general public outside the theatre, offered to erect a nine-foot fence to eliminate the "visibility," only to have the local zoning authority refuse to grant an exception to the existing zoning regulations limiting fences to three feet in height.[17]

Investigatory power may also be a source of governmental influence on exhibition. In Houston, a justice of the peace exercised a seldom-used power of Texas justices of the peace and held a court of inquiry on whether obscene films were being shown at two art theatres in Houston. The subpoena power was used to obtain testimony from the theatre managers.[18]

Restrictive Action Not Technically Aimed at the Content of Films

Enactment or enforcement of laws relating to public order, safety, or morality can often be devices by which public authorities attempt to influence exhibition policies of local theatres. They may also be a means of punishing uncooperative exhibitors not easily reached by legal attacks on the content of their films. The instances of restrictive action which follow may or may not have been so motivated. Yet in many of the cases there were reports of complaints against the types of films which had been playing at the theatres in question. In some of the cases, of course, the restrictive action is transparent in its purpose.

In Columbus, Ohio, the city fire department, conducting a "routine" inspection a few days after the manager of an art theatre was arrested for showing *Les Liaisons Dangereuses,* found several fire hazards in the theatre and ordered it closed. The fire inspectors claimed that the theatre had bad projection booth wiring, that the fireproof shutters (in front of the projectors) were out of order, that the exit lights in the auditorium had not lit, and that "some other miscellaneous violations of fire division regulations" were found.[19]

In Lancaster County, Pennsylvania, the county attorney succeeded in ending Sunday exhibition at three drive-ins by invoking a state blue law enacted in 1794. The three theatres involved had been showing films on Sundays for twelve, seven, and six years respectively. The county attorney reported that he had received "numerous" anonymous complaints against films being shown at two of the three theatres.[20]

In an admitted effort to reduce attendance of juveniles at films he generally regarded as suitable only for adults, the New York City commissioner of licenses in 1965 began strict enforcement of a city ordinance requiring theatres to maintain separate supervised sections for unaccompanied children under the age of sixteen. Little or no attempt had been made to enforce this regulation previously.[21]

In a number of cities, attempts have been made to effect sharp increases in theatre or occupational license fees, in some cases by more than 100 per cent. In Scranton, Pennsylvania, two theatre chains succeeded in having a license fee increase ruled illegal on the ground that it was "a revenue-raising measure in the guise of police and safety regulations." The city council had raised the annual fee from twenty to fifty cents per seat.[22]

Drive-in theatres have been subject to various restrictions based on local zoning and public nuisance laws. In many communities permits for construction of drive-ins, petitions for amending zoning laws to allow construction, and requests to move drive-ins have been denied. A number of bills were introduced in state legislatures in 1965 and 1966 either aimed specifically at drive-ins or affecting their operations in an indirect way. In Ohio it was proposed that no drive-in be allowed to operate after one-thirty a.m.[23] Since exhibition cannot begin until nine or nine-thirty p.m. during the summer months with daylight saving, such a proposal would probably have made drive-ins unprofitable during those months. An even more destructive measure economically was a proposal in the Indiana Assembly to require drive-ins to hire a guard for every carload of patrons.[24] A bill barring anyone under eighteen from attending a theatre that let out after ten p.m. was defeated in Nebraska.[25] Similar laws have actually been enacted in several cities and towns in other states. In Parma, Ohio, an ordinance later held unconstitutional had required all drive-ins to close by 12:01 a.m.[26] In several instances authorities have proceeded against patrons of drive-ins under morality laws. Police in one city were able to secure the withdrawal of an objectionable film by threatening to prosecute patrons for fornication.[27] Along the same lines, the mayor of Grand Prairie, Texas, invited to speak to a local Rotary on "Curbing Lewd Movies," was able to tell his listeners that "our police arrested forty-four characters on morals charges in one foray."[28]

There is at least one reported instance of public authorities apparently attempting to undermine the business of a theatre—in this case, an indoor theatre—by themselves going into the exhibition business. In Red Wing, Minnesota, a local exhibitor lost a seven-year struggle in the courts to keep the city's municipal auditorium from being used as a motion picture theatre. The exhibitor had succeeded in stopping the city from operating the movie enterprise itself, but failed later in an attempt to keep the city from leasing the auditorium to a private party.[29]

An unusual instance of punitive action that may have been based on a censorship interest involved the dismissal of a San Francisco medical social worker from his job at the city-run General Hospital in October, 1964. The social worker, one Saul Landau, was the head of a group which had sponsored a showing of the Jean Genet film *Un Chant d'Amour* at a local hotel. The film, which has a homosexual theme, had been the object of censorial action and pressure in a number of cities. At an earlier San Francisco showing, also sponsored by Landau, the film had been seized by police, but was later returned by the district attorney's office. However, the day after its hotel exhibition, Landau was dismissed from his job for what his lawyer said was the "exercise of his constitutionally guaranteed rights." Hospital officials, though admitting they had objections to Landau's sponsorship of the film, maintained that he was fired for absenteeism.[30]

Miscellaneous Official Pressure

Exhibitors are subject to a wide variety of direct threats or attempts at "persuasion" by public officials. The examples of this that follow do not include those threats made in connection with (usually in advance of) the cases of official action already described.

As Table 12 shows, miscellaneous pressures against exhibitors take the form of "demands," "warnings," "advice" or mere "requests." The possibility of raids, confiscation, arrest, theatre license revocation, and injunction are among the official actions reported as threatened. Agents of these pressures have included prosecuting attorneys, police chiefs, sheriffs, city councils, mayors, and rank-and-file members of police forces. Usually the object of the pressure is a single film and often, though not always, a nudist or "nudie" film. In some cases an entire exhibition policy—usually a nudist or "nudie" policy—is the source of complaint. In other cases, admission of children to "adult" films is the only issue. In every case but one in Table 12, the major concern was with the effects of erotica. In the one exception, involving *Black Like Me* in Miami, Florida, the chief of police based his ob-

TABLE 12 *Reported Miscellaneous Pressures Against Exhibitors by Governmental Authorities, January, 1962, through December, 1966*

Location	Date	Agent	Object	Pressure
Montclair, N.J.	Feb., 1962	police commissioner	single film	request for withdrawal
New Orleans, La.	Feb., 1962	"city authorities"	single film	demand to view
Houston, Tex.	July, 1962	justice of the peace	exhibition policy	court of inquiry

TABLE 12, *Continued*

Location	Date	Agent	Object	Pressure
Asheville, N.C.	Jan., 1963	city council	exhibition policy	"advising change"
West Memphis, Ark.	March, 1963	city council	exhibition policy	threat of raids
Rochester, N.Y.	Oct., 1963	city attorney	admission of children	"warning"
Pittsburgh, Pa.	Nov., 1963	city, county attorneys	single film	threat of injunction
East Cleveland, Ohio	Dec., 1963	law director	single film	threat of prosecution
Atlanta, Ga.	March, 1964	asst. city attorney	single film	threat of arrest
Lewiston, Me.	March, 1964	county attorney	single film	request for withdrawal
Atlanta, Ga.	June, 1964	mayor	submission of three films for review	threat of confiscation
Braintree, Mass.	June, 1964	police chief	single film	threat of license revocation
Cleveland, Ohio	July, 1964	city prosecutor	single film	request for withdrawal
Chattanooga, Tenn.	July, 1964	mayor, amusement board	exhibition policy	request for change
Albuquerque, N.M.	Jan., 1965	city commissioner	exhibition policy	request for change
East Chicago, Ind.	Feb., 1965	justice of the peace	admission of children	"edict" and "investigation"
Coral Gables, Fla.	Aug., 1965	city commission	exhibition policy	request for cooperation
St. Louis, Mo.	Sept., 1965	state senator	exhibition policy	threat of injunction
Kansas City, Mo.	March, 1966	member of recreation dept. staff	admission of children	"order"
North Miami, Fla.	Nov., 1966	city council	exhibition policy	resolution urging change
Los Angeles, Calif.	Dec., 1966	police	single film	threat of prosecution

Table is based upon the following publications and periods covered: *Variety*, Jan. 1, 1962, to Jan. 1, 1967; *Boxoffice*, July 1, 1964, to Jan. 1, 1967; *Motion Picture Exhibitor*, July 1, 1964, to Jan. 1, 1967; *Motion Picture Daily*, Sept. 1, 1964, to Jan. 1, 1967; and *Motion Picture Herald*, Sept. 1, 1964, to Oct. 1, 1965.

jections on the danger of a race riot.[31] The film, however, contains dialogue related to sex questions, including those of an interracial character. In one other case, involving the New Orleans premiere of *Walk on the Wild Side,* the adaptation of the Nelson Algren novel which is set in a seamy section of the city, local officials were concerned about damage to the city's image.[32]

Sometimes the communication between officials and exhibitor is by telephone, but more often than not it is through face-to-face contact, usually with the officials visiting the theatre. Occasionally, local exhibitors are asked to meet with city officials. From these meetings "agreements" are sometimes announced in which the exhibitors have usually made promises to cooperate.

In most instances of pressure noted in Table 12, initial compliance with the official requests or demands was obtained. This usually meant withdrawal of a film in question. Where an entire exhibition policy was under attack, compliance meant a change in the policy, though, here at least, occasional lapses into the former policy have been reported. Situations in which exhibitors have resisted, to one degree or another, have been discussed elsewhere in this section, since such resistance has often been met with official action going beyond mere threat: for example, arrest, confiscation, license revocation, or some punitive action not aimed directly at the exhibition policy.

Compliance, either immediate or after some initial resistance, appears to be the rule in the cases of official pressure. During a seven-year period in Madison, Wisconsin, in which about forty movie complaints arose, the city ordinance authorizing the police department to ban an obscene or immoral film was reported never to have been invoked. The police inspector charged with viewing films about which complaints were received credited this record to the fact that local theatre managers consistently concurred with police suggestions. In fact, the managers reportedly often *asked* the police to preview questionable movies they had scheduled. Apparently they then went along with whatever the police decided.[33]

Private Action and Pressure Against Exhibitors

Though the effective restriction of exhibition is usually at the hands of governmental authorities, the source of almost all censorial energy related to the exhibition of films in the United States is private. In many, if not most, of the instances of official action or pressure against exhibitors noted in the preceding sections, the authorities said they were acting or were reported to have been acting only after receiving N-number of complaints, telephone calls, names on petitions, etc. In many cases, there had been earlier trade-press reports of complaints by private individuals and groups, or of other forms of private pressure in the same community or against the same theatre. Generally speaking, private action or pressure, whether organized or unorganized, represents an early stage in a censorship controversy. At later stages where official action has been stimulated, private action may also be in evidence. And in some cases, private pressure or action continues where official pressure or action was apparently refused or where it had failed.

Some of the private groups attempting to influence exhibition are *ad hoc* organizations such as Combat, a group formed by the representatives of various churches and church-connected organizations in Wauwautosa, Wisconsin, or the Mothers of Minnesota, or the Atlantic City–Cape May County (New Jersey) Citizens Committee. Yet most of the pressure groups in the field appear to be established groups, that is, groups not organized primarily to fight obscenity. These groups have many other functions, and often the motion-picture control activities are handled by sub-units. Examples of such organizations or their sub-groups are the High Point, North Carolina, Ministerial Alliance, the Bridgeport, Connecticut, Pastors Association, the Louisville, Kentucky, PTA, the Do Something About It Committee for the Moral Safety, of the New Orleans Council of Catholic School Cooperative Clubs, the Connecticut Catholic War Veterans, the Fort Lauderdale, Florida, NAACP Youth Council, the Fort Lauderdale, Florida, chapter of the International Longshoremen's Association. A few groups or "citizens committees," such as the Gaston County, North Carolina, Sheriff's Committee on Obscenity, have quasi-official status.

The pressure groups usually operate at one or more of three action levels. They may address other groups or the general public, public officials, or exhibitors directly. Speaking to the public may take the form of circulating or publishing film ratings, providing speakers for the meetings of other groups, writing letters to newspapers, etc. At the second level, the groups may try to interest local, state, and even national authorities in some kind of executive or legislative action against an exhibitor or against movie exhibition generally. Positive results at this pressure level have been described in preceding sections.

Direct action against an exhibitor usually involves an attempt to induce cooperation from him in an atmosphere that may range from cordiality to outright hostility. Occasionally it includes picketing of the theatre, and in some cases an attempt to boycott it for a period of time. Sometimes children or adolescents are used in the picketing. One unusual instance of direct action involved the closing of an art theatre in Fort Wayne, Indiana, after the owner of the building housing the theatre terminated the exhibitor's lease. There was some indication that the pressure did not originate with the landlord, who maintained that although the termination would cost him $27,000 on the lease, the action was still worthwhile since "I live here." Termination of the lease occurred at the same time the city's mayor threatened to revoke the exhibitor's business license.[34]

Individuals or groups have also taken legal action against exhibitors. In Louisville, Kentucky, local PTA groups sued to enjoin an exhibitor from showing allegedly obscene films.[35] Several hundred residents of Marion County, Indiana, appealed a ruling of the county board of zoning appeals in an effort to block construction of a drive-in theatre. An attorney for the residents produced a sixteen-page list of films shown at two *other* drive-ins owned by the applicant for the zoning permit. The attorney described the films as "offensive" to the community's morals.[36]

Organized Roman Catholic Pressure

The Roman Catholic Church probably ranks as the most important single group in the control of movies in this country at any level: production, distribution, or exhibition. As censorial pressure, Catholic strength rests on numbers, a potential for militancy, and a programmatic development which includes a moral evaluation and a systematic rating of all leading commercial films shown in the country. (Catholic influence on production and distribution will be examined in Chapter 8. Here we will consider only the Church's action with respect to exhibition.)

The National Catholic Office for Motion Pictures, formerly the Legion of Decency, rates films as "A-I," morally unobjectionable for general patronage; "A-II," morally unobjectionable for adults and adolescents; "A-III," morally unobjectionable for adults; "B," objectionable in part for all; and "C," condemned. There is, in addition, a special "A-IV" rating for films which, though not being morally offensive, require some explanation and analysis as a protection for the uninformed against wrong interpretations. These ratings, circulated in all dioceses and also to a limited extent to the general non-Catholic public, are considered moral guides by church officials. Decisions to implement the ratings through organized activity, and the choice of methods to be used, are left with the bishop in each diocese and, to a lesser extent, with local priests.

Implementation may take several forms: encouragement of individual Catholics to observe the ratings, pressure on public officials to take formal or some kind of informal action against exhibitors showing "C" or, in some cases, "B" films, and direct organized action against the exhibitor who shows "C" or "B" films.

Encouragement of individual church members to observe the ratings in their own movie-going habits is the most sustained method of giving force to the Church's position on particular films. This observance is realized mainly through a pledge to support the ratings, offered annually in every parish. In addition to the pledge, church publications often reflect concern about certain films and stress the importance of individual Catholics not patronizing them. For example, *The Evangelist,* the official weekly of the Albany, New York, diocese, editorially criticized the showing of *Poor White Trash* at several local drive-ins, and suggested that "theatres that prefer such questionable fare should be avoided by all who have a respect for moral standards and an appreciation of their worth as intelligent creatures of God."[37] Stronger church pressures on individual Catholics may exist in some communities. According to one film proprietor whom I interviewed, a condemned film was withdrawn from a Dobbs Ferry, New York, theatre for lack of patronage, after a local priest stationed himself at a table in an empty store across the street from the theatre and wrote down the names of parishioners who entered. In areas with large Catholic populations, organized church pressure may have particular force. In Montclair, New Jersey, *Les Liaisons Dangereuses* was withdrawn from a local theatre at the request of the city's police commissioner after the film had been denounced at local masses the Sunday before.[38] In Warwick, Rhode Island, the city's board of public safety threatened to suspend the business license of a local theatre if the proprietors did not cancel a booking of *Kiss Me, Stupid,* which had been condemned by the Legion of Decency. The board cited a promise by the exhibitor, at the time his original license was issued, not to book condemned films.[39]

Direct Catholic pressure on or action against an exhibitor may take several forms. Parishioners may be asked to write letters demanding that a film be withdrawn. In Newark, New Jersey, the archdiocesan office of the Legion of Decency once distributed "decency kits" outlining procedures for a campaign against indecent films, which included committees to call upon theatre managers.[40] Often action is limited to particular films. The management of a Staten Island, New York, theatre cancelled a booking of the condemned *Boccaccio 70* after it reported receiving "hundreds" of letters from irate citizens citing the Legion's rating.[41] In California, four foreign films which had received condemned ratings were withdrawn from a film festival of a local fine arts association in San Luis Obispo, following the protests of two local priests who threatened a boycott of the theatre which sponsored the festival.[42]

Actual boycotts against theatres are organized either to protest a continuing exhibition policy or to punish the theatre management for exhibition of a condemned film in the past. In Albuquerque, New Mexico, a diocesan boycott of an indoor and of an outdoor theatre, each having a nudist and "nudie" policy, was sustained for three months and was lifted only after the theatres returned to more conventional exhibition.[43] A boycott of a Lancaster, Pennsylvania, art theatre lasted more than five years and extended, intentionally or unintentionally, to other activities held at the theatre from time to time.[44] In a well-known boycott staged several years ago, Catholics in the Albany, New York, diocese were forbidden to attend any theatre for six months which had shown the condemned *Baby Doll*.[45]

In many areas Catholic influence is great, though overt pressure is slight —that is to say, there is considerable cooperation between church authorities and exhibitors. In St. Paul, Minnesota, a city with a very large Catholic population, nudist or "nudie" pictures are never booked; and even some popular foreign films, such as *Never on Sunday*—probably assured of a profitable run in almost any location—were reported never to have played in the city.[46] In Milwaukee, an exhibitor who had signed a booking contract for the condemned *Kiss Me, Stupid* before it was completed, and therefore before it had received the Legion of Decency's rating, actually contacted a local Catholic priest to get his opinion on the film before showing it. The exhibitor agreed not to schedule the film during the Christmas holidays, the most popular moviegoing period of the year.[47] In Albuquerque, New Mexico, where there had been an earlier Catholic boycott, a group of exhibitors, representing seventeen of twenty-one local theatres, drew up a code of ethics in which they agreed not to book any film condemned by the National Catholic Office.[48]

Church authorities have occasionally shown sympathy for the economic situation of the local exhibitor and have been alert to encourage exhibition of favorably rated films. In recent years the National Catholic Office (Legion of Decency) has annually cited a number of films for excellence or wholesomeness in entertainment. In some communities where Catholic pressure has resulted in the withdrawal of a film, an effort has been made to organize moviegoing support for either the substitute film or for approved films shown at the theatre in question. In Augusta, Georgia, for example, 200 of 311 students of the local Catholic high school turned out to see a film held over as a substitute for the condemned *Kiss Me, Stupid,* which the local exhibitor had withdrawn upon the presentation of a Catholic-sponsored petition with 1,500 names.[49] On a somewhat different level, church authorities in Lake Placid, New York, once offered an exhibitor $350 in lieu of receipts, and their assistance in obtaining a substitute movie, if he would withdraw the Brigitte Bardot film *And God Created Woman*. His refusal resulted in a six-month ban against the theatre.[50]

Direct Catholic action alone has been an important local control on motion pictures. When such pressure has been exercised in concert with official action, the result is often a very formidable community force. As shown by the experience of Nico Jacobellis, described in the next section, its effect can be substantial not only on an exhibitor's work but on his personal life as well.

The Jacobellis Syndrome

On June 22, 1964, the United States Supreme Court held the film *The Lovers* not to be obscene, and reversed the conviction of Nico Jacobellis, a theatre manager who had shown it at the Cleveland Heights, Ohio, Art Theatre on November 13, 1959.[51] Though libertarians were heartened by the outcome of this controversy, Jacobellis' personal experience as an exhibitor willing to resist attempts of local authorities and private citizens to control the content of films was anything but reassuring. His situation illustrates the kinds of powerful pressures that can be brought against a local exhibitor by the coincidence of official and private action within a community.*

That resistance for Jacobellis was possible at all was due to the willingness of his employer, Louis Sher, owner of the theatre and of several other art theatres in Ohio, and Daniel Frankel, distributor of the film, to see the controversy go into the courts, underwrite the legal expenses, and appeal initial adverse decisions to the Ohio Supreme Court and later to the United States Supreme Court. Ultimate success was also due in no small measure to their decision to retain Ephraim London, probably the country's leading film censorship attorney. Frankel estimated that the trial and appeal costs of Jacobellis' case and of a concurrent case involving the conviction of a theatre manager in Dayton, Ohio,[52] also for showing *The Lovers,* totaled $70,000. The distributor believes that Cleveland Heights authorities attacked Jacobellis, rather than himself or Sher, because Jacobellis was the only one of the three lacking the personal resources with which to defend himself. According to Frankel, Jacobellis had nothing whatever to do with the booking of *The Lovers.* He was merely the theatre manager, and had he refused to play the film "he could have been fired on the spot."

Jacobellis, described by Ward Marsh, film critic for the Cleveland *Plain Dealer* and a prosecution witness at his trial, as "amiable, friendly, and utterly sincere,"[53] emigrated from Italy in the early 1950's and had managed the Heights Art Theatre for several years before his arrest. The theatre itself was opened in 1954, the same year state censorship was terminated in Ohio. It is located near a quiet intersection of two residential streets lined with apartment houses and older homes converted into multi-family dwellings. It is a neighborhood housing a suburban upper middle class. The theatre is small even by art theatre standards. Its balcony is no longer in

* I am particularly indebted to Nico Jacobellis and to Daniel Frankel, president of Zenith International Films and distributor of *The Lovers,* for supplying many of the details of the controversy noted in this section; and to Mrs. Marion Kelly, reporter for the Cleveland Heights *Sun Press,* for making available her personal files on the matter.

use and the balcony lobby has been converted into the manager's office. There are no large displays in the downstairs outer lobby, and modern art hangs on the walls of the inner lobby, where Jacobellis serves coffee between performances. The atmosphere is subdued and nothing whatever suggests sensationalism. The theatre has never had a children's admission.

According to Jacobellis, several officials in Cleveland Heights had been against establishment of an art theatre from the beginning and tended to associate foreign films with salacity. Before eruption of *The Lovers* controversy, local police had occasionally asked to view films before opening, and Jacobellis obliged in these instances. Apparently the only occasion in which the police had attempted to overtly influence exhibition policy occurred during the run of *The Snow Is Black*. At that time they had asked Jacobellis to put up a sign saying that no one under twenty-one would be admitted. He refused, and arrived at the theatre the next day to find that such a sign had been put up at the box office window anyway. He removed the sign and later refused a police request that such a notice be included on the marquee.

The theatre manager was arrested on November 13, 1959, during a performance of *The Lovers*. He was fingerprinted, photographed, booked on charges of possessing and of exhibiting an obscene motion picture, and released on $100 personal bond. The episode was reported the next day in the Cleveland *Plain Dealer* as the lead story with a banner headline and three pictures of the arrest. The arresting officer was quoted as saying that Jacobellis had been warned three years earlier about showing obscene films at the time a Swedish film had played. "We told him that we expected theatre managers to do their own censoring, but that we would make spot checks."[54]

The arresting officer said the police had received several complaints, but he did not know whether any of the callers had actually seen the film. The chief of police was clear about the role of the police in local movie exhibition: they viewed films about which "questions" were raised, and the theatre managers were then asked to cut those scenes which the police regarded as harmful to public morals. "Up to this point we have merely sought—and received—the cooperation of the movie house operators. We don't act as censors and we don't propose to."[55]

Jacobellis believes the motivating force behind the arrest and seizure was pressure from local Roman Catholics, particularly from several members of the parish Citizens for Decent Literature group. Indeed, in the week following his arrest the diocesan *Catholic Universe Bulletin* called attention to the fact that the Art Theatre, in its early years, had run many films formerly barred by the state board of censors, and added that the theatre "has habitually screened films condemned by the Legion of Decency."[56]

After his arrest, the theatre manager was the object of varied and persistent harassment. He and his attorneys received crank calls. One man phoned Jacobellis at two and at four a.m. several consecutive mornings. The callers were threatening, often obscene, and occasionally referred to him as a Jew, though he is, in fact, a Roman Catholic. He eventually had his telephone removed. Deliverymen, taxi-cabs, television repairmen whom he had never summoned, regularly turned up at his apartment. He also received several anonymous and threatening notes. Eventually he stopped answering his door.

Later, the police searched his apartment in an attempt to discover obscene materials. They bore a warrant issued by a municipal court judge on the basis of an *anonymous* letter received by the police, which claimed that Jacobellis had shown lewd films. According to the theatre manager, he had to sit in his underwear and watch while police officers "tore up" his apartment. The only finding of interest was a recording of Carl Sandburg's *The People, Yes* which the police at first believed might be a "party" record. Coincidentally, reporters and photographers from the local and the Cleveland press had learned of the search and were waiting in front of Jacobellis' building when the police arrived. The judge who had issued the warrant was later criticized in an editorial in the local *Sun Press*. However, he said he didn't think any of Jacobellis' rights had been violated, and added that it would be well not to make a "fuss" about the raid because it might hurt Jacobellis' case.[57] Shortly after the raid, Jacobellis quit his apartment and for several weeks lived in his office at the theatre.

According to the theatre manager, the Cleveland *Plain Dealer* refused to accept any ads from the Art Theatre for a number of weeks following his arrest. Finally, during the Christmas week the paper took an ad for the film *Albert Schweitzer,* and continued to accept ads after that, though no reason was given for the earlier refusals.

Jacobellis also claims that punitive measures were taken against him by the local Roman Catholic Church of which he was a member. Some time after his arrest he married a young woman from Verona, Italy, who had been visiting the United States. An Italian bishop, also from Verona and who had known Jacobellis' fiancee, was, coincidentally, visiting the local parish at the time. The bishop agreed to say a mass himself for Jacobellis and his fiancee. However, Jacobellis claims that an order came from diocesan headquarters cancelling the mass and that "there was even some feeling that I should not set foot again in the church." At this time, also, he had not yet obtained American citizenship, and according to Frankel there was "talk on the part of some of the clerical people of having him deported."

On June 9, 1960, after a seven-day trial before a three-judge court, Jacobellis was convicted on both the counts of possessing and of exhibiting an obscene film. He was fined $500 on the first and $2,000 on the second, and was then held six days in the county jail while a probation report was prepared.

Admittedly, Jacobellis' experience with community censorial forces was extreme, yet the pattern of restriction is not unique. Its various elements are familiar to many exhibitors. Jacobellis' eventual exoneration four years after his conviction and four and one-half years after his arrest can offer slight encouragement to other exhibitors faced with the coincident pressures of local authorities and of powerful community religious groups.

Informal Censorship: Effectiveness

In strict legal terms, informal control always involves a voluntary act. That is to say, where public officials or private groups have succeeded in informally restricting exhibition they have been able to *persuade* an exhibitor to yield to their wishes (rather than forcing him with a legal order such as that resulting from an adjudication of the obscenity issue). Such persuasion is hard to trace, partly because it is often covert, and is intended to be so by the parties involved. Even when it is overt, the circumstances are usually such that each of the parties has an interest in exaggerating the relative effectiveness or ineffectiveness of the influence.

In the case of exhibition, persuasion—that is, successful informal control —can function at two levels. The one is that of overt controversy, where persuasion is aimed at effecting an immediate objective against a degree of resistance. The objective is usually the withdrawal of a particular film from a run already under way, cancellation of a future booking, or a change in an exhibition policy itself. In the last, the objectionable policy usually has been one of frequent or exclusive exhibition of nudist or "nudie" films, though occasionally, as in the Jacobellis situation, objections have been made to American or foreign films of quality. In a few instances, the immediate aim of informal control is merely that of persuading the exhibitor not to admit children or younger adolescents to a particular film.

At the second level, persuasion is self-operating and reveals itself only through anticipation. An exhibitor who feels the edge of informal control once in an overt controversy, for example, may be especially reluctant to experience it again in that form. In such cases censorial influence becomes self-operating and very likely leaves no trace at all. Undoubtedly, in many local situations, informal control has always operated at this level; that is, the exhibitor has merely anticipated the limits of pressure-free decision-making, or at least has not been anxious to find out what the actual limits might be.

For these reasons, reliable estimates of the efficiency of informal control are hard to make. Probably only some kind of survey of exhibitors, local law-enforcement authorities, and perhaps even of the leadership of local pressure groups would begin to yield rigorous data. Yet even here, because of the element of anticipation, perhaps only more probing studies of decision-making of the various individual exhibitors would actually lay bare the grip of informal influence on exhibition.

Though conclusive evidence is not available, some speculation about the force of informal censorship can be made on the basis of information that is available. And from this it appears that informal censorship is probably a far more effective restriction on exhibition than many libertarians either realize or are willing to admit, and that it is probably a far more effective restriction than either of the two leading formal controls: prior censorship and criminal prosecution.

For example, if the twenty-five reports of miscellaneous official pressure against exhibitors in Table 12 are taken as evidence, they reveal exhibitor compliance with the pressure in all but five or six instances. And, of these five or six, in only two was there any suggestion of formal resistance on the part of the exhibitor. In both instances the exhibitor was reported preparing to ask for an injunction against the harassment. The situation in Madison, Wisconsin, may or may not be typical, but in that city—the home of a great university and therefore a community in which an exhibitor might expect relatively strong public support for the free speech side of a censorship issue —the local police reported that exhibitors were *always* willing to go along with police suggestions about particular films.

Trade press reports reveal somewhat greater incidence of exhibitor resistance when local authorities went beyond threats or "advice" and actually took some kind of action, even though the action was not technically aimed at control of exhibition. For example, some exhibitors were reported to have enjoined or to have attempted to enjoin attempts to revoke business licenses. One exhibitor was also reported to have brought an antitrust action to prevent a municipality from allowing a public auditorium to be used as a movie theatre in competition with his own. But these instances of resistance appear to be exceptions to the rule, at least as informal censorship is reported in the trade press. They may indicate unusual resistance situations, since all of them involved the overt governmental action which often marks a relatively late stage in a censorship controversy.

The extensive compliance that accompanied the reports of miscellaneous official pressure in Table 12 is all the more striking when it is realized that such censorship is likely to find its way into trade-press reports only when an exhibitor has offered considerable resistance, at least initially. How much more widespread are instances of informal censorship in which there is little or no resistance on the part of the exhibitor can only be imagined.

Though there have been a few reports of the attempts of various non-

Catholic groups to secure exhibitor cooperation, most of the available data on the effectiveness of purely private pressure involve Roman Catholic influence. Indeed, since Catholic pressure is tied to the National Catholic Office ratings, these ratings provide a ready standard against which effectiveness may be assayed. Catholic influence on exhibition may be effective at the level of overt controversy, in which some exhibitor resistance has been offered, as well as at the second or self-operating level.

At the former level, Catholic influence may sometimes be devastating. In the Lake Placid, New York, situation, the town's only theatre closed following a punitive boycott by local Catholic Church officials and parishioners. In Lancaster, Pennsylvania, Catholic pressure was credited with helping to turn a potentially profitable art theatre into a "touch-and-go" operation, and with leading to the eventual closing of the theatre.[58] Catholic boycotts have been reported to have caused declines in business at theatres for months after a condemned film had been shown.[59] Direct Catholic pressure has also effected changes in exhibition policies, and the withdrawal of particular films.

In spite of many apparent successes, overt direct Catholic pressure on exhibition often risks a self-defeating consequence. A well-publicized loss of Catholic patronage may be more than made up for by the increased non-Catholic patronage, resulting either from the greater publicity given to the supposedly sensational aspects of the film in question or from a possible annoyance of non-Catholics with the application of ecclesiastically based pressure.

Generally stated, the effectiveness of direct Catholic pressure not accompanied by governmental action or threat probably depends on the degree of economic deprivation that can be inflicted on the exhibitor, minus whatever self-defeating potential there is to the publication of Catholic pressure. The amount of economic punishment that can be meted out, in turn, probably depends on the relative size of the local Catholic community and on the degree of militancy that diocesan and parish leadership can generate. From the exhibitor's side, two other factors may be important to whether or not Catholic pressure—or for that matter, any kind of pressure—is successful. One of these is the estimated box-office potential of the film in question. A condemned film with demonstrated drawing power, such as *Never on Sunday,* has been known to furnish exhibitors with unusual courage. Another factor operating with less frequency is the chronic shortage of films with apparent profit-making potential. Because of this a few exhibitors have taken chances on condemned films they might otherwise have shunned.

Overt Catholic influence usually represents a failure of other modes of Catholic influence, just as overt governmental action usually represents the failure of other official attempts at persuasion. All of this is to say that much Catholic influence as well as the most effective Catholic influence is probably of the self-operating kind. Many exhibitors never book condemned films and probably have never even given thought to booking such films. Other exhibitors may actually consult with the local Catholic clergy before making final arrangements for a condemned film, or even for one given a "B" rating ("morally objectionable in part for all"). Generally speaking, the circuits (the large theatre chains) do not book condemned films at all. In addition to this, according to a trade publisher interviewed, many exhibitors who "have never even seen a Catholic" will not book condemned films, apparently out of fear that such films are of a type that would provoke general censorial reaction.

In general, it can be said that self-operating Catholic influence is probably greatest in those cities and towns with a relatively high proportion of Catholics in their populations, such as Milwaukee, Wisconsin, and St. Paul, Minnesota, and is probably greater in the smaller rather than in the larger of those cities and towns. A booking agent for theatres in small towns in Wisconsin, particularly those in the eastern half of the state where the percentage of Catholics in the population is relatively high, told me that in these towns there is probably a high correlation between the National Catholic Office for Motion Pictures rating for a film (that is, the degree of approbation, beginning with "A-1—morally unobjectionable for general patronage," etc.) and the film's gross receipts. However, whether this supposed correlation is due to Catholic discipline or merely to the cinematic preferences of persons living in small towns, is not clear.

Self-operating Catholic influence is probably also greater in the case of large theatres (many of which are in the circuits)—theatres which play large-budget, first-run films which depend on large audiences to return a profit. Conversely, self-operating Catholic influence is probably least significant in the case of small theatres specializing in art or foreign films, which generally do not depend on large audiences. Not surprisingly, then, these smaller theatres have been the ones most often reported to be the object of overt Catholic pressure.

Informal Censorship and Licensing: a Comparison

Though informal censorship tends to be a somewhat haphazard, hit-or-miss pattern of control, its successes can have a highly restrictive effect on motion pictures. Procedurally, most forms of informal censorship are markedly deficient in anything approaching due process, while the substantive aims involved are often freewheeling by current constitutional standards. Today such censorship compares unfavorably in a number of points with control by licensing.

First, the mainspring of censorial action in the case of licensing is always the motion picture itself. In licensing, the censors always view the film, while in informal censorship those who play the censors' role often have not seen the film at all. In the latter situation censorial action is often precipitated by advertising, trailers (previews of the coming attraction), reviews, or by the nature of previous films shown at the theatre in question. For example, in Fox Point, Wisconsin, a suburb of Milwaukee, more than 200 women were reported to have circulated petitions calling upon public officials to ban a scheduled showing of *Sex and the Single Girl*. The protesters admitted they had not seen the film and were basing their objections on advertising, reviews, and on the title.[60] In Cleveland, Ohio, a scheduled booking of *The Molesters* was cancelled after many protests, based entirely on the showing of a trailer of the film, were received by the theatre management. A Cleveland *Plain Dealer* columnist wrote, "from what is shown in the trailer, *The Molesters* is not a movie that should be shown in a reputable downtown theatre such as Loew's State."[61] Censorial reaction to a film on the basis of its ads and trailers is a source of special irritation in the film industry. However, here at least, the industry would appear to have only itself to blame, since it is well known that ads and trailers often accent sensational aspects of a film to a point of unrepresentativeness.

Second, the substantive standards applied in informal censorship are likely to be far broader than those with which licensing boards must work. The boards today are limited to the restriction of obscenity, but informal censors may, and often do, find a film objectionable for moral, religious, or racial reasons. Even when informal censors confine their objections to erotica, their applied standards are likely to be far broader than the relatively narrow ones now permitted by law. In addition, the informal censor, even though he may be a county or city attorney, may not see many films in the course of a year. In fact, in some instances he may have seen no other film than the one involved in the controversy at hand. For example, in a Madison, Wisconsin, controversy over an attempt by the local police to cut a scene in *Phaedra,* the police inspector who ordered the deletion and who generally served as the police department's specialist in such matters said that he never went to the movies or even watched television except for football games. The inspector, a machine-shop foreman before joining the police force, said his decisions on film censorship were guided by a controversial pamphlet, *Who Is Tampering with the Soul of America?,* written by Jenkin Lloyd Jones, a conservative Oklahoma editor, and by a wish to "please the Madison populace."[62]

The informal censor may therefore lack the extensive frame of reference for comparing films that is available to most members of licensing boards. When the informal censor is a police chief, sheriff, police inspector, detective, or member of a private group, the censorial standard applied may be highly subjective. In the case of a religious group, the applied standards may be based on a sectarian morality. The aim of National Catholic Office ratings, for example, is not merely to control obscenity, but to control "immoral" expression as that expression is judged by a Roman Catholic view of life. In all cases, informal censors are likely to lack the qualifications of either a judge or jurors, or even those of carefully selected members of licensing boards.

Third, procedural safeguards are non-existent. Though certain legal remedies may be available to an exhibitor faced with informal censorship, the exhibitor has no procedural protections in the process of informal censorship decision-making itself. No burden of proof is carried by the informal censor. No hearing, defense, or appeal is available to the exhibitor. Restraint is apt to be determined by political, social, or ecclesiastical power rather than by any legal or constitutional principles. In addition, the obscenity issue remains without authoritative determination. In contrast, under the *Freedman* requirements, a licensing system now affords a number of important procedural safeguards: a prompt judicial review of the obscenity issue, a burden of proof carried by the government, and a prompt judicial determination of the obscenity issue.

Fourth, informal censorship attacks the proprietary interest in motion pictures at its weakest point, the person of the exhibitor. While licensing involves the distributor, whose responsibility it is to submit the film for review and to pay the licensing fees, informal censorship—and, indeed, even the complete use of the criminal process itself—is aimed at the exhibitor on the scene. The exhibitor, particularly if he is only a hired manager, is apt to be in a far less favorable financial position than a distributor. When he is a local man, which he is in most cases, his vulnerability to informal community pressures is substantial. In most communities his reputation and personal goodwill are factors, in many cases crucial ones, in his being able to realize a profit from the theatre operation. Public backlash against a particular film is felt primarily by the exhibitor and only remotely by the distributor, producer, director, screenwriters, players, or others who may be connected with it. And even where the criminal process is employed—either to completion in the case of a trial and verdict or only incipiently as in the case of confiscation alone—an exhibitor may lose in reputation even though he wins in law, because of the popular notion that where there is smoke, there somehow must be fire.

Moreover, in any controversy, an exhibitor also has contractual obligations to the distributor of the film, and normally may not even make deletions without the distributor's permission. One distributor interviewed said it was his policy to agree to changes where he, the distributor, was convinced there would be serious community action against the exhibitor, but that he would not agree to changes where the exhibitor was merely "nervous." The prospect of being caught between contractual obligations and community pressures may discourage many exhibitors from booking controversial films at all. In situations of community pressure, the respective interests of an exhibitor and a distributor may not coincide. For example, it is usually in the distributor's interest to see the exhibitor willing to go to trial where the chances seem good that the film will be found nonobscene. Such a decision can be of considerable judicial and nonjudicial advantage to the distributor elsewhere. But, as noted above, an exhibitor's best interest in the long run may be in not having any invocation of the criminal process against him at all.

The exhibitor's problem is not one of the lack of remedies. On free speech grounds, for example, he may be able to enjoin officials from instituting proceedings against him for unrelated offenses or enjoin them from taking extralegal action against him. In *Bantam Books* v. *Sullivan,* the Supreme Court itself upheld a proprietor's claim to injunctive relief against informal coercive activities of a state commission created to investigate the sale of "corrupting" literature, even though the commission had no formal powers of its own. Several types of proprietary actions are possible against the pressures of private groups. Damages may be claimed against those employing economic sanctions, or an injunction may be obtained against interference with reasonable business expectations. An exhibitor might have a cause of action for malicious prosecution if a group's referral of information to prosecuting officials was without probable cause, or for defamation if a group had referred to him, say, as a purveyor of "obscene" or "filthy" films.[63] Yet, as a practical matter, these various proprietary remedies against public officials and groups do not provide an adequate defense. The typical exhibitor is simply not in a strong enough position financially or reputationally to invoke them, and he remains, by that measure, the most vulnerable of film proprietors.

It is true that a distributor may be inhibited in resisting a prior censorship order. Yet this restraining aspect of licensing is modest in comparison with counterparts for the exhibitor in informal censorship. For the distributor in the licensing situation, community social pressures are largely absent; the process of resistance is formal and routinized; and the *Freedman* doctrine, in effect, builds resistance into the licensing system itself by requiring the government to seek adjudication where a licensing board has ruled a film obscene.

Wherever freedom of speech is threatened, eventual vindication of the speech in question almost always depends on the willingness of some private party—the proprietor, or at least *a* proprietor of the speech—to resist the encroachments and to lay claim to First Amendment rights. In comparing informal censorship and censorship by licensing, the chance of an exhibitor resisting the former is much less than the chance of a distributor resisting the latter. In situations of informal censorship of the sort described in this chapter, it is unreasonable to expect an exhibitor to be a champion of civil liberties very often.

Control of the movies by informal censorship does offer one advantage, at least in theory, over control by licensing. With licensing, a film may never receive exhibition at all—that is, it may never enter the "marketplace of ideas." In informal censorship the film may have at least a chance of being shown. This may occur where an exhibitor is determined to resist informal censorship, but more likely where it does occur it will be because the film had begun its run *before* the censorial forces began to exert pressure. In either case, however, this advantage over licensing may be diminished or lost entirely if local authorities confiscate the film or enjoin its exhibition.

In practice, this entry-into-the-marketplace-of-ideas advantage of control by informal censorship is minimal. First, most informal censorship is probably self-operating; that is to say, the exhibitor has anticipated a censorship situation and has not even booked the film, which means that it is kept out of the marketplace of ideas as effectively as if it had been denied a license by a board of censors. Second, judging from the reported instances of informal censorship, the formation of public opinion in support of the threatened speech—the great advantage of entry into the marketplace of ideas—is rare, and cannot be considered a reliable presence in the informal censorship controversy.*

It seems clear that when the effect of control of movies by licensing is compared with the effect of control by informal censorship, the former method today is likely to provide the more stable and promising environment for freedom of speech. The important question remaining, however, is whether the two methods are in fact alternatives, or, in other words, what is the relationship between licensing and informal censorship?

Informal Censorship and Licensing: An Inverse Relationship?

Comparison of the severity of informal censorship with that of licensing has meaning for public policy only if the two forms of control are, in their actual operations, real alternatives, that is, only if some sort of inverse rela-

---

* One striking exception to this rule occurred in Madison, Wisconsin, where police ordered deletions in *Phaedra*. Newspaper publicity given to this order eventually resulted in the appointment by the mayor of a citizens committee to view the film. The committee decided the film was not obscene, and the deleted parts were restored. The film then ran for three additional weeks. This model outcome appears all too infrequently in informal censorship.

tionship exists between them. Though conclusive evidence on this point is not available, data that are available strongly suggest that such a relationship does in fact exist.

First, in the opinion of many exhibitors—heard in private more often than in public—licensing is a form of insurance against other controls. And in large measure their behavior appears to reflect this perception. Though a certain orthodoxy on the licensing question prevails throughout the film industry today, exhibitors, individually or in their regional and national associations, have not often been conspicuous in the front ranks of anti-licensing efforts. In fact, exhibitors, whom one distributor has characterized as "the most frightened people in the world," have occasionally sought substitutes for licensing where licensing itself was not available. One group of exhibitors in New York actually hired the former director of the state's defunct board of censors as a consultant, "to tell us what he would have done about a particular picture when the board was in operation."[64] It is not uncommon in some areas for an exhibitor to *request* that the chief of police or city attorney view a questionable film in advance and, should the film be found objectionable, ask that he suggest changes that might allow it to be shown. Moreover, in the case of the Milwaukee Motion Picture Commission, the only censorship operation examined in this study to which no legal powers attach, local exhibitors have consistently gone along with its recommendations. This is all the more striking since an exhibitor's insistence upon playing a film in defiance of the commission's recommendations is the only way the commission's censorship-in-fact can be effectively challenged.

Second, in the handling of a film, a certain obvious incompatibility exists between the operation of prior censorship and the use of criminal prosecution or other, informal, methods of control. In New York State this incompatibility had statutory recognition: exhibitors there had immunity from an obscenity prosecution when the film in question had been licensed by the state Motion Picture Division.[65] And in other licensing jurisdictions a public prosecutor, as a matter of practice, is unlikely to undertake or threaten to undertake action against a film judged not to be obscene by professional public censors.

Perhaps the most persuasive evidence of an inverse relationship between licensing and other forms of control is that provided by the quantification of trade press reports of prosecutions, arrests, business-license revocations, official action not technically aimed at the content of films, new control laws, miscellaneous official action, group pressures, etc. These instances of censorship, based on a survey of the trade press for the five-year period 1962–1966, are collected in Tables 13 and 14. Three jurisdictional categories are compared: (1) licensing—those states and cities with operating licensing systems; (2) former licensing—those states and cities which once had licensing systems but in which licensing was found unconstitutional in

TABLE 13   *Reported Official and Private Action Against Exhibitors in Licensing, Former Licensing, and Nonlicensing Jurisdictions, January 1, 1962, to June 30, 1965*

	Licensing[a]		Former licensing[b]		Nonlicensing		Total
	No.	%	No.	%	No.	%	
Population (1960 census, in millions)	32.6	18.1	27.1	15.1	120.3	66.8	180
Prosecutions	1		17		12		30
Arrests and confiscations[c]	0		6		11		17
Use of criminal process, totals and percentages	1	2.1	23	48.9	23	48.9	47
New control laws[d]	0		1		5		6
Business license revocation or conditions attached	0		1		7		8
Restrictive action not technically aimed at content of films	1		5		5		11
Miscellaneous official pressure[e]	1		7		13		21
Official action other than use of criminal process	2	4.3	14	30.4	30	65.2	46
Official action, totals and percentages	*3*	*3.2*	*37*	*39.8*	*53*	*57.0*	*93*
Private action alone[f]	*3*	10.7	6	21.4	19	67.9	28
Censorial action, totals and percentages	*6*	*5.0*	*43*	*35.5*	*72*	*59.5*	*121*

Table is based upon the following publications and dates of coverage: *Variety*, Jan. 1, 1962, to June 30, 1965; *Boxoffice*, July 1, 1964, to June 30, 1965; *Motion Picture Daily*, Sept. 1, 1964, to June 30, 1965; *Motion Picture Exhibitor*, July 1, 1964, to June 30, 1965; and *Motion Picture Herald*, Sept. 1, 1964, to June 30, 1965.

   [a] Kansas, Maryland, New York, Virginia, Chicago, Detroit, Milwaukee, Memphis, and Fort Worth.

   [b] Massachusetts, Ohio, Pennsylvania, Atlanta, Ga., and Portland, Ore. Though licensing in the two cities was declared unconstitutional *during* the period surveyed, there were no reports of instances of nonlicensing censorial action in those cities while licensing was in force.

   [c] Does not include those where prosecution was reported to have followed.

   [d] Does not include new licensing enactments.

   [e] See Table 12.

   [f] Figures include only incidents in which there was no reported accompanying official action. Where there were reports of official action and private action together in the same controversy, the incident is tabulated under the appropriate category of official action.

TABLE 14 *Reported Official and Private Action Against Exhibitors in Licensing, Former Licensing, and Nonlicensing Jurisdictions, July 1, 1965, to January 1, 1967*

	Licensing[a]		Former licensing[b]		Nonlicensing		Total
	No.	%	No.	%	No.	%	
Population (1960 census, in millions)	9.8	5.4	50.6	28.1	119.6	66.4	180
Prosecutions	0		7		10		17
Arrests and confiscations[c]	0		7		9		16
Use of criminal process, totals and percentages	0	0.0	14	42.4	19	57.6	33
New control laws[d]	0		2		4		6
Business license revocation or conditions attached	0		5		6		11
Restrictive action not technically aimed at content of films	0		2		1		3
Miscellaneous official pressure[e]	0		1		6		7
Official action other than use of criminal process	0	0.0	10	34.6	17	65.4	27
Official action, totals and percentages	*0*	*0.0*	*24*	*39.0*	*36*	*61.0*	*60*
Private action alone[f]	1	20.0	3	60.0	1	20.0	5
Censorial action, totals and percentages	*1*	*1.5*	*27*	*41.5*	*37*	*56.9*	*65*

Table is based upon the following publications and dates of coverage: *Variety*, July 1, 1965, to Jan. 1, 1967; *Boxoffice*, July 1, 1965, to Jan. 1, 1967; *Motion Picture Daily*, July 1, 1965, to Jan. 1, 1967; *Motion Picture Exhibitor*, July 1, 1965, to Jan. 1, 1967; and *Motion Picture Herald*, July 1, 1965, to Oct. 1, 1965.

[a] Maryland, Chicago, Detroit, Milwaukee, Dallas, and Fort Worth.

[b] Massachusetts, Kansas, New York, Ohio, Pennsylvania, Virginia, Atlanta, Memphis, and Portland, Oregon.

[c] Does not include those where prosecution was reported to have followed.

[d] Does not include new licensing enactments.

[e] See Table 12.

[f] Figures include only incidents in which there was no reported accompanying official action. Where there were reports of official action and private action together in the same controversy, the incident is tabulated under the appropriate category of official action.

the years following the *Miracle* case; and (3) nonlicensing—those states and cities which have not had licensing at all, or at least not since before the *Miracle* case. The 5-year period is divided into an earlier 42-month period, January, 1962, through June, 1965 (Table 13), and a later, 18-month period, July, 1965, through December, 1966 (Table 14), to take account of the termination of licensing in three states and one major city during 1965.

In both periods, reported instances of official or group action against exhibitors are proportionally far greater in former licensing areas than in licensing areas. With a population only 85 per cent as large as that of the licensing areas, the former licensing areas had more than *seven* times as many reported instances of censorial action in the January, 1962, through June, 1965, period. In the later, July, 1965, through December, 1966, period, the former licensing areas, with slightly more than five times the population of the licensing areas, had twenty-seven reported instances of censorial action compared with one for the licensing areas.

The contrast between licensing and nonlicensing areas is no less striking. With slightly more than three and one-half times the population of the licensing areas, nonlicensing areas accounted for *twelve* times as many instances of reported censorial action in the earlier period. In the later period, with the nonlicensing areas slightly more than twelve times as populous as the licensing areas, there were thirty-seven instances of official or private action compared with a single instance in the licensing areas.

Moreover, of the seven instances of censorial action in licensing areas in the entire five-year period, three actually involved marginal circumstances. The single instance of the use of the criminal process against an exhibitor was the result of an error on the part of Rochester, New York, officials, who seized *Bell, Bare and Beautiful,* apparently unaware the film had been duly licensed by the state Motion Picture Division and that the exhibitor therefore had statutory immunity from an obscenity prosecution in connection with its exhibition. The case was eventually dismissed and the film returned to the theatre.[66]

The only reported instance of censorial action in a licensing area falling into the category of "official action not technically aimed at the content of films" involved an indirect attempt to effect a form of classification, rather than an attempt to have a film withdrawn or altered. In this instance the New York City commissioner of licenses began strictly enforcing an ordinance which requires theatres to maintain a supervised section for unaccompanied children under sixteen. The commissioner made it clear that he was acting in response to parental complaints that children were being admitted to some films "not designed for children."[67] The action was not aimed at preventing a film or a part of a film from being *shown*.

And, one of the four instances of group pressure reported in licensing areas—in this case in Milwaukee—involved merely the postponement of a booking. The film, *Kiss Me, Stupid,* which had been given an "adults only" rating by the city's Motion Picture Commission, had been condemned by the Legion of Decency, and the exhibitor, under Catholic pressure, agreed to cancel the originally scheduled opening during the Christmas holidays and to reschedule the film at a later date.[68]

Finally, in those jurisdictions in which licensing was terminated *during* the five-year period—New York, Virginia, Kansas, and Memphis—reported instances of official or group action against exhibitors jumped from four in the earlier forty-two month period to twelve in the later eighteen-month period.

To the extent that the figures in Tables 12 and 13 represent censorial reality, two general conclusions may be drawn. First, the comparison of licensing with former licensing areas suggests that termination of licensing as a control agency for motion pictures may result in vastly increased use of other control agencies, such as the criminal process and informal censorship. Second, the comparison of licensing with nonlicensing areas suggests that the existence of a licensing system may inhibit the use of other control agencies generally.

These conclusions tend to draw even greater force if it is further assumed, as it is logical to do, that most informal censorship is self-operating, and that self-operating censorship is rarely, if ever, the subject of trade press reports or those of any other kind of publication. Therefore reported instances of overt official or group action very likely reflect much more pervasive informal censorship that is self-operating or not publicized. If this is so, then the differences between licensing and former licensing areas, on the one hand, and between licensing and nonlicensing areas on the other, are probably even greater than the figures in Tables 13 and 14 would indicate.

I make no claim that the data presented in this section conclusively demonstrate an inverse relationship between licensing and other censorship. Indeed, conclusive evidence might be provided only by inquiries of a more direct nature into both attitudes and practices, perhaps in the form of comparative surveys in two or more states. But the data presented here do create a strong presumption of such an inverse relationship.

8

Nongovernmental Censorship: Advisory Ratings and Self-Regulation

Some students of politics and of the film medium believe that motion pictures can and should be controlled mainly by their patrons and their proprietors. Controls that are entirely nongovernmental and private in their origin and operation have always played a part in the censorship of the movies. Such controls are also part of a well-established American tradition of preferring nongovernmental to governmental regulation, if, indeed, any regulation is necessary at all. But, as a closer look at them will show, the values of patron and parental sovereignty, on the one hand, and proprietary sovereignty, on the other, are more impressive in theory than in practice.

The basic idea in patron sovereignty is that the best way to control motion pictures is to have each moviegoer make his own decision whether to see a given film, with the sanction of such a regime being felt through the box office. Accordingly, objectionable films will not be patronized, will not show a profit, and hence will not be imitated. A variation on this idea is that parents can make similar moviegoing decisions for their children.

Such a system relies on information about the content of films being available to the individual moviegoer and, especially, to the parents of youthful moviegoers. Advisory ratings, therefore, play a central role. Such ratings ordinarily provide a grade or classification for a film according to age suitability or general moral content. With such information the individual moviegoer or parent can make a rational decision whether or not to attend or to allow his children to attend a particular movie.

Though advisory ratings no doubt operate in the prescribed manner for some patrons, a system of patron sovereignty based upon them breaks down at a number of points. For one thing, it ignores the basic fact that for most moviegoers films are still escapist entertainment and are therefore improbable objects of rational decision. Secondly, with the changing structure of the American family, it is doubtful that many parents have the requisite authority over the moviegoing habits of their children, and perhaps even more doubtful that many have the necessary interest in the matter to seek out and examine advisory ratings.

Furthermore, in practice, the effectiveness of advisory ratings tends to increase with their coerciveness. This is true of the most influential of all advisory ratings today, those of the National Catholic Office for Motion Pictures, which have a definite coercive dimension. Indeed, it is the ecclesiastical connection that, in large measure, makes them effective. Yet, in this instance at least, the more effective such ratings are, the less they are advisory and the less they rely on the judgment of the individual patron and, in turn, the more they tend to function as a phase of pressure group action. In fact, as shown in the preceding chapter, the drive to make such ratings effective also tends to blur even the governmental-nongovernmental distinction since, inevitably, attempts are made to enlist the support of public officials.

Finally, there are several classes of films which are relatively immune from the kind of punishment at the box office that advisory ratings are presumed capable of meting out. These films—usually of the so-called exploitation variety—are hard to attack through a system of advisory ratings because, being cheaply produced, they do not need a large audience to be profitable, and because the audience that supports them either is not reached by such ratings or is affected by them in a way opposite of that intended.

In the light of these considerations, the idea of individual patron decision-making as a main source of control—an ideal that the film industry officially and piously embraces—must be viewed with considerable skepticism.

The basic idea in proprietary, as opposed to patron, sovereignty is that motion pictures can and should be controlled largely through self-regulation. Such control can take the form of a formal apparatus, like that of the Motion Picture Code and its Production Code Administration, which would operate for the entire industry or at least for a large segment of it; or it can take the form of an informal exercise of self-restraint by the proprietors of a film in its production, distribution, and promotion.

In theory, *formal* self-regulation by the industry, through the Motion Picture Code, for example, will head off "outside" censorship while at the same time holding down the less responsible elements in the industry. The theory of *informal* self-regulation is that individual proprietors will act with restraint because they will be governed by equivocal box-office returns and because they are responsible citizens who have no wish to harm the public.

In actual practice, formal self-regulation has inhibited other forms of censorship to a degree in the past, and has been somewhat effective within the industry in discouraging sensationalism. But in the latter task, at least, this form of censorship has become much less efficient in recent years. One reason for this is that formal self-regulation functions largely as a response to other forms of censorship, especially governmental action and the pressure of powerful groups, particularly if the latter can be applied through the box office. Another reason for its retreat before sensationalism is that it functions in the first instance as an instrument of the industry's economic self-interest, and that such self-interest has been increasingly interpreted as requiring less effective formal self-regulation. Hence, this form of control has also become less effective in averting "outside" censorship.

In practice, informal self-regulation almost always depends upon outside factors; that is, in most instances it does not rest on an inner sense of public responsibility. It operates when other forms of restraint, especially that of formal self-regulation, the pressure of private groups, and the "box office" (patron and parental sovereignty), are operating effectively. It is not surprising, then, that informal self-regulation should be attenuated today.

The functioning of nongovernmental control can be better understood by exploring it in three areas: advisory ratings, including those of the National Catholic Office for Motion Pictures; formal self-regulation through the Motion Picture Code; and informal self-regulation, largely through examination of new film-making liberties.

Film Rating

The Green Sheet

The Green Sheet is a monthly consensus of evaluations of current films. It is perhaps the oldest and, except for the ratings of the National Catholic Office for Motion Pictures (Legion of Decency), the best known and most widely circulated of all advisory motion picture ratings. In fact, since its first appearance in 1933, it has been a model for other private film ratings. Yet the Green Sheet itself is the product of an unusual organizational amalgam of private groups and the motion picture industry. The publication's ratings are the work of the Film Board of National Organizations, which has ten member groups. The organization's expenses, including those of the publication and distribution of the Green Sheet, are underwritten by the Motion Picture Association of America (MPAA), which represents the interests of the major American production and distribution companies. In addition, the editor of the Film Board, Mrs. Marie Hamilton, is an employee of MPAA, and has her office in the organization's main complex in New York.

The ten organizations represented on the Board are the American Jewish Committee, the American Library Association, the Daughters of the American Revolution, the Federation of Motion Picture Councils, the General

Federation of Women's Clubs, the National Congress of Parents and Teachers, the National Council of Women of the United States of America, the National Federation of Music Clubs, the Protestant Motion Picture Council, and the Schools Motion Picture Committee. Conspicuously absent is Roman Catholic representation. Catholic interest in film rating instead is channeled through the church's National Catholic Office for Motion Pictures. According to Mrs. Hamilton, the Office is welcome to join the board and, in the past, has been invited to do so.

The main object of the Green Sheet is rating for age groups, though it also provides a brief description of the content of each film rated. The ratings used and their "suggested audiences" are "A," adults; "MY," mature young people; "Y," young people; "GA," general audience; and "C," children (unaccompanied by adults). A film may have more than one rating, as was the case with *A Man for All Seasons,* which was rated "A-MY-Y." The "suggested audience" is actually based on education level as well as age. For example, "adults" are those beyond high school, "mature young people" are those in high school, "young people" are those in junior high school, and "children" are those under twelve.

In the rating process each member organization sends three or four reviewers to a screening. Each of the reviewers writes a report and each organization then constructs a composite review and rating based on its own reviewers' reports. These composite reviews and ratings are sent to Mrs. Hamilton who, in turn, constructs the Green Sheet's composite review and rating. Though disagreements with the proposed final composite may be worked out in an "executive" session with representatives of all the groups, the entire process described above apparently leaves considerable discretion in the hands of the editor. Minority reports may be appended to the final composite review and rating, but they are not common.

Standards used in arriving at the various audience designations vary with the member organizations, if not with the individual reviewers themselves. Yet, according to the editor, reviewers have had experience with families and "after a while they develop a 'feel' for what is of interest to persons at various stages of development." Except for the representative of the American Library Association, all the reviewers are women. Though it is debatable how much of a cross-section of American opinion the reviewers of the member organizations represent, the composite nature of the evaluations has the advantage of not being vulnerable to domination by any particularist doctrine.

In the three-year period 1964–1966, exactly 600 films were reviewed and rated. Of these, 130 or 21.7 per cent were rated for adults; 222 or 37 per cent, for "adults—mature young people"; 130 or 21.7 per cent, for "adults—mature young people—young people"; 118 or 19.7 per cent for a general audience or for a young audience particularly.

Supposedly, the Green Sheet is "objective" in its reviews and does not deal in criticism. However, this neutrality would appear to be realized only if "criticism" means negative evaluation, for Green Sheet reviews are often rich in positive terminology such as "splendid," "delightful entertainment," etc. *My Fair Lady,* for example, was described "objectively" as "one of the best of all possible pictures."

The major shortcomings of the Green Sheet as a source of advisory classification rest in its limited coverage and in the limited circulation of its ratings. Until 1963, only films with the MPAA seal of approval—that is, mainly those made or distributed by member companies—were reviewed in the Green Sheet. The coverage has since been enlarged to include a few non-seal films, mainly foreign productions aimed at wide distribution in the United States. Now, about 20 per cent of the films covered in the Green Sheet are those without the MPAA seal. Though the publication probably reviews and rates most films of general circulation today, its coverage is still far less than that of the National Catholic Office for Motion Pictures, which reviewed 805 films in 1964–1966, and far less than that of the average state or municipal licensing board.

Though the Green Sheet is aimed at moviegoers generally, its distribution has been limited mainly to the mass media, schools, libraries, churches and exhibitors. These institutions and groups are relied upon to circulate the ratings more widely by republication and by posting, though apparently their response here is irregular. Until 1964, total circulation was limited to 30,000 copies. Under growing pressure for governmental classification that year, circulation was expanded to 60,000 copies, which now go to 900 daily newspapers, 14,000 exhibitors, and 13,000 libraries and branch libraries. Exhibitors may also purchase copies in quantity for distribution to patrons. Even though demand for copies has regularly outrun supply, distribution to individuals on a regular basis is discouraged, apparently for reasons of cost. Total readership is estimated to be only two or three times larger than the circulation.

Although it is true that the Green Sheet is a more extensive undertaking today than in years past, it is also true that the MPAA had to be coerced into the expansion, and this fact reveals the fundamental weakness of the entire operation. The MPAA's acting president at the time asserted that the "real significance" of the Green Sheet expansion was that of "a strong affirmation of the family's right to govern what their children will see,"[1] but actually the MPAA was responding to a long-standing threat of the New York state legislature to enact a classification law. When the MPAA agreed to expansion, two pending classification bills were sent back to the rules committee. The chairman of the Joint Committee on Offensive and Obscene Material then praised the MPAA's decision, at the same time warning that if the industry did not "fulfill its moral obligation to the people of this State, the Joint Committee will consider further action."[2]

It is perhaps not surprising, then, that MPAA officials should be somewhat evasive about the costs of financing the Green Sheet. At the time of the expansion agreement, however, the association's acting president was willing to estimate the annual cost of printing and postage for the expanded operation at more than $50,000.[3] This figure is probably considerably less than the organization spends to lobby state legislatures on the classification question, and perhaps less than it spends to represent itself to the New York state legislature alone. By almost any measure, it is not a great sum for an industry as large as that embraced by the major American companies.

The fundamental problem presented by the Green Sheet operation is that the MPAA, representing the largest film companies, has not only been against governmental classification but against almost any meaningful classification at all. On the one hand, MPAA members produce and distribute "major" productions, expensively budgeted films, requiring a large audience and in the sociology of today's moviegoing this means extensive reliance on teenage viewers. On the other hand, the Green Sheet represents a form of classification, though a mild and merely advisory form, to be sure. In dealing with the New York legislature or with any other authority debating compulsory classification, the Green Sheet operation is an asset to the industry. Yet, insofar as the publication actually functions as classification, it tends to reduce the audience for all but the most broadly rated films. For the industry, then, the Green Sheet has political and public relations utility at the same time that it is a potential economic liability. From the standpoint of the MPAA's interest alone, this dilemma could be resolved by a Green Sheet that is viable in form but largely ineffective in substance.

The Green Sheet controversy is a manifestation, as is the continuing debate over the Motion Picture Code, of the dynamic relationship between governmental pressure or action and self-regulation. Self-regulation depends for its very life on the presence of governmental threats or very strong private pressures. Without such threats or pressures, it is likely to resolve itself into a minor part of a public relations program.

Other Non-Catholic Ratings

Several other publications in addition to the Green Sheet systematically rate films on their suitability for different age groups and interests. Among these are *Parents Magazine, Consumer Reports,* the *Parent-Teachers Asso-*

ciation magazine, *Consumer Bulletin,* the *Protestant Motion Picture Bulletin,* the *Daughters of the American Revolution* magazine, and the *Christian Science Monitor.* The DAR ratings, which are included in the Green Sheet composite, are also published in newspapers and broadcast over radio in several southern and border states.

In addition to these publications, private reviewing agencies have been established in a number of cities. These organizations, often dominated by lay church representatives, may also have formal or informal connection with the film industry. In Columbus, Ohio, film ratings prepared by the Interfaith Committee for Better Entertainment in Columbus are printed weekly in the city's newspapers. The Greater Milwaukee Better Films Council rates films, using categories similar to those employed by the Green Sheet, but also attempts to evaluate critically the same films, using the designations "poor," "fair," "good," "very good," "excellent," and "outstanding." In 1965, the Greater Detroit Motion Picture Council began distributing ratings to women's clubs, church groups, and local film exchanges (distribution agencies). The ratings, accompanied by a short description of each film, follow the Green Sheet pattern of categories. The organization does not mention films which have met with its disapproval. Instead, according to the chairman of the council, the ratings are a "white list" of films which deserve support.[4]

One rating organization which attempts state-wide coverage is the Texas Motion Picture Board of Review, composed of twelve women volunteers representing various church denominations. The ratings, which employ Green Sheet categories, are published in a number of Texas newspapers. Publication and distribution costs are underwritten by the largest film industry group in the state, the Texas Council of Motion Picture Organizations, which apparently hoped the enterprise would be a publicly acceptable alternative to governmental censorship. In January, 1964, the group's executive director praised the board's activities, claiming optimistically that "since initiating the program in Dallas, complaints from censor advocates have dwindled almost to naught."[5] Yet fifteen months later the city passed a classification ordinance and set up an official review board.

Perhaps the most unusual film-rating agency is the profit-making Dial-A-Movie, begun in Chicago in 1963 and now operating in a number of other cities as well. Dial-A-Movie provides a recorded telephone message listing ratings for current films. It is an outgrowth of successful Dial-A-Stock and Dial-A-Saint ventures, and relies on sponsors, who have included insurance companies, savings and loan institutions, and funeral directors' associations. When initiated, the ratings appeared to be based on a moral evaluation with categories including a "condemned" classification, which closely paralleled those of the Legion of Decency. Though no sources of evaluations were mentioned in the messages, the proprietors admitted that the entire scheme had the "concurrence" of the Roman Catholic Church.[6] The format was later changed, so that now Dial-A-Movie usually lists films by three rating categories—"suitable for family," "suitable for adults and teenagers," and "viewing of these movies should be restricted to adults"— which reflect more a concern with age interest than with general morality.

The effectiveness of all of these rating endeavors is in all likelihood quite limited. In almost every instance a positive and interested act is required to inform oneself of the evaluations, a circumstance clearly limiting their audience. For this reason, their influence on local exhibition is probably slight. And, as a result, their possible role as a stand-in for official censorship or for other forms of control is probably infrequently realized, or lost altogether as in the case of the Texas Board of Review.

The National Catholic Office for Motion Pictures

Today, the most influential film ratings by far are those of the National Catholic Office for Motion Pictures, which until 1966 was known as the Legion of Decency. The importance of these ratings rests on the persuasive power they have with individual Catholic moviegoers, who are given an opportunity to take an annual pledge in the churches to support the ratings, and on the ability of the Church itself to organize effective action to implement the ratings. The force of the ratings, in turn, has provided the National Catholic Office with considerable direct leverage on producers and distributors.

Development. The National Legion of Decency, the first of forty-two world Catholic film offices, was established by the nation's Catholic bishops in 1934 out of exasperation with the American film industry. In the early 1930's the moral content of movies was a source of great concern among the clergy of all three major faiths. Though the film industry had drawn up the Motion Picture Code in 1930 in response to complaints, the code, by itself, was merely an advisory document. With no effective enforcement provisions, it failed to halt sensationalism in films. In fact, one of the code's co-authors, the late Martin Quigley, Sr., a trade publisher, admitted that the code would not work at all unless there was "sufficient pressure and support of public opinion to encourage or compel the industry at large to conform with the letter and spirit of the regulations."[7] This pressure was supplied by the Legion of Decency. Its establishment was widely hailed, and in this early period the agency was able to enlist the active support of a number of Protestant and Jewish groups. The film industry responded to this mobilization and its potential for boycott by setting up the Production Code Aministration as a quasi-independent, self-supporting body charged with enforcing the code.

Current Organization. Today, as in the past, the Catholic Office rates films not only with regard to suitability for children and adolescents, but also for adults. This means that some films are judged not to be worthy of any commercial exhibition whatever. And it is here that the Office's ratings and review differ fundamentally from those of most of the other private groups providing advisory evaluations. Catholic film rating is aimed at the realization of "a wholesome screen against which there can be no objections on moral grounds."[8] Until 1958, four rating categories were used: "A-I, morally unobjectionable for general patronage"; "A-II, morally unobjectionable for adults and adolescents"; "B, morally objectionable in part for all"; and "C, condemned." That year two other categories were added: "A-III, morally unobjectionable for adults," and a "separate classification, morally unobjectionable for adults, with reservations," for films which "require caution and some analysis and explanation as a protection to the uninformed against wrong interpretations and false conclusions." In 1963, the title " separate classification" was changed to "A-IV."

Administratively, the Office is responsible to the Episcopal Committee for Motion Pictures, Radio and Television, composed of five bishops. The Office itself is under the supervision of its executive secretary, the Rev. Patrick J. Sullivan, who succeeded Monsignor Thomas F. Little when the latter returned to the pastorate in 1966 after nineteen years at the Office–Legion of Decency. Reviewing and rating is done by three groups: the motion picture department of the International Federation of Catholic Alumnæ, the Office's New York Board of Consultors, and the board of consultors to the educational division of the Office's National Center for Film Study in Chicago. The New York Board of Consultors is comprised of men and women, laity and clergy, of various ages. It includes educators and professional film critics, as well as doctors and lawyers. The National Center for Film Study group, made up mainly of persons engaged in film education work in high schools and colleges, participates in the rating of films the Office considers especially important.

Most of the Office's review work is still performed by the International Federation of Catholic Alumnæ reviewers, who at one time made up the only reviewing and rating group. These women are required to have had academic training in Catholic ethics and philosophy. Recruits undergo a six-month training period during which they attend weekly screenings. A discussion is led by a veteran reviewer at the end of each preview. According to Mrs. James F. Looram, Chairman of the Motion Picture Department of the Federation,

A very important qualification . . . of a reviewer is her appreciation of wholesome motion picture entertainment. (An open mind is most essential.) The reviewer's yardstick is *traditional* standards of morality upon which the sanctification of the individual, the sacredness of the home and ethical foundation of civilization necessarily depend. . . . Under the guidance of experts in the field of morality and decency, they continue their training for many years before they are considered skilled reviewers.[9]

Many of these reviewers now participate in annual university film-education conferences as well. In recent years the Office has gone out of its way to counter the once popular impression that its reviewing and rating is the work of "old maids." The Office's final rating for most films is actually based on a consensus of participants from all three review groups. The rating of *Peyton Place,* for example, was said to have involved the opinion of more than 150 persons, and *La Dolce Vita* more than 120.

In recent years the Office has reviewed between 250 and 300 films annually. These include all major productions, domestic and foreign, and any other films intended for wide distribution. Certain types of films—particularly "nudies" and nudist camp movies—are not viewed or rated at all. On the basis of the Office's rating standards, it is likely that all such films would be condemned. The Office believes that moviegoers who see such films probably would not be affected by ratings anyway.

The Office's great influence is with MPAA-member companies, that is, with most of the large American producers and distributors. With these companies the agency may actually enter the production process itself. Many of the major companies routinely screen their films for the Office *before* they are released so that, if need be, changes may be made that would save a film from a condemned or perhaps a "B" rating. The Office may also be asked to give opinions on scripts, though this is not common. In addition to the major companies, a few independent producers also submit films for prerelease evaluation. In contrast, importers of foreign films rarely submit their motion pictures for such examination, though of course they may be reviewed anyway. In these cases, Catholic Office reviewers usually see the film in a theatre during a regular performance.

Some distributors of foreign films have tried to avoid being rated, and have refused the Office's request to review. In these cases, the film in question has usually either been placed in saturation booking* or opened in other cities before being brought to New York. Opening a film outside New

---

* Saturation booking is the risky but sometimes highly profitable practice of opening a film simultaneously at a great many theatres in a given area, usually to the accompaniment of an advertising bombardment, often sensational in character. It is most often a strategy aimed at obtaining large gross receipts before the film—which is often a poor one—can be hurt by bad reviews or by word-of-mouth criticism. Hence, it is also a technique that can be used to offset the ill effects of a condemnatory rating, at least for a while.

York has been a means of delaying damaging advisory ratings, since most rating of the Office, the Green Sheet, and of a number of other agencies is done in the city. The Office has countered this maneuver by having a local representative view such films wherever they are opened, a practice resorted to reluctantly, since the agency prefers to maintain the collective character of its rating process wherever possible.

In terms of circulation, Office ratings are probably brought to the attention of most of the nation's nearly 50,000,000 Catholics through local churches. There are, in addition, about 15,000 paying subscribers, many of whom are non-Catholics.

Standards. In general terms, the Office applies the Ten Commandments and "basic Judeo-Christian standards" in judging films. According to both Msgr. Little and the Rev. Harold C. Gardiner, a leading Catholic writer on the problem of censorship and obscenity, the Office is primarily concerned with treatment rather than subject. For Father Gardiner, sin must be recognized for the varied things it may be objectively, such as

an offense against God, a violation of the social order, or a degradation of the individual. If a film glosses them over or says that this or that objective evil is really a good, then the film has sinned against the moral and artistic order. This is what the Legion of Decency has in mind when condemning a film for not presenting "moral compensation."[10]

In film rating, in the view of Msgr. Little, there can be "no compromise with evil, wherever it is."

Where a "B" rating (morally objectionable in part for all) or condemned rating is given, the Office usually states its reasons. For example, a film may receive a "B" because of "casually presented immoral behavior" (*Girls on the Beach*), "obscene gestures for their own sake" (*What Did You Do During the War, Daddy?*), or because of gratuitous suggestiveness in dialogue (*Honeymoon Hotel*), costuming (*The Cincinnati Kid, Marriage on the Rocks*), dancing (*From Russia with Love, The Return of Mr. Moto*), or in situations (*The Money Trap, Our Man Flint*). A "B" may also be given for "excessively graphic emphasis on cruelty and horror" (*Curse of the Living Corpse*), "exploitation of criminal activity" (*Young Dillinger*), etc.

Fairly typical of the explanations for the "C" or condemned rating were the evaluations for the Italian *Love and Marriage:*

This cinematic quartet of highly suggestive and questionably humorous stories is essentially a burlesque of marital fidelity. The film resorts in its treatment to gross vulgarities, exhibitionism in costuming and multiple evidences of voyeurism.

For the French *La Bonne Soupe:*

The film's graphic presentation of the details of prostitution is considered totally unacceptable for a mass medium of entertainment.

For the Italian *Mondo Pazzo:*

This film, which makes a pretense at being a documentary, is completely unacceptable as motion picture entertainment because the photography and editing concentrate, almost to the exclusion of positive comment, upon nudity, semi-nudity, erotic behavior, sadism, masochism, human indignity, and self-destruction. Moreover, the commentary also tends to be bitterly cynical and offensively suggestive to the point of obscenity.

For the French-British *Mademoiselle:*

Any ironic comment which this film may intend to make is so weak as not to compensate for its sordid story of evil and its frequently offensive treatment. Moreover, the development of its theme is wrapped in such ambiguity that one could conclude that from the author's viewpoint this is a story, not so much about an individual woman, but about womankind, with the inadmissable assertion that she is the personification of evil.

Nudity, of which more will be said, brings an almost automatic condemned rating.

Spokesmen for the Office have maintained that evaluations are based essentially on moral standards common to the three major faiths in the United States. Though this is no doubt true in many instances, it is probably also true that evaluations are often based on conceptions of morality *not* shared by many Protestants and Jews. This may often be the case today where divorce, abortion, birth control generally, suicide, and religion are dramatic subjects. For example, according to Mrs. Looram, a Catholic film reviewer must be

careful to check if the film treats marriage lightly, if it reflects the acceptability of divorce . . . if suicide is shown whether it is presented as justified or as plot solution or if it is presented as double effect under the guise of heroism.[11]

A film may be given a "B" rating for portraying suicide as an heroic or acceptable act (*Space Ship, Seven Women*), for "sympathetic presentation of the hero's complicity in mercy killing" (*Duel at Diablo*), for "offensive use of Christian symbols" (*Masque of the Red Death*), for offensiveness to the "religious sensitivity of the viewer" (*Yesterday, Today and Tomorrow),* or for ridicule of "authentic religious values" (*Diary of a Chambermaid*). A more striking example of particularistic evaluation is evident in prerelease discussions relating to certain scenes and dialogue in *The Nun's Story*. The Legion of Decency had urged the removal of a scene in which a mother superior urges a nun to fail an academic examination intentionally.

The Legion reasoned that the scene might create the impression that the behavior of the mother superior was typical. In this instance, the director of the film, Fred Zinnemann, refused to give in and the Legion agreed to let the scene stand.[12]

In the last ten years, and particularly in the last two or three, the Office–Legion of Decency has become more liberal and flexible in its evaluations and ratings. In 1957, the "A-III" rating (morally unobjectionable for adults) was added, as was the "Separate Classification," later to become "A-IV" (morally unobjectionable for adults, with reservations). Those who speak for the Office tend to be equivocal on the question of whether the standards for the older ratings—"A-I," "A-II," "B," and "C"—have also undergone change. Whether they have or not, it seems clear that many films that might have been given a "B" or perhaps even condemned in an earlier day now receive an "A-III" or "A-IV" designation. According to Msgr. Little, the "A-III" and "A-IV" ratings were added to meet the increasing maturity and sophistication of American Catholics in the last thirty years, reflected particularly in the greater numbers of Catholics going to college. Many observers of the film industry believe the Office ratings and evaluations today are often more flexible than those of the film industry's Production Code Administration. Perhaps the most telling evidence of liberalization is that the agency's work has come under attack from some conservative Catholic sources. The veteran Catholic film critic, William Mooring, recently charged that a "hard-core majority" of "non-rigorists" had gained control of the Office's machinery and had pushed out the so-called rigorists and "prudent moderates." According to Mooring, the Office "should renew its once realistic guidance of the Catholic rank and file by dropping its emphasis upon ideological, ofttimes antireligious drama as superior 'art' for mature sophisticated people. This confuses not only the unlettered, but many genuine intellectuals also."[13]

The liberalization is also reflected in increasing Office emphasis on "encouraging worthwhile films through critical approval and awards, by patronizing or jointly sponsoring theatres operated by . . . responsible managers."[14] Part of this more positive approach is the publication of the monthly "Catholic Film Newsletter," which recommends several current films and usually accompanies its selections with detailed reviews, often of high quality. Although this list includes many of the innocuous movies that so often mark the "A-I" and "A-II" ranks, it also includes many films of critical acclaim. In recent years the Office has presented annual awards to films whose "artistic vision and expression best embody authentic human values." Among these have been such adult films as *Darling, Juliet of the Spirits, Georgy Girl,* and *The Shop on Main Street.* Moreover, the agency's change of name from the "Legion of Decency" has itself been explained in terms of the need for a name that reflected the "broad transformation" of the Catholic approach to motion pictures.

All the same, liberalization cannot hide the fact that many films of merit, in some cases with recognition of the highest rank, are to be found on the Office's condemned list. In recent years, for example, the Polish *Knife in the Water,* Ingmar Bergman's *The Silence,* the Japanese *Woman in the Dunes,* the Swedish *Dear John,* the British *Blow-Up,* and the American *The Pawnbroker* were given "C" ratings. At the same time, such efforts as *Godzilla vs. the Thing, Robinson Crusoe on Mars,* and *Goliath and the Sins of Babylon* received "A-I" ratings.

The Office's major concern in recent years has been the nudity vogue in both American and foreign films. In 1965, the five bishops who form the Episcopal Committee for Motion Pictures, Radio and Television, the policy-making body for Catholic film reviewing, came out in opposition to any nudity in motion pictures at all:

> In itself nudity is not immoral and has long been recognized as a legitimate subject in painting and sculpture. However, in the very different medium of the motion picture it is never an artistic necessity. The long history of film production proves that dramatic and artistic effect has been achieved without recourse to nudity in motion picture treatment.
>
> The temptation for film-makers to exploit the prurient appeal of nudity in this mass medium is so great that any concession to its use, even for otherwise valid reasons of art, would lead to wide abuse.[15]

Father Sullivan has explained the Office's present application of this policy:

> By nude treatment we mean full breast, derriere or genital exposure of an adult woman; also genital exposure of the male. We have not objected to the brief derriere exposure of the male as in *Zorba the Greek, Ulysses,* and *Marat/Sade.* However, should such male exposure be pitched for obvious homosexual titillation, it would also be unacceptable.[16]

The award-winning *The Pawnbroker* was condemned in 1965 solely because of two brief, dramatically integrated scenes in which women's breasts were exposed. The Office issued a lengthy explanation of the rating, which was apparently arrived at after considerable discord among the reviewers. The ruling was rationalized on pragmatic rather than on purely moral grounds, an unusual position for the Office to take on the record.

> . . . The good of the motion picture industry as well as of the national community requires that a marked effort on the part of some producers to introduce nudity into film treatment be discouraged, for such treatment is open to the gravest abuse.[17]

After a year in release, distributors of the film agreed to remove the objectionable nudity, apparently to get a better rating and even wider bookings. The Office then reclassified the film "A-III" (morally unobjectionable for adults), making an exception to its general policy of not reclassifying a movie after it has received national distribution, in this instance "because of the film's extraordinary value."[18]

On the question of nudity, it seems clear that the Office, with a sense of urgency, comes close to seeing itself as the major moral guardian of the entire nation. Yet there is ample authority that regards the kind of moral guardianship furnished by the original *Pawnbroker* condemnation as altogether inappropriate. The film was on most of the "ten best" lists in 1964 or 1965, including that of Philip T. Hartung, film critic of the Roman Catholic monthly *The Commonweal*. Moreover, the Broadcasting and Film Commission of the Protestant National Council of Churches chose the film as the best American film of 1965 in its category, "Honest and compassionate portrayal of human nature." The dilemma for the National Catholic Office in its evaluation of films like *The Pawnbroker* is summed up in one film critic's rhetorical question: "If the . . . [Office] considers itself the guardian of morality in films, how can it expect its rating system to be taken seriously when it condemns one of the few significantly moral films made by Hollywood?"[19]

The fact is, however, the Office's ratings are taken seriously by a great many persons and, as a result, the judgments have considerable restrictive force not only at the exhibition level already discussed, but also at that of production and distribution as well.

The Issue of Favoritism. Films receiving the Production Code Administration's seal of approval are rarely condemned by the Office, though they may occasionally receive "B" ratings. The Office–Legion of Decency, the major goad in the creation of the Production Code Administration, has often been a kind of "gun behind the door" in that agency's administration of the Motion Picture Code. In the words of Msgr. Little, "the Code sometimes uses us as a stick. They'll say, 'Gee, you'll have trouble with the Legion if you put that nude in.' "[20] The Production Code Administration and the Office–Legion have seen eye-to-eye to such an extent over the years that only a handful of films produced by major American companies and bearing the code seal have been condemned by the Catholic agency. Part of the explanation is that the large American companies, most of which are members of the MPAA and therefore usually do not release films without the seal, also consult the Office before release if there appears to be a possibility of a "B" or "C" rating.

Yet in some quarters the Office is suspected of bias in its evaluations, particularly the favoring of the large American companies. According to one distributor of foreign films whom I interviewed, "It's more than just a coincidence that major company films are rarely, if ever, on the Legion's condemned list, especially considering the salacity of such major company features as *Irma la Douce, The Carpetbaggers,* and *Of Human Bondage,* none of which was condemned." In commenting on the Office's original *Pawnbroker* condemnation, Ephraim London, the censorship attorney, raised an even more serious charge:

> The Legion thinks nothing of approving a picture where every part of the human body is revealed through clinging or wet dresses, but let a woman's breast be exposed and it becomes something different. The Legion's actions lend credence to the rumors that they will sometimes compromise where sufficient contributions are made to the church.[21]

Yet an executive officer of a film importer's association told me he did not believe the Office has shown much, if any, favoritism, though "they are probably quite impressed by the fact that a film has gotten a seal."

Influence on Production and Distribution. A film can be hurt by either a "C" or a "B" rating, particularly if it is a large-budget production aimed at a wide audience, as are most films of major American companies. A condemned rating will almost always keep a film out of the circuits (the large theatre chains which include most of the largest theatres in the country). In addition, in areas with large Catholic populations few theatres of any size will book condemned films. Moreover, a "C" rating will usually prevent a later sale to television, often the source of substantial second-stage income from a film. Likewise, airlines tend to avoid condemned films in their selections for in-flight showings. For these reasons, distributors and producers of major films are reluctant to have such films receive condemned ratings or even "B's". It follows that the Office can exert formidable leverage directly on major producers and distributors.

All major American companies maintain some kind of liaison with the Office through which the Catholic agency can be sounded out on a controversial film while it is still in production. According to Msgr. Little,

> Sometimes a company may show us a film a long time in advance. If it's a hot potato, they may ask us what we think. Sometimes they want to get a better rating. It could be a family picture, but may contain something of interest to the boys in the front row. An adult situation may preclude an "A-I" rating. In its original form, *The Carpetbaggers* would have been condemned. Did we say, "You can't make the picture"? No, they came to us and asked, "What do you think is objectionable?" They didn't want a "C" rating, so there was a compromise for pragmatic reasons. The exhibitors want to keep in our good graces.[22]

The Office denies that it is ever the initiatior of such negotiations or bargaining sessions. It is known that Geoffrey Shurlock, the Production Code Administration director, or John Vizzard, his chief assistant, who was once a seminary student, often act as intermediaries. These negotiations are seldom made public, but one such session, involving Legion of Decency objections to the adaptation of the Tennessee Williams play *A Streetcar Named Desire,* has been described by Elia Kazan, the director of the film:

We did not see eye to eye. . . . At the meeting I had a hostile attitude. It is hard to suppress anger when you are being judged about something you think worthwhile. The leader of the legion group at these talks was always stressing that he was not a censor; that he was not demanding, just talking. He had a sorrowful attitude. Very soft-spoken. So sorrowful. He was damned patronizing. "I am not asking you to do anything," he would say, "I'm just telling you what we think." I had the impression that they had watched the picture in a different way from anyone else. Williams and I told Feldman [Charles K. Feldman, the producer] we were not going to do what they wanted.[23]

Yet in this case, twelve deletions were eventually made in the film when Kazan was overruled by Warner Brothers, under whose auspices the film was produced. Kazan has described the interests of the two sides:

. . . Warners just wanted a seal. They didn't give a damn about the beauty or artistic value of the picture. To them it was just a piece of entertainment. It was business, not art. They wanted to get the entire family to see the picture. They didn't want anything in the picture that might keep *anyone* away. At the same time they wanted it dirty enough to pull people in. The whole business was an outrage.

. . . . .

. . . The legion's point of view is also clear: they believe that certain things should be seen and others should not be seen by those who follow their dictates. If a picture, especially an important picture, can be brought into line with their code, they are naturally pleased. That leaves the public, the author and myself to be considered.[24]

A somewhat different experience with the Legion was described to me by Robert Gurney, Jr., an independent producer. He had asked the agency to rate his film *Edge of Fury,* a factually based story of a mentally ill rapist "whose condition society has done nothing to prevent." According to Gurney,

A priest and a monsignor visited me and saw the film. Then we talked a long while. Afterward, the priest said that he really believed I was serious in my intent in this film. I felt the talk was really a kind of interview for the purpose of assessing my own character and that upon this hinged their approval of the film.

In the case of foreign films, the Office deals with the American distributor who, having purchased the North American distribution rights, has full authority to make deletions. One such distributor described his dealings with the Office as "reasoning together," while another told me that Office negotiations were "pure blackmail."

Sometimes films that have not been shown to the Office in advance are re-edited *after* going into release—that is, after their premieres—in order to escape a "C" rating. Such was the case with the British *The Small World of Sammy Lee* and the Italian *The Conjugal Bed.* This practice brought a sharp reaction from New York film critics who had based their reviews on the uncut versions shown at the premieres and who claimed, therefore, that the films in distribution were not the same ones which may have received favorable reviews.

The Office has apparently been able to persuade the proprietors of certain films to advertise them as unsuitable for children lest they receive a condemned rating. Yet spokesmen for the Office doubt that most "C" films could be given "B" ratings merely by their being advertised as unsuitable for children.

Except for *The Pawnbroker* condemnation, the best-known and perhaps most significant Office–Legion action in recent years was the condemnation of United Artists' *Kiss Me, Stupid,* in 1964. The film, which received almost universally poor reviews as an artless exercise in vulgarity, was the first major American film condemned since *Baby Doll* in 1956. United Artists made what it described as extensive deletions in the film after the Legion's original objections, but the edited version was also unacceptable. Declaring that further changes suggested by the Legion would have meant reshooting scenes, the company accepted the "C" rating and released the film under a subsidiary, Lopert Films. This move was seen as a confrontation with the Legion and a challenge to Catholic influence on the medium. A number of previously scheduled bookings were cancelled and the film is generally regarded to have performed poorly at the box office. In fact, according to one estimate, the film would not even earn back its initial cost of $2,000,000.[25] Shortly afterwards, the poor showing of *Kiss Me, Stupid,* was cited as the reason for the willingness of the producers of *The Amorous Adventures of Moll Flanders* to cut five minutes of scenes from the film at the Legion's request.[26]

Producers and distributors are naturally reluctant to admit they have yielded to Office "suggestions," less for reasons of pride, perhaps, than belief that such reports would hurt the film's chances at the box office. Compromises by the proprietors are thus seldom publicized. Yet there is a relatively simple way of determining whether or not a film has been altered as a result of negotiations with the Office. In the Office's annual booklet listing all films reviewed for the year, those marked with an asterisk are ones for which the Office's rating is "applicable only to prints shown in the United States." According to Office spokesmen, this denotation is an indication that changes have been made in the film. It is, in effect, a warning that the deleted portions may have been restored for foreign distribution.

The potential restrictive impact of National Catholic Office ratings on adult viewing is indicated in Table 15. For the three-year period 1964–1966, Office "censorship"—condemnation and changes made at the

TABLE 15 *National Catholic Office for Motion Pictures—Legion of Decency Ratings with Restrictive Effect for Adult Viewing, 1964–1966*

	1964		1965		1966		Total	
	No.	%	No.	%	No.	%	No.	%
Films reviewed	258	—	285	—	262	—	805	—
Condemned	16	6.2	15	5.3	12	4.6	43	5.3
Other rating after changes in film	20	7.8	19	6.7	13	5.0	52	6.5
"Censored"	36	14.0	34	11.9	25	9.5	95	11.8
"B" (morally objectionable in part for all")ᵃ	34	13.2	36	12.7	27	10.3	97	12.0
Restricted	70	27.1	70	24.7	52	19.8	192	23.9

Figures in table are compiled from the Legion of Decency annual report of films rated and reviewed, 1964, and the National Catholic Office for Motion Pictures annual reports of films reviewed and rated, 1965 and 1966. The classifications "A–II" and "A–III," not included in the table, are also restrictive in their effect, but only upon children and adolescents, respectively.

ᵃ Figures in this line do not include films which received a "B" rating after changes were made. Such films are included in the category "Other rating after changes in film."

agency's request—affected ninety-five films, or 11.8 per cent of those viewed. With "B" rated films, which some exhibitors will not book on weekends or holidays and which others are reluctant to book at all, added in (minus those rated "B" after changes), the Office was restrictive in the case of 192 films, or 23.9 per cent of those viewed. Going beyond restrictiveness for adult viewing, if films with "A-II," "A-III," and "A-IV," ratings, all of which are meant to be restrictive in one degree or another on children and adolescents, are included, then the Office can be said to have been restrictive in the case of 611 films, or 75.8 per cent of those reviewed.

However, the figures in Table 15 also indicate that, as highly restrictive as Catholic ratings have been, the percentage of restrictiveness on adult viewing has decreased in every category during the 1964–1966 period—probably a fundamental reflection of the Office's new liberalism.

Comparisons of Office–Legion restrictiveness with those of the state boards of censors must be made with caution. For one thing, the fiscal and record keeping calendars of the Catholic agency and the various licensing boards do not correspond exactly. For another, if there has been re-editing, the boards usually see the film after it has taken place. For still another, the licensing boards view many films—including the "nudies" and nudist films—which the Office does not rate at all. Finally, the figures of most of the licensing boards include shorts—cartoons, serials, and short subjects—as well as features, while the Office views only feature films. Keeping these differences in mind, a rough comparison can be made for 1964, the last full year in which all four of the state licensing boards were operating. That year the boards denied licenses to 0.62 per cent of films examined and approved 2.93 per cent after changes, for a censorship percentage of 3.55 (see Table 4). The same year the Legion of Decency condemned 6.2 per cent of films it reviewed and gave less restrictive ratings to an additional 7.8 per cent after changes were made, for a total "censorship" percentage of 14.0.

A better basis for comparing the restrictiveness of licensing boards and the Office would be the compilation of the number of condemned films licensed and the number denied licenses. Unfortunately this particular information is not available from the licensing boards. However, since almost all films rejected entirely by the censor boards today are "nudie," nudist, or other exploitation films—the very sort the Office usually does not bother to rate at all—it is very likely that most films actually condemned by the Office are licensed by the boards.

Considered above, of course, are only instances of controversy, that is, situations in which Office influence is applied in the face of some kind of resistance. Not taken into account is self-operating Office influence in the form of anticipation by film proprietors. Such self-operating influence may have vitality not only in the executive offices of the major companies, but also in the minds of some producers at all stages of the film-making process. When this is considered, then the real extent of Office censorship may be truly remarkable, overshadowing any quantitative indications of influence in overt controversies.

The Motion Picture Code

The Motion Picture Code and the Production Code Administration make up the self-regulatory apparatus of the Motion Picture Association of America, the organization of the major American film companies. The operation of this censorship has never been free of criticism, nor its purposes free of ambiguity. Its maligners and defenders represent a diversity of interests and in each camp there are improbable comrades. The code has been attacked by those who view it as a kind of sieve, largely ineffective at keeping erotica and other sensationalism off the screen. It has been indicted by others for whom it is an oppressive restriction on freedom of speech and a bar to honesty and maturity in the Hollywood film. On the other hand, the code has been defended by those who see it as a kind of bastion against harmful matter in films. Still others, who believe some method of control over the film medium is inevitable, consider it a kind of compromise censorship, one which places a lesser burden on freedom than would other restrictive agencies.

Notwithstanding the richness of this debate, the code should be placed in a somewhat fuller perspective at the outset. The first task of formal self-regulation over the years has actually not been that of censorship at all, but the protection of the industry against loss. By holding down extremes of sensationalism and vulgarity, or at least appearing to do so, the code not only creates an image of a responsible industry, but also tends to reduce pressure for "outside" control and to cut any loss of confidence in (and hence patronage of) the industry on the part of the moviegoing public.

Thus, like the Green Sheet, the code must be viewed not only in terms of freedom of speech and the protection of the public from harmful matter, but also in the third dimension—its economic utility to the film industry. With this in mind, formal self-regulation can be examined, in the extent to which it actually does control motion pictures today, its effect on freedom of expression in the medium, and its relation to other forms of censorship.

Development

The film industry first got into the business of self-regulation in the 1920's. Faced with growing public criticism of the content of films and the threat of more extensive and restrictive governmental censorship, the largest studios and distributing companies formed the Motion Picture Producers and Distributors of America (MPPDA), later to be called the Motion Picture Association of America (MPAA), and named Will Hays, the former postmaster general, as its head. As the industry's first regulatory act, the directors of the association passed a resolution discouraging the purchase of questionable books and plays as source material for the screen. Later, in 1927, a series of resolutions known as "Don'ts" and "Be Carefuls" were adopted as a caveat for the production of sound films. These guidelines failed to have much of an effect on the content of movies, and hence did little to allay public criticism of the industry. In 1930, to appease its attackers, the industry asked Martin Quigley, Sr., a Catholic layman and trade publisher, and the Rev. Daniel Lord, S.J., to draft what came to be known as the Production Code. Yet since no effective provision was made for its enforcement or interpretation, the code was merely an advisory document. As such, it, too, had little effect on either the content of films or on the industry's shaky public relations. The turning point in self-regulation came in 1934, when American Catholic bishops formed the Legion of Decency to review and rate films. At the same time, they threatened the industry with a general boycott by Catholic patrons if the moral tone of films did not improve. This pressure resulted in the MPPDA's formation of the Production Code Administration (PCA), as a quasi-independent, self-supporting body charged with enforcing and interpreting the code.

Authority of the PCA was based on a provision for a $25,000 fine of any MPPDA member who sold, distributed, or exhibited a film not bearing the PCA's seal of approval. The force of this sanction rested, in turn, on the oligarchical character of the industry. The MPPDA and hence the PCA were dominated by the five largest companies in the industry—the "majors." These companies controlled 70 per cent of the first-run theatres in major cities. In turn, these theatres accounted for 45 per cent of all film rentals in the country.[27] Since the vast majority of other theatres showed only films which had proved their earning power in the first-runs, they were the theatres in which all but the most cheaply produced films had to play if they were to recover their costs and realize a profit. In this way, non-MPPA members—the independents—were regulated along with the larger studios and distributors. The PCA and the code became, in effect, the private government of the industry.

This system of control was seriously weakened in 1948 by the antitrust decree in *United States* v. *Paramount Pictures,* which forced producers to divest themselves of interest in theaters. This ruling thus unhinged the source of power by which the major companies had dominated the industry. Earlier, the fine for exhibition without the PCA seal had been quietly rescinded for fear that it would be the basis of an antitrust action. The provision for a fine for the sale or distribution of a film without the seal was rescinded after the *Paramount* decision. Today, the only sanction likely to be imposed on a noncooperating MPAA member is loss of a seat on the MPAA board of directors.

The antitrust decision, however, was only one factor in the erosion of the code's authority. Changes in the constitutional status of movies and a narrowing of the legal concept of obscenity, on the one hand, and stiff competition from television and foreign films, on the other, all added to the decline of formal self-regulation. Nevertheless, as can be seen from what follows, some economic disadvantage still attaches to a film not bearing the

PCA's seal of approval, in spite of these developments, particularly if it is a large-budget production.

Standards

The original Production Code, which had been amended several times since its inception in 1930, was replaced entirely by a newer and somewhat streamlined code in 1966. By its own terms, the new code is "designed to keep in closer harmony with the mores, the culture, the moral sense and the expectations of our society." But two unstated reasons for the change were that some of the specific prohibitions in the old code, such as those of nudity and profanity, had become increasingly inconvenient artistically and commercially; and that repeated stretchings of the provisions of the old code, as well as the practice of some member companies of releasing through wholly owned subsidiaries films denied the seal of approval, had weakened public confidence in the seriousness and integrity of self-regulation itself.

The original code had proscribed a variety of matter under such titles as "Crime," "Brutality," "Sex," "Vulgarity," "Obscenity," "Blasphemy and Profanity," "Costumes," "Religion," "Special Subjects," "National Feelings," "Cruelty to Animals." Specific prohibitions extended to subjects such as abortion, to the manner of treatment of several other subjects such as mercy killing, kidnapping, adultery, the clergy, childbirth, etc., and to a host of particular words including "chippie," "fairy," "goose," and several derogatory references to racial, religious, and ethnic groups. In terms of the motion picture reality of the 1960's the most limiting feature of the old code was the ban on nudity.

In 1956, the prohibitions against narcotics, prostitution, and miscegenation as subjects had been rescinded, and five years later the code was amended again to allow homosexuality and other sexual aberrations to be used as subjects, provided they were "treated with care, discretion, and restraint." A further *de facto* revision was effected when seals were issued to *The Pawnbroker* in 1965 and *Who's Afraid of Virginia Woolf?* in 1966, which contained nudity and profanity, respectively.

The new code not only revised the standards of the old, but also authorized the labeling of certain approved films as "suggested for mature audiences," an innovation much disputed in the industry. The new code's standards are set out in ten brief paragraphs:

The basic dignity and value of human life shall be respected and upheld. Restraint shall be exercised in portraying the taking of life.

Evil, sin, crime and wrong-doing shall not be justified.

Special restraint shall be exercised in portraying criminal or anti-social activities in which minors participate or are involved.

Detailed and protracted acts of brutality, cruelty, physical violence, torture, and abuse, shall not be presented.

Indecent or undue exposure of the human body shall not be presented.

Illicit sex relationships shall not be justified. Intimate sex scenes violating common standards of decency shall not be portrayed. Restraint and care shall be exercised in presentations dealing with sex aberrations.

Obscene speech, gestures or movements shall not be presented. Undue profanity shall not be presented.

Religion shall not be demeaned.

Words or symbols contemptuous of racial, religious or national groups, shall not be used so as to incite bigotry or hatred.

Excessive cruelty to animals shall not be portrayed and animals shall not be treated inhumanely.[28]

These standards are marked by far less detail than those of the original code. For example, the latter contained ten paragraphs dealing with the treatment of crime alone, ranging from suicide to "excessive flaunting of weapons by criminals," with one paragraph setting out six specific prohibitions on the depiction of drug addiction. Under the title "Sex," there were eight paragraphs of prohibitions, including the forbidding of "lustful and open-mouth kissing, lustful embraces, suggestive posture and gestures," and the use of seduction or rape as material for comedy. The new code contains no separate standards for the labeling of films "suggested for mature audiences," nor is any age mentioned to designate a "mature audience."

The major effect of the abbreviated and more generally phrased standards, as well as the labeling provisions, is to give the Production Code Administration more discretion in ruling on the acceptability of motion picture content. For example, the new arrangements allow the PCA to approve nudity in one film and to rule it indecent in another. It was the absence of such flexibility in the old code that required a special exemption in the case of *The Pawnbroker*. Unfortunately, however, information about specific code rulings is no easier to obtain under the new code than under the old, since the PCA has never made public its decisions or their rationalizations. Information that has become public under either code has usually been supplied by dissatisfied film proprietors. It is known, for example, that in the production of *Lolita* in 1962 the PCA forbade any mention of Lolita's age and any amorous scenes between the girl and her middle-aged lover,

Humbert.[29] The year before, the seal of approval was refused the much-acclaimed British film *The Victim,* the story of a blackmailed homosexual, because of the use of the words "homosexual" and "homosexuality," and because the film supposedly dealt too clinically with the subject.[30] In 1962, *The Case of Patty Smith* failed to receive the seal because its main theme was abortion and because the word itself was used.[31] Under the new code these three films would probably have received a different treatment from the PCA.

The new standards and their apparent flexibility may also ease adaptations from books or the stage. In the past such transformations often required major story changes to conform to the requirements of the code. The effect on the integrity of the original story was sometimes severe. For example, before the old code was revised in 1961 to allow homosexuality as a dramatic element, the entire motivation of the chief characters in *Tea and Sympathy* and *Cat on a Hot Tin Roof* had to be altered in order to make those films acceptable.[32]

The PCA's new authority to designate certain films as "suggested for mature audiences" marks a departure from the MPAA's previous adamant opposition to labeling of any kind. Distributors of films so designated may be asked by the PCA to carry the "suggested for mature audiences" line in their first-run advertising. Otherwise, however, the label is binding on no one. The designations, then, are actually advisory ratings rather than an equivalent of classification. The MPAA's official position that the moviegoing habits of children are the responsibility of parents and not that of the industry or the state remains unchanged. Whatever obligation the industry has, it is discharged with the single advertised line in first-run copy that a particular film is "suggested for mature audiences."

It is no secret that the labeling provisions were added to the new code in the hope of heading off further governmental classification, proposals for which were being made with increasing frequency in many states and cities in the mid-1960's. As with the Green Sheet, the MPAA is likely to get considerable mileage from the "suggested for mature audiences" lines without the advisory labeling being very effective in separating the mature moviegoers from the immature.

In contrast to the advisory designations, a really effective self-administered classification is possible, though perhaps not altogether feasible. It would probably require a labeling system that would be binding on all exhibitors through contractual provisions in the rental agreements with distributors. Such an arrangement was used by Warner Brothers for *Who's Afraid of Virginia Woolf?* in 1966. It gave the distributing company the right to withdraw the film if an exhibitor admitted anyone under eighteen who was not accompanied by a parent. Effectiveness of this sort of arrangement depends on both the information available to the distributor and on his determination to enforce the contractual right.

Publication of the new code was accompanied by an extensive MPAA public relations campaign stressing the integrity of the code seal and the responsibility of the "suggested for mature audiences" designation. Yet in the light of the ease with which the industry circumvented the code in the past, the new effort was received in many quarters with considerable skepticism. One fact that cast doubt on the industry's apparent good intentions was that the new code was silent on member companies using wholly owned subsidiaries to release films denied the code seal. A proposal to eliminate this hypocritical practice was voted down during the drafting sessions on the new code.[33] As had been the case with the old code, the nature of the substantive standards may be less significant in the long run than the fact that there appears to be one set of them when it is commercially convenient and another when it is not.

The Censorship Process

The PCA is active in several stages of production. All MPAA members are obliged to submit scripts to the agency, but often its actual work begins earlier with advisory opinions on novels, unpublished stories, or plays that are being considered for purchase and adaptation. Besides passing on the script, the PCA may also examine costumes, dance sequences, and film clips during actual production. (Frequently—in the case of non-MPAA members, for instance—the PCA sees only the completed film.) A final review is made of the finished film and, if approved, the seal is issued. Advertising and titles are examined by units of the PCA for conformance with principles of the Advertising Code, a sister document to the Production Code.

The PCA also compiles rulings of various domestic and foreign official censors, which are shared with producers. In addition, the agency acts as a coordinator through which recommendations and complaints from various pressure groups may be brought to the attention of the studios.

With a senior staff of ten, which includes the code administrator, Geoffrey Shurlock, and six assistant censors, and an annual budget of approximately $350,000, the PCA now issues between 150 and 200 seals annually for feature films, and processes more than 200 scripts. Though there is apparently much informality among the agency's staff, the dominant force in the organization is Shurlock, who may be the most important nongovernmental censor in the world. Though the agency is often criticized for being too permissive, and sometimes for not being permissive enough, Shurlock himself remains a respected figure in the industry. Now in his seventies, he is the fourth chief censor the code has had, having succeeded the late Joseph I. Breen as director in 1954. A Briton by birth, he had been a screenwriter and script reader in Hollywood before joining the PCA from the ranks of the unemployed in the 1930's. He is generally praised for his intelligence and judgment by students of Hollywood.

Though the work of the PCA is not open to public scrutiny, it is known that there is considerable give and take between the agency and the producers of the films being judged. These negotiations often see Shurlock and his assistants taking part in the creative process itself, making suggestions on how scenes may be handled to make them acceptable.

Where differences between the PCA and a producer remain, the latter may take an appeal to the MPAA Motion Picture Code Board in New York. The board is composed of the MPAA president, the heads of MPAA-member companies, four independent producers, and six representatives of theatre owners. Relatively few appeals are taken—there were only six in the 1954–1964 period—and reversals are uncommon. The three major reversals in recent years involved *The Pawnbroker* (nudity) in 1965, and *Who's Afraid of Virginia Woolf?* (profanity) and the British *Alfie* (abortion) in 1966. All three rulings were made under the old code, and the first two were actually contributing factors in the drafting of the present code.

As far as the industry's self-regulatory apparatus is concerned, the code board's decision is final. When the board upholds the PCA, the only avenue open to a producer who refuses to make the required changes is release of the film without the seal of approval. Often in the case of MPAA-member companies, denial of the seal is not appealed at all, and the film is released anyway through non-member subsidiaries functioning as "fronts." This strategy allows the member company to remain a member in good standing while sharing in the profits of the film in question. According to an admission of the MPAA president, thirty-nine such releases or releases of films which were not even submitted to the PCA took place in a recent three-year period.[33]

Industry Influence

Because industry economics and public relations (which ultimately affect the economics) have been dominant factors in both the creation and the shaping of the code and the PCA, many critics—those whose main interest is in widening freedom in the medium, as well as those concerned primarily with protecting the public from harmful films—have been led to question the integrity of self-regulation.

The industry has long been charged with manipulating the code and its administration to suit its own ends. For example, some critics observe that the code revision in 1961 to allow homosexuality and other sexual aberrations as subjects was made *after* several major companies had gone into production with large-budget films dealing, at least in part, with homosexuality—*Advise and Consent, The Children's Hour,* and *The Best Man.* According to Max Youngstein, a former vice-president of United Artists, an MPAA-member company, most of the charges of laxity against the PCA in recent years have probably involved instances where "Shurlock has been overruled by the pressure groups on the top executive level of the various companies."[34]

In some quarters the PCA has been accused of favoring films of MPAA-member companies against those of non-member companies. These charges are most frequently made by small independent American producers and by distributors of foreign films. For example, Robert Gurney, Jr., the producer whose film *The Prude and the Parisienne,* described as a "sophisticated spoof on nudism," was denied a seal, believed the nudist camp scenes in the film were analytically no different from nudist camp scenes in *The Prize* and *Shot in the Dark,* two major-company films that received the seal.[35] Leo Handel, producer of *The Case of Patty Smith,* which was refused a seal because of an abortion theme, charged the PCA with discrimination, since the agency had granted seals to *Blue Denim, One Plus One,* and *Splendor in the Grass,* major-company films which also dealt with illegal operations.[36] This lack of confidence in the PCA, whether merited or not, is summed up by one independent distributor of foreign and art films who told me that submitting his company's pictures to the agency would be allowing "the competition to judge our product."

From time to time, the PCA has also been charged with discrimination of another sort—the favoring of, or at least the giving in to, demands of particular groups. Here, the Roman Catholic Church is frequently mentioned, though a number of racial, religious, and ethnic groups are often included in this criticism.[37] Catholic influence on major producers has probably had an inevitable and significant spillover into the offices of the PCA over the years. At least it is a striking fact that only five motion pictures with the PCA's seal have been condemned by the Legion of Decency–National Catholic Office in the more than thirty years the two control agencies have coexisted.*

Whether or not any or all of the charges against the PCA are true, they have helped to undermine public confidence in the entire self-regulatory effort. For these reasons, there have been suggestions, from time to time, that

---

* They are *Son of Sinbad,* 1955; *Baby Doll,* 1957; *Kiss Me, Stupid,* 1964; *The Pawnbroker,* 1965 (though later reclassified "A-III" in 1966 after deletions); *Hurry Sundown,* 1967.

the film industry loosen its control over the regulatory operation and give more publicity to the censorship decisions. Ruth Inglis, an advocate of industry self-regulation as the method of controlling films, proposed such a course in her study of the PCA in 1947. She suggested creation of an advisory body

composed of distinguished and responsible citizens. Important groups in the community should be represented so that it can serve as a cross-section of the total American population, including current movie fans. The group should include rural as well as urban members; and educators, social scientists, artists, public leaders, critics, and religious groups of the principal denominations should be represented. The motion picture industry should be represented not only by producers but by writers, directors, actors, and exhibitors.[38]

Such a body would report annually to the public on the number and the kinds of rejections and changes which were made in films during the production process. It would also serve as a kind of appeal board to which writers or pressure groups could take complaints. In addition, it would have responsibility for recommending amendments to the code. Proposals for public involvement in the code's censorship have been made several times since. Just before the 1966 redrafting, Bosley Crowther, film critic of *The New York Times,* speaking of the need for revising the code, argued that such change should come about by assembling "a representative group of sociologists, psychologists, educators and progressive clergymen whose judgment and articulation of the basic values would command public confidence and respect."[39]

Whatever the merits of these or similar suggestions may be, it seems unlikely that the major companies, that is, the MPAA, would give up any control over the code and its administration. Yet supporters of the Inglis type of proposal sometimes cite the British censorship arrangement as a working example of the separation of the film industry from a nongovernmental regulatory process. Since 1913 the regulatory agency for the film medium in Britain has been the British Board of Film Censors, a private, self-supporting rating organization. The industry's only formal connection with the board lies in the selection of its president, who is usually a man well known in public life. A vital dimension of the British system is that the board's ratings are given legal effect through local ordinances relating to exhibition. Yet such an arrangement in the United States with the present Motion Picture Code would almost certainly raise a First Amendment question, since the code's proscriptions go far beyond that of obscenity, to which official censorship is largely limited today. In any event, the difficulty of persuading the American film industry to support proposals like those of Miss Inglis is enough to make such suggestions largely irrelevant.

Coverage

In the years before the *Paramount* decision, when the MPAA could make policy for the entire film industry, about 95 per cent of all films shown in this country were made with the cooperation of the PCA. Not only did MPAA-member companies, the so-called majors, make and distribute many more films than they do today, but most non-member companies, too, submitted their films to the PCA to keep from being shut out of the most lucrative exhibition markets. Today, in contrast, the PCA examines a much smaller number of films and a much smaller percentage of all films exhibited in the United States. For example, in the eleven years 1935–1945, during its 95 per cent period, the PCA issued seals to an average of 528 feature films a year,[40] while in the five years 1960–1964, seals were issued to an average of only 205 a year. During the latter period the New York State Motion Picture Division licensed an average of 812 feature films annually, of which only an average of 179, or 22 per cent, had PCA seals.

Despite this absolute and relative decline in coverage, the MPAA maintains that films with the seal still account for nearly 90 per cent of the total exhibition time in the country and for about the same percentage of motion picture gross receipts. However, in the view of one trade publisher interviewed, this figure for total playing time may be somewhat high, a more realistic estimate being between 80 and 85 per cent. If coverage is measured by the number of films shown that have the seal, the percentage is even lower. Of 285 films released in the United States in 1966, including imported films, only 168, or 59 per cent, had the seal.[41] Furthermore, MPAA claims of broad coverage receive a moral, if not significant quantitative, setback by the organization's own admission that during the 1963–1965 period, thirty-nine films of member companies that either had been denied the seal or had not been submitted to the PCA at all were released through wholly owned subsidiaries.[42]

Today, the vast majority of foreign films are not submitted to the PCA at all. In the four-year period 1961–1964, the New York state censors licensed 2,376 foreign-made feature films, of which only 132, or 5.6 per cent, had the PCA seal. During the same period, New York censors licensed 873 American-made features, of which 583, or 66.8 per cent, had the seal. According to Shurlock, many films are not submitted to the PCA, because the producers know they cannot get a seal of approval. These films include the "nudie" and nudist variety.

Yet it is also true, at least in the past, that many films have not been submitted to the PCA simply for reasons of economy, since a $500 minimum fee was charged for examination of a feature film. In an effort to induce independent distributors, including those handling foreign films, to submit their product to the PCA under the new code, the MPAA planned to reduce the examination fee to as low as $250, scaled to the cost of the negative.

Though PCA coverage falls far short of 100 per cent by any measure, there are instances of extra-industry application of some of the code's provisions. This has been the case for several years in Milwaukee, where the city's Motion Picture Commission, functioning as a board of censors even though it has no formal authority, has occasionally used certain provisions of the code as standards in viewing films which have not been submitted to the PCA. Of particular concern are the provisions dealing with ridicule of religion, race, and national origin, and those dealing with brutality and crime.

Effectiveness

As the foregoing indicates, the effectiveness of the PCA as a censorship agency has declined measurably in recent years. Yet this is not to say that the code seal has no meaning or effect at all. Under certain circumstances, a film without the seal may be seriously handicapped.

Before 1953, no member-company film submitted to the PCA and rejected by it had ever been released. That year *The Moon Is Blue*, denied a seal because of allegedly light treatment of a proposed adultery which did not take place, was exhibited without the seal. In 1956, *The Man with the Golden Arm*, an adaptation of the Nelson Algren novel on drug addiction, was also released and exhibited without a seal. Both films had highly profitable runs, the former, in fact, earning gross receipts eleven times greater than its production costs.[43] Reception of the films shattered the then prevailing belief that a costly major production was financially doomed without the seal. And the success of these two films was also the main stimulus for revising the code in 1956.

Though lack of a seal may substantially weaken an independent producer's bargaining position when he seeks a distributor, today it usually will not keep a film from getting distribution and exhibition. It may, however, keep it from getting wide exhibition, or at least exhibition on as wide a scale as it might have had with a seal. In the case of a large-budget film, this may make the difference between profit and loss. Many exhibitors are still reluctant to book non-seal films, since such films are more likely to be objects of informal censorship in many communities. Yet where it is clear from the early box office returns that the film is likely to be a triumph, absence of a seal may not make much difference at all. In recent years this was the case with *Room at the Top* and *Never on Sunday*, each of which returned large profits and had wide circulation extending into second, third, fourth, etc. runs. The general rule is that exhibitors will abandon an unsteady ship, but have few reservations about sailing on a financially promising one of any flag; one more indication that in the film industry the prospect of immediate profits is likely to be the ultimate persuasion, stilling fears and principles alike.

With the publication of the new code in 1966, the MPAA tried unsuccessfully to persuade leading groups of exhibitors to pledge themselves to play only films with the PCA seal. At the same time, independent distributors warned that any meaningful formal pledge of this kind would raise antitrust questions and invite litigation—another indication of the essential incompatibility of effective self-regulatory coverage and an economically decentralized industry.

The code seal still has considerable force today in specialized exhibition. Films without seals are not shown at military bases nor are they screened by most television stations. The few stations which make exceptions are apt to confine such films to very late viewing hours, away from so-called prime time. In fact, one of the ironies of movie censorship is that United Artists, the company which financed both *The Moon Is Blue* and *The Man with the Golden Arm* and which backed Otto Preminger, the producer of both works, in defying the PCA, should very quietly in 1961 request seals for both films. It was believed the company had eventual television exhibition in mind in making this move.[44]

In recent years legal sanctions have been proposed that would indirectly give new force to the code seal. Bills have been introduced in several state legislatures to require the seal as a condition of exhibition, though by mid-1967 no state had yet enacted such legislation. Yet one municipality, Lee's Summit, Missouri, in 1964 actually passed an ordinance prohibiting exhibition of any film not bearing the seal of approval.[45]

In contrast to a fusing of the seal and legal sanctions for more vigorous censorship, the seal can also function as an anticensorship device. As licensing procedure rather strikingly illustrates, approval by one censorial agency can be used as a counterweight to other censorial interests or pressures. In this respect the code seal can actually have a legitimating effect on a film. In the case of *The Pawnbroker,* which had received a condemned rating from the National Catholic Office for Motion Pictures, a major breakthrough in bookings was reported after the film was given a seal by the MPAA on an appeal from the original PCA denial.

The seal is probably most effective today in the preproduction stage of the motion picture business. Failure to get "go ahead" approval from the PCA can dry up investment capital, turn a planned large-budget film into a shoe-string operation, and even result in cancellation of production plans altogether. The producers of *Lolita,* the film based on the novel by Vladimir Nabokov, found that until the PCA had tentatively approved a second and revised shooting script, bankers were unwilling to risk underwriting the enterprise.[46] In the case of *The Prude and the Parisienne* and its independent producer, Robert Gurney, Jr., failure to get "go ahead" approval meant failure to get established stars, which in turn eliminated chances for large-scale financing. Gurney had hoped to use a major actor in the film, but the actor declined when the PCA refused to promise a seal based on the shooting script Gurney had submitted. Thus, according to Gurney, the want of PCA approval eventually forced him to cut his budget from $1,000,000 to $300,000 and to spend more than a year in raising that sum.[47]

There is little question that the PCA can still apply considerable leverage to producers in particular circumstances. It may take unusual private resources and unusual determination to make a middle-sized or large-scale film in this country in the face of PCA opposition.

Restrictiveness

Comparisons of the code, in its effect on freedom of expression, with licensing, prosecution under obscenity laws, the pressures of private groups, and other informal methods of control discussed earlier, are difficult for two reasons. First, code censorship takes place at the production stage rather than at that of exhibition; and, second, there is little public information on the substantive character of the PCA's decisions, or even on the identification of films submitted to the agency but denied the seal of approval.

Whether or not censorship at the production stage is inherently more restrictive than control on exhibition is open to debate. At first glance, at least, integration of censorship with the production process would seem to allow opportunity for far greater influence over the content of a film. Yet it may be argued that the earlier the stage at which objections to content are raised, the more likely they can be met or compensated for without seriously affecting what the film-maker is trying to communicate. In contrast, post-production cuts may severely alter the meaning and effect of a film. It may also be argued that the staff of the PCA is likely to have greater understanding of and sensitivity to the creative element in film-making than are most other censors.

Nevertheless, PCA censorship ultimately rests in the hands of a very few persons. Their decisions are not ordinarily subject to any kind of public review. And, except for the generalized terms of the Motion Picture Code itself, very little is known about the censorship standards employed. Moreover, as the frequent charges of manipulation suggest, the industry's control of the PCA can result in the agency's decisions reflecting the economic interest of the industry, and perhaps even the interest of the MPAA-member companies as against their non-member competition.

PCA censorship has always been more restrictive than formal governmental control—licensing or prosecution under obscenity laws. For example, a 1957 study revealed that apparently no film with the PCA seal had ever been the object of an obscenity prosecution.[48] And after surveying motion picture obscenity prosecutions in recent years, I know of none involving a film approved by the PCA.

The same general pattern prevails with regard to licensing. Satisfying the PCA is likely to be a far more formidable task than gaining a permit from a governmental censor board. None of the state or municipal censors whom I interviewed could recall a case in which a license had been denied a film bearing the seal. In fact, there are apparently few instances in recent years in which even changes have been ordered in PCA films. The Milwaukee Motion Picture Commission has sometimes given "adults only" ratings to films with the seal, but it has not required deletions in any, nor has it given a "recommended not be shown" rating to any. The pattern is hardly surprising. Though the code has been liberalized several times in recent years, its modifications have lagged far behind changes in the legal concept of obscenity. In fact, most of the films rejected or cut by licensing boards today —the "nudie," sado-masochistic, or other exploitation feature—are not even submitted to the PCA, because they would stand no chance at all of getting the seal. Therefore, as in the case of films reviewed and condemned by the National Catholic Office, it can probably be said that almost any film actually submitted to the PCA and denied a seal is also apt to be routinely licensed by the major state and city boards of censors today.

Extensive comparison between films denied the seal and National Catholic Office ratings is not possible, again, because of the lack of data on the identity of films in the former group. Yet some comparison is possible for films with the seal. As we have seen, very few such films—five in all—have been condemned by Catholic rating. This represents an extremely small fraction of 1 per cent of all the films released by MPAA-member companies and rated by the Office–Legion of Decency since that organization was founded in 1934. At first glance this might seem to indicate that PCA review, which precedes Catholic rating, is the more restrictive of the two. Yet, since Catholic influence among major producers can be considerable during the production process itself, the remarkable Catholic-PCA "consensus" may actually indicate the very opposite, in terms of restrictiveness. In any case, there appears to have been little to choose from between the ultimate sanctions applied by the two agencies: condemnation and denial of the seal. Catholic restrictiveness, of course, is not limited to films condemned, but may extend also, in some degree or other, to films given the "B" rating (morally objectionable in part for all). Many MPAA-member-company films have fallen into this category over the years.

The Motion Picture Code and its administration is a form of censorship set up by the major companies of the industry under a plea of protecting moviegoers from harmful films. But the censorship actually has had as its first purpose the protection of the economic position of the industry through improved public relations.

The code is less of a limitation upon freedom in the film medium today than perhaps at any time in the past. In its substantive standards it has been liberalized through revision and reinterpretation. In addition, its sanctions, which once rested on the oligarchical power structure of the industry, have been weakened by decentralization and by a new pluralism in the medium.

Yet the code's substantive standards are still far more restrictive than those employed in licensing censorship or control through prosecution under obscenity laws. They are probably no less, or at least not much less, restrictive than those of the National Catholic Office for Motion Pictures. In terms of sanctions, the seal decision continues to have some force, though far less than in the past. In occasional circumstances, it can still affect the size of a film at the production stage and the extent of its circulation once in distribution.

Another factor weakening the code as a major control on motion pictures is that its coverage is far more limited than in the past. It still deals with major films, but today it deals largely with these films alone, and they now account for a much smaller percentage of all films exhibited in the United States than perhaps at any time in the past. It is doubtful that code coverage could be expanded easily, since submission to it is voluntary. Any attempt to extend its authority by economic coercion would probably raise antitrust questions.

The main effect of code censorship today, then, is to keep major films out of the courts and out of police stations. For this reason, the code cannot be considered a general alternative to licensing or to other forms of control, which for the most part are concerned with the sorts of films never submitted to the PCA at all. In effect, the code can function as a re-channeler of censorship energies only with regard to major films.

Nonetheless, this still leaves room for an inverse relationship between code censorship and other forms of control in one area—that of classification. This censorship—whether in the form of licensing or advisory ratings partially coercive through group pressure—usually focuses on major films. Films of the "little" industry—the American independents and the distributors of foreign films—are already largely, though not entirely, classified *de facto.* That is to say, the audience for these films is already largely one of adults. On the other hand, films of the "big" industry (mainly MPAA-member companies), which are large-budget productions in need of mass audiences, are seldom part of *de facto* classification. They usually play at theatres which ordinarily provide for moviegoers of all ages without discrimination. For these reasons, binding classification administered by the PCA, in contrast to the merely advisory "suggested for mature audiences" designation, would probably allay much of the censorship interest now directed at major films. Also, such classification could have some effect on pressure for general censorship where such pressure has been the undiscriminating reaction to the absence of classification.

Yet the PCA does not now classify films, and MPAA resistance to classification, until now at least, has been unshakable. This situation again reflects the expediential character of code censorship and the fundamental disadvantage of industry self-regulation as a reliable response to the control problem in the medium. Industry self-regulation affects industry economics, and the MPAA has consistently resisted attempts to separate the one from the other. This means that classification through the PCA is unlikely to come about until greater censorial pressures—those from government and those from private groups, especially the Roman Catholic Church—are built up. Yet the building up of such pressures is probably harder today than ever before because of the liberalization that has taken place in all institutions of control.

Informal Proprietary Restraint

The last of the major components of movie censorship are the decisions of those who make the films. The choice of subject, the manner of treatment, and the way in which the finished film itself is promoted largely determine, at least in the first instance, whether there is likely to be a censorship controversy at all. Few persons or groups concerned with the moral content of films today believe that informal proprietary restraint can be the effective method of control, though many such persons who happen also to feel uneasy about governmental controls may sometimes long for a kind of if-men-were-angels solution in which film proprietors would all be sufficiently circumspect. Proprietary restraint merits examination, not because of any possibility that it will become an alternative to other forms of restriction—its chances of that are slim, indeed—but in order to note its limitations and, by that means, to identify some of the forces involved in *maintaining* motion pictures as a medium of controversy. This is not to say, of course, that self-restraint does not operate at all. Where exercised, it is obviously the most effective of all controls, though in many instances it has also tended to inhibit the maturating of the film as an art form. In fact, until recently, any discussion of proprietary restraint would probably have had to dwell largely on its restrictiveness. Its salient feature today, however, is its relative incapacity.

The term "proprietary" is not used here in the strict legal sense of ownership, but rather in the broader sense of referring to any interest having a voice in determining the subject, specific content, or promotion of a film. The proprietary interest includes the producer, the company risking its assets to finance the film, the distributor (if it is not the foregoing company), the bankers who advance the capital, the director, and, rarely, the players and the writers. It is hard to generalize about the exact locus of ultimate decision-making. This is apt to vary from film to film, and even from time to time in the case of each specific film.

Nevertheless, two points can be noted. The first is that the influence of the bankers is often overrated. A commercial bank makes loans from funds on deposit and is not involved in investments. Such a bank is usually prevented by law from having a profit interest in a film or in any other venture on which it lends money. Though a bank may still have a degree of informal influence, since it evaluates the assets of those taking the risk and makes loans secured by the risk-takers, bankers today are not often great unseen pullers of strings where the substantive character of a film is at issue.[49]

Second, those involved in the most creative aspects of film-making—the director, the performers, and the writers—have the least influence. Ultimately, writers have almost none. Among the performers, only the biggest stars can demand dialogue or story changes. A director cuts (edits) the film, but only a few of the most established directors today—Elia Kazan, Otto Preminger, George Stevens, for example—are likely to have final cut rights, that is, ultimate control over the content of the film. In fact, most major decisions are likely to involve many persons, of whom the director is but one. Probably the greatest proprietary influence is exerted by the producer and the sales management or distribution executives, who for most Hollywood films are connected with the risk-taking movie company.

Self-restraint may involve several motivations: fear of financial loss on a film, that is, fear of a poor box office; fear of spurring the forces of censorship; fear of damaging the public relations of the film industry and thus its long-run economic position; and a real concern over the possible harmful effects of the film on viewers. Where self-restraint breaks down, it is almost always because it was believed to stand in the way of greater immediate profits or in the way of artistic freedom and integrity. Of the two values, the former is by far the more significant.

Proprietary restraint has tended to break down with increasing frequency in recent years. This is merely another way of saying that in subject matter, its treatment, and in promotion, films have become more daring, particularly in the portrayal of erotica and violence; and that, as a result, they have become more controversial. The several factors in this development have been discussed, but may be summarized again here. The film industry had found itself in an economic strait after television succeeded in capturing the mass entertainment audience. As a matter of survival, it became necessary to offer something that television could not. At the same time, a new permissiveness developed both in the law of obscenity and in the level of public tolerance of discussion and representation of erotica in the media of communication. These changes were complemented by a weakening of formal regulation within the film industry itself, when the handful of major Hollywood companies lost their near-dictatorial powers in the wake of antitrust decrees decentralizing the entire industry. Finally, interest in film-making widened, particularly film-making as an art, and with this came the knowledge and skills needed to make films at relatively low costs.

The new economic imperatives, the new freedom, and the new pluralism combined to provide opportunity for greater self-expression and artistry, as well as for a renewed exploration of the money-making possibilities of sensationalism. Many film proprietors have traveled one or both of these paths. Their enterprise has produced four types of motion pictures that have provoked censorship controversies: the exploitation film, the art film, the major film with an adult theme, and the experimental film. Each of these types will be considered below.

The Exploitation Film

"Exploitation film" is a general trade term referring to several kinds of third-rate movies, the common characteristic of which is shock or salacity. The least sensational in the genre are the nudist camp films, usually plotless, short on professional actors, but abounding in volleyball, ping pong, and other motion-filled activities. Not to be confused with these are the "nudie" films, usually comedies with burlesque overtones. These ordinarily have a rather simple plot contrived to call for a generous and frequent display of female breasts and buttocks. Most nudist and "nudie" films are American made. Another exploitation group, usually foreign made, deals with provocative subjects such as perversion, abortion, teen-age drug addiction, wayward girls, wife-swapping, the vice dens of Europe, etc. These films, sometimes pretending to be documentaries, often feature nudity as well. Still another group, usually American made, traffics in sadism and violence, frequently in an erotic context. All exploitation movies are turned out quickly at low cost by small independent companies. Today, films of this variety account for most of the restrictive action of licensing boards and for much of the informal movie censorship in the country.

It is fair to say there have always been exploitation films. Until recent years their exhibition was confined to a handful of "skid row" theatres located mainly in the largest cities of the country. In the 1960's, however, these films scored what the trade termed a "breakthrough." A significant audience developed and the films got wider and better bookings. By 1964 it was estimated that there were 700–800 theatres in the country playing exploitation films all or part of the time.[50] In some instances, theatres which had formerly shown only family or only art films switched over completely to exploitation features. This "breakthrough," of course, has meant increased profits and, in many instances, truly spectacular returns. In turn, the box office success has influenced not only other independent producers, but the major film companies as well.

One or two exploitation successes have already become legend in the industry. *The Immoral Mr. Teas,* a "nudie" shot in 1959 without professional actors or script, at a reputed cost of $24,000, had gross receipts of more than $1,000,000 in four years.[51] It played continuously for more than two years in Hollywood under the very eyes of the "major" industry. Another "nudie" classic, *Not Tonight, Henry,* with original costs of $40,000, has done almost as well at the box office. Both films have been involved in licensing controversies and obscenity prosecutions.

The economics of foreign-made exploitation films can be equally impressive. For most of these films, the American rights can be purchased and the film set up in distribution for a total cost of not more than $25,000. This means that the distributor's initial investment can often be paid off by a very few bookings. One such film, *Daniella by Night,* had gross receipts of $80,000 from an eight-week run at a single theatre in New York City alone.[52]

The "breakthrough" has also resulted in an upgrading of exploitation films. While their producers once hid behind pseudonyms, success has brought respectability and an unembarrassed defense of their enterprise. According to Dave Friedman, a leading producer of exploitation films today, the higher quality of "nudies" not only makes booking easier to obtain, but also makes it easier to claim that these films have "redeeming social importance" should there be an official obscenity charge. According to Friedman, patrons feel less guilt when nudity is not inserted gratuitously, and particularly when it is done with humor.[53]

According to Radley Metzger, probably one of the most candid and least apologetic figures in this sector of the movie industry, many exploitation films have broken out of the "all-male" audience pattern and now attract some general patronage, mainly "the date crowd," especially if the films have "a light touch." Metzger's company, Audubon Films, has handled such imported features as *Soft Skin on Black Silk, The Weird Lovemakers, Sexus, Twilight Girls,* and *I, a Woman.* Many of his imports Metzger admits to "doctoring"—the shooting and insertion of extra footage—in order to increase the film's exploitation value for the American audience. In fact, because censorship restrictions are now generally more stringent in Europe than in the United States, Metzger has resorted to producing films of his own, like *The Dirty Girls* and *The Alley Cats,* for the American market.[54]

In spite of the refinement of some "nudies," exploitation films are still highly competitive, and proprietors miss few opportunities to bring to the screen the sorts of lurid subjects that for years have been the staple of the confidential magazines. For example, the *Christine Keeler Story* was in production only months after the first news of the Profumo scandal. And, in a double dose of exploitation, plans were announced for a European production of *Fanny Hill,* featuring Mandy Rice-Davies, *la deuxième femme* in the Profumo affair, in the title role.[55]

Among the most sought after themes are prostitution, wayward youth, promiscuity, and nymphomania. Lesbianism is believed to have particular commercial appeal, and is preferred by many exploitation-film proprietors to all other themes. On the other hand, male homosexuality is usually avoided in the belief that it is too disturbing a subject, for most persons, to be popular on the screen. Of nonerotic themes, dope smuggling and the Negro who passes for white are said to have high probability of success, though a certain amount of violence in their treatment is usually desirable. Most exploitation-film proprietors, and for that matter a great many film proprietors of any sort, believe that they are merely providing a moviegoing public with what it wants.

Whether this is a valid claim or not, there is no question that the exploitation film is a permanent source of fuel for censorial fires. The proprietors of such films deal in the forbidden, and, to the extent that standards of acceptability change and become more permissive, they must press against the new boundaries. This imperative contributes to a continuing disequilibrium between freedom in the film medium and pressure for its control.

The Art Film

The art film, or "quality" film as it is sometimes called, makes up a rather amorphous category probably more easily described by its representative films than by any attempt at a definition. Among the leading art films in recent years have been the French *Hiroshima, Mon Amour, La Guerre Est*

Finie, and *The 400 Blows;* the Italian *L'Avventura, 8½,* and *The Organizer;*
the Swedish films of Ingmar Bergman; Poland's *Knife in the Water;* the
British *Saturday Night and Sunday Morning, The Servant,* and *A Taste of
Honey;* India's *Pather Panchali* trilogy; the Czech *Shop on Main Street;*
Japan's *Woman in the Dunes* and *Rashomon;* and *Ulysses,* played by actors
of Dublin's Abbey Theatre. Some works of American independents—*David
and Lisa, One Potato, Two Potato, The Cool World, The Pawnbroker*—
can also be included in this class of film. If there is a touchstone of the
art film it is probably that of a modest budget and a director of origi-
nality.

In the past, art films have been the subject of much formal and informal
censorship. A list of leading censorship controversies of the last ten or fifteen years would find an impressive stable of such films: *The Miracle, La
Ronde, Miss Julie, Game of Love, Lady Chatterley's Lover, The Lovers,
Les Liaisons Dangereuses, The Virgin Spring, The Silence, A Stranger
Knocks,* etc. For many proprietors of art films, as well as for many students
of the film medium, freedom for this class of film is the key to the entire
censorship struggle. Yet, notwithstanding its embattled past, the art film is
only infrequently the object of formal censorship today. In fact, if the films
we have listed were now to be submitted for the first time, most of them
would be routinely licensed by every board of censors in the country. It is
doubtful that the art film is quite so secure from informal censorship, but
even here it is likely to have less difficulty than in the past.

Though the art film does not inherently press against the limits of acceptability as does the exploitation film, its potential for becoming a source of
censorship of one kind or another remains. "Artistic sovereignty," taken seriously by many art film proprietors, is an uneasy companion to self-restraint, if in fact the two elements can coexist at all. Also, it is no secret
that it is easy to inject nudity or other sensationalist elements into an art
film strictly for box office purposes, while rationalizing such inclusion in
terms of artistic integrity. Furthermore, any change in the prevailing pattern
of exhibition limited to adult audiences, and fairly select ones at that, would
no doubt restore the art film to status as a major source of censorial interest. The fact that most art films do not have wide exhibition is rarely a matter of choice on the part of their proprietors. In fact, many believe that in
order to offset the always-present possibility of large losses on other films,
exhibition to the "big audience" must be sought where the opportunity is
presented. Finally, because it is the main expression of intellectuality and
thematic sophistication in the film medium, the art film will often be critical
of the conventional and the established, and by that measure is likely to
continue to be the occasional object of informal censorship.

The Major Film with an Adult Theme

The same factors which have worked to undermine the effectiveness of the Motion Picture Code have worked to loosen the bonds of proprietary restraint among the major film-makers. In the last few years Hollywood films have been marked by both an increasing maturity and an increasing sensationalism, the latter reflected in bolder portrayal of erotica, nudity, and violence. In fact, the very success of the art film and the exploitation film have spurred a kind of imitation by the major industry. Yet while the art film and the exploitation film are made on low budgets and have relatively few bookings, playing mainly in small theatres and to audiences of adults, the major film, with high production costs, is booked into the circuits and plays to a general audience. When major films feature adult themes, particularly when such themes are sensationalized, they generate censorship pressures. The objective of these pressures is usually classification, though in many instances, where the censorial reaction is less discriminating, the objective becomes one of generalized restriction.

Increased erotica and sensationalism have not characterized all major-company films, of course. Many producers have foregone the new opportunities for injecting heavier doses of sex, nudity, or violence into their films. In fact, motion picture trade journals frequently contain items in which a Hollywood figure has criticized the lack of self-restraint among his fellow film-makers, and the general movement away from family or general audience films. It should also be noted that some film proprietors who have made adult films have actually specified that such films be limited to audiences of adults.

Nevertheless, the temptation to sensationalize or eroticize major films in subject or treatment or both is very strong. In an industry of unpredictable fortunes and the always-present possibility of large losses, erotica has often seemed one of the few reliable forms of investment insurance. This view, and the recent spectacular profits made by some exploitation films, have given full flower to the Hollywood imitation. Reflecting this trend is the fact that almost every sensationally exploited book in recent years—*Lolita, Fanny Hill, Tropic of Cancer, Candy, Sex and the Single Girl, Valley of the Dolls,* or the popularly salacious works of Harold Robbins—has been purchased by Hollywood for cinematic adaptation. In fact in the case of *Sex and the Single Girl,* a non-fiction book of advice, Warner Brothers paid $200,000 for the movie-making rights and then used only the title! The company commissioned studio writers to think up a plausible story to accompany it.[56]

The man who has shown Hollywood the way to the adult film is Joseph E. Levine, who in ten years rose from an obscure New England exhibitor's station to become perhaps the most respected and envied figure on the business side of the American film industry. Levine got his start, and at the same time demonstrated the value of new promotional techniques, by purchasing *Hercules,* an Italian film which was to receive uniformly poor reviews. He bought it for $100,000, spent $1,500,000 on its promotion—largely through sensationalized "hard sell" advertising and saturation bookings—and then eventually reaped more than ten times that amount in profit. Later, he went on to fortune with the much acclaimed Italian film *Two Women,* which he purchased after watching the movie's rape scene. As a result of these and like successes, the words "Joseph E. Levine presents" have become the most influential credits in the industry. Though it is sometimes said, with a mixture of envy and disdain, that Levine will present anything that makes money, he has in fact taken chances (and losses) with some films of quality, such as *Long Day's Journey into Night.* The things that make money, according to Levine himself, are "sex, violence, and action."[57] A recent Levine film which had heavy doses of these ingredients, particularly the first, and which made a great deal of money, was *The Carpetbaggers,* an adaptation of the Harold Robbins bestseller of the same name. The film more than recouped its entire production cost of $3,300,000 in the first five weeks of its run in the New York metropolitan area alone.[58] In doing so, it also set a record for receipts for a short run in the area. Experience with this film is offered as dramatic proof that spectacular profits can await a sensationalized major production given sensationalized promotion. Robbins and Levine wasted no time. Robbins' next book, *The Adventurers,* was purchased for the movies by Levine for $1,000,000 before it was written![59]

Until they are proven wrong in their economics, promoters like Levine and films like *The Carpetbaggers* will have imitators. The main question with regard to censorship and proprietary restraint lies in whether these films will be classified. To limit such movies to adults would be to cut into their profit potential, in some cases sharply. On the other hand, as long as such films remain available to a general audience, they will be a major source of censorship pressures of one form or another.

The Experimental Film

The giving way of self-restraint in the name of artistic freedom marks this fourth category of films. The experimental film, sometimes called the avant-garde or "underground" film, is the highly expressionist product of a small group of dedicated and usually insolvent amateurs clustered in New York's Greenwich Village and Lower East Side and, to a lesser extent, in San Francisco. Their works, which range from very short shorts to full-length features, are often turned out on 16 mm film (compared with the 35 mm commercial standard) with hand-held cameras at costs of often less than $100 and seldom more than $1,000 a film. The subjects and techniques are diverse. Some films involve social protest; others are merely exploration of lights, colors, geometrical shapes, the synchronization of sound and movement, etc. And some, whatever they are, would appear to be intelligible only to their creators or to psychoanalysts of their creators. Experimental is an apt term. One of the best-known of the genre, Andy Warhol's *Empire,* is an eight-hour film of a view of the Empire State Building from the street outside. Though a few experimental films have received critical attention, most have been dismissed as amateurish—"home movies with pretensions."[60] Yet diversity of form and technique aside, the one element more than any other that has attracted attention to this class of film is the fact that the source material is often erotica and deviation.

In the past, experimental films were exhibited mainly in private homes, to film societies in rented auditoriums or theatres, and on a few college and university campuses to relatively small groups. In some cases the showings were clandestine. Probably not more than one moviegoer in ten thousand had ever seen an experimental film. Now, the pattern of limited exhibition is changing. The Film-makers Cinematheque, a nonprofit rudimentary distribution organization for experimental films in New York, has opened its own "showcase" in a basement theatre in midtown Manhattan which once housed off-Broadway stage shows. The theatre is open to the public six nights a week for repertory screening of the works of new film makers and those of such underground-film stalwarts as Andy Warhol, Kenneth Anger, Jonas Mekas, and Stan Brakhage. Moreover, some of the works of the latter have begun to be shown in a few of the city's commercial theatres. In fact, so much have exhibition opportunities increased, that some of the leading underground works have actually become profitable, and many experimentalists believe that eventually as many as one hundred commercial theatres in the country will play "underground" films on a regular basis.

It is not surprising that many of the most popular of these films have been the most daring with erotica. For example, Kenneth Anger's *Flaming Creatures,* which Arthur Knight, a leading student of the film, has called "close to pornography," is the film record of a transvestite orgy in which male genitals are exposed.[61] In another Anger film, *The Story of O,* a naked girl is dominated by a young man. She is chained, blindfolded, and wears a leather dog-collar about her neck. Her back is scarred from a whipping. Arthur Knight has described still another Anger film, *Fireworks.*

. . . it is the dream wish of a pervert, filled with his ambivalent fear of and desire for the male. From the first shot of a monster erection under the sheets to its final, horrifying sequence in which a gang of sailors mercilessly beats and tortures the hero (with a strong suggestion of castration as well), the images have a compulsive, nightmare quality. A brawny sailor exhibits his muscles at a bar, then attacks the boy. Another lashes him with chains. Still others break his nostrils, slash him with broken glass, pour a trickle of suspiciously symbolic cream over his bloodied face. At the climax, a single sailor tall against a black background stands for a moment fiddling with his fly. It falls open, and what seems to be a huge phallus appears. The sailor holds a lighted match to its tip, and, as the thing shoots off sparks and flame, we see it is only a Roman candle. The final shot reveals that it was all a dream, but the specific nature of the dream is underscored by a view of the sailor lying prone, inert on the hero's cot.[62]

It is possible to record any human behavior or event or simulation thereof on film, just as it is possible to hold theories of art according to which no subject or behavior should be proscribed from cinematographic observation or representation. Some of the experimental film makers have approached these limits. In Stan Brakhage's *Thigh Line Lyre Triangular,* amidst constant interruption by a bewildering array of flashing lights, colors, configurations of spots, and geometrical patterns perhaps randomly obtained, a view of a woman's genitalia is repeatedly flashed on the screen. A manipulating hand appears and a finger is inserted. The scene turns out to be in an obstetrical context and the film is an expressionist depiction of the birth of a child. Yet, to the audience, this is not clear until later in the film. In Brakhage's *Wedlock,* a man and a woman are shown in intercourse, entirely in negative film, that is, the black and white images are reversed. Finally, in still another Brakhage film, *Vein,* a young boy masturbates in front of the camera. Though there are other shots, including that of his face, most of the film is a closeup of the penis being fondled.

There is little doubt that the experimental film is on a collision course with censorship. Though still leagues behind the art film and even the exploitation film in its distribution and exhibition, the experimental film is far ahead of either in daring. Films of this type are sure to have wider circulation and larger audiences in the future and probably, to some degree or other, make their way into conventional commercial exhibition. The makers of these films, accustomed as they are to financial straits and to real or fancied establishment slings and arrows, are apt to be the least compromising of men and women in the film medium.

The four types of film discussed here are the major sources of censorship interest today. Products of changing conditions in the medium, they mark a decline in proprietary restraint, and indicate that such restraint is not today, if indeed it ever was, an effective antidote to other forms of control. On the contrary, these films are likely to be a continuing stimulus to censorship. What is acceptable, what is felt must be expressed, and what is profitable are all dynamic forces, and much film-making can be expected to be shaped accordingly. Given this stimulation, it is unlikely that censorship interest in motion pictures will be put to rest.

Even assuming that greater restriction at the proprietary level is possible, it is a fair question whether it would even be desirable. Serious reservations can be held from the standpoint of the maturation of the film medium, or at least of a sector of the medium. The changing conditions which have encouraged some of the most sensationalistic and, in qualitative terms, some of the worst films, have also opened the doors to some of the most creative works, and these in turn have lent reinforcement to claims made on behalf of the film as an art form. The new fluidity in the medium is a mixed development. Low sensationalism and high art alike are borne by its current.

From the standpoint of freedom and censorship, however, films of both sorts, particularly of the former, are often the source of public tension. In the search for ways in which this tension can be managed, the individual film proprietor is unlikely to be a reliable ally.

V

CONCLUSION

9

Freedom of Speech in a Mass Medium

Motion pictures can hardly avoid being a major object of censorship in a mass democratic society that is officially dedicated to realizing as wide a freedom of speech as possible. The censorship interest in the medium seeks to keep from the screen that which it perceives to be threatening or offensive, and in attempting to do so, operates through a number of controls— governmental, nongovernmental, legal, and extra-legal—which vary in frequency and effectiveness of sanction. This interest is rooted sociologically in a disequilibrium between the content of films and their audience. In the past, such imbalance was held to a minimum by governmental boards of censors, the film industry's own self-regulatory apparatus, and Roman Catholic pressure. This triad of controls successfully enforced a common denominator of content called the "family" film, though the extraordinary profit in such movies made the censorship task an easier one. When this pattern of control was eventually broken up by the decline of the censor boards and industry self-regulation, on the one hand, and the arrival of television, on the other, the content of movies underwent a radical change that, until now at least, has far outpaced changes in the audience pattern. Today, as in the past, the movies are a mass medium playing to a largely undifferentiated mass audience in which youth is especially well represented. At the same time, unchecked by advertisers, they have come to deal in sex and manners with a freedom traditionally reserved for the elite media of hardcover books and the stage.* The resulting lack of balance arouses a censorship interest at the same time that traditional modes of control are less re-

* Some magazines and paperback books today are also marked by the same audience-content disequilibrium, and it is not surprising to find them subject to some of the same censorship interest and pressures. There is a difference in degree, however, with movies traditionally regarded as a far more powerful communicating device and therefore one having a special capacity for harm.

sponsive to that interest. This has resulted in the partial frustration of censorial energies on the one hand, and the finding of new, often highly effective accommodation for some of these energies on the other.

Of the traditional controls, prior censorship administered by governmental licensing boards has been unquestionably the most controversial, even if not the most effective. Its form as a prior restraint has made it the target of libertarians, and in fact in much of the debate this peculiar institution has been cast as the major obstacle to true freedom in films. Though it was clearly a highly restrictive and often abusive censorship at one time, it does not remain so today. Its reformation by the courts in the last fifteen years makes comparison with the past especially difficult. Gone are the vague substantive standards and the freewheeling procedures which so often gave the censors leverage far beyond their statutory powers. The governmental censors of today, subject to close judicial supervision, actually "control" motion pictures only in the first instance. Moreover, elimination of almost all censorial standards except obscenity, and the liberalization of obscenity doctrine itself, have completely altered the substance of prior censorship.

Today the boards are faced with the question of, not whether the camera should play upon a woman's face as she is presumably having intercourse with her lover (*Ecstasy*), but whether entire bodies should be shown in intercourse (*A Stranger Knocks*); not whether a heroin needle should be shown entering a man's arm (*The Man with the Golden Arm*), but whether a man's leg should be shown after he has been drawn and quartered (*Two Thousand Maniacs*); not whether a woman should be portrayed as finding happiness in adultery (*Lady Chatterley's Lover*), but whether she should be shown about to have sexual congress with a large dog (*491*). Today most nudist camp films, nudity in documentaries, run-of-the-mill "nudie" films, much sado-masochistic violence, and much that is suggestive in dances, dialogue, and situations is routinely passed, in most cases for viewing by a general audience. In fact, it can almost be said that anything censored as late as the early 1960's would be licensed today, and that almost anything censored today would not even have been produced for public exhibition as late as the early sixties.

Though prior censorship is now more of a disadvantage in form than in substance, some film proprietors have maintained that it still sets movies apart in a kind of second class status among the media of speech. However, evidence indicates that the movies exercise an actual freedom of content that is far greater than any of the other mass media—newspapers, magazines, radio, or television. Though free of governmental prior restraint, these media are all subject to very powerful internal restraints in the form of advertisers' influence, which is almost always exercised in the defense of conventional values and decencies. In the portrayal of erotica, control by advertisers actually functions as a kind of broker mechanism that adjusts the rigorous official free speech ethic prescribed by the First Amendment to the level of popular acceptability. It is just such a broker mechanism that the movies have never had. Hence control of the latter has always been more "public," inevitably involving government to a much greater degree than that of the other mass media.

A striking example of the relatively greater freedom exercised by movies can be seen in the 1962 censorship case involving the film *The Connection*. The New York Court of Appeals held that the word "shit," used several times in the sound track as slang for heroin, was not ground for denying an exhibition permit, and the film was then shown intact in the state. However, neither the trade nor the general press mentioned the word at all in their reporting of the decision, though some verbal gymnastics were necessary to avoid doing so.* Other examples of the freedom differential abound, not the least of which result from the widespread practice of newspapers and radio and television stations editing movie advertising copy, and in some cases rejecting it altogether.

This greater *de facto* freedom in the movies would be less remarkable if they had developed some kind of audience stratification. Yet, with few exceptions, this has not been the case. Some foreign, art, and exploitation films do play in selected theatres or to audiences with special interests, but this division is an unreliable one, since it tends to break down wherever there are strong proprietary economic temptations to enlarge the audience. Another possible stratification, that of classification, has been resisted by most of the film industry despite recent changes in the Motion Picture Code. In effect, then, the movies exercise a new freedom of content while remaining a mass medium without either the inhibition of functioning internal restraints or an established audience stratification. In these circumstances, the charge that today's highly limited prior censorship casts the movies as an underprivileged medium of speech appears to be a hollow one indeed.

Though partially blocked by the declining responsiveness of both the boards of censors and the industry's self-regulation, the censorship interest aroused by the new freedoms still exercises a coercive and often clandestine control on films. However, its energies have definitely not been channeled primarily through individual patron decision-making buttressed by advisory ratings, nor through use of the criminal process—the two methods

---

* *The New York Times* substituted "an Anglo-Saxon word" and "a four-letter word," leaving some doubt in the reader's mind about exactly what word was involved. *Variety*, the show business weekly which takes pride in a certain hardboiled sophistication and which has few, if any, youthful readers, was more informative if not less euphemistic, describing the word as "the second-most tabooed in polite society."

of control preferred by film-makers and libertarians. On the one hand, advisory ratings (excluding Catholic ratings, which because of their coercive dimension and relation to organized group power are not merely advisory in character) are too diffused in their effect to win recognition as an important and realistic means for controlling movies. On the other hand, the prosecuting power, though invoked more often than in the past, is frequently frustrated on appeal by the liberalized obscenity doctrine, with the result that the power is probably used far more often to intimidate than to indict. Indeed, if advisory ratings, obscenity prosecutions, and prior censorship were the only controls on movies, partisans of free speech would have little need to fear. Libertarian and proprietary forces have managed to win one courtroom battle after another. But the real war over freedom of speech in the medium today is less one of a conventional set-piece struggle against boards of censors or prosecutors than one of an anti-guerilla campaign against scattered, frequently unseen, but often highly effective opposition.

Except for Catholic influence on production and distribution, most censorship of movies today is effected informally within the community against exhibitors. Its forms include a variety of extralegal acts by public officials at the demand of community groups, and direct action by groups themselves. Sometimes officials have also employed legal but noncensorship powers— such as that of occupational licensing—for censorial purposes. In many instances, informal censorship is or becomes self-operating through the exhibitor's anticipation of unwanted consequences. Whatever its form, the aim of informal censorship is to effect changes in motion picture exhibition as quickly, cheaply, and effectively as possible. Such censorship is almost totally lacking in anything resembling standards of due process and often comes close to being an *in rem* lynching. Proscriptive objectives invariably range far beyond the narrow legal standard of obscenity, and the informal censor is often an infrequent moviegoer or a non-moviegoer lacking the sophistication or experience necessary to distinguish the artful or merely unconventional from the exploitative or pornographic. It is not surprising, then, to find many films—such as the award-winning *Who's Afraid of Virginia Woolf?* which was routinely licensed by boards of censors—kept from exhibition at certain theatres, or in entire communities, by informal censorship.

Under these circumstances, the significant question about prior censorship today is not whether it is bad, but whether it does any good. The answer here would seem to depend on whether licensing can be further reformed and, more importantly, on whether it is a real alternative to informal censorship. Clearly, further improvements are needed to ease the burdens on the film proprietor and on free speech. For example, judicial review of censorship orders should be speeded up even more, so that it takes place in a matter of days rather than weeks; fees charged to film proprietors should be eliminated entirely; and fairly rigorous qualification standards, accompanied by an attractive pay scale, need to be developed for the selection of censors. These minor reforms added to the major ones already effected would leave prior censorship, from the submission of a film to a court order on it, a routinized control process offering a quick public review according to requirements of due process of law, in a proceeding in which the values of free speech are likely to receive an extraordinarily high priority.

If prior censorship and informal censorship are inversely related, as available evidence seems to suggest, then the former control probably functions to rechannel a large amount of censorship energy. On the other hand, though reconstructed within, licensing remains a censorship institution in form and can still be an effective limitation on films fairly raising the question of obscenity.

For films approved, prior censorship actually functions as a form of insurance against other controls; issuance of a license has a kind of legitimating effect upon a film. This protection may not necessarily prevent all other censorial action, but it is likely to reduce the probability of such action and to increase a proprietor's will to resist where such action does occur. In this way, licensing may actually serve to insulate some nonobscene yet unconventional expression from community pressures or interdiction.

Finally, the systematic coverage of films, which distinguishes governmental licensing from the film industry's self-regulatory apparatus, could also mean that prior censorship might come to play an important role in any eventual stratification of the medium. Licensing is particularly well suited to the classification of films, should legislative bodies decide to require such audience restriction. Whether undertaken as a supplement to general licensing, as a substitute for it, or initiated without general licensing, an enforceable systematic rating of films according to their suitability for young persons appears to be a promising way of reducing censorship pressures in almost every community in the nation.

As the apparent utility of prior censorship today is an ironic testament to libertarian victories of the past, the entire problem of freedom in the mass medium raises a number of questions concerning the traditional libertarian approach to free speech. Among many libertarians and not a few film proprietors, there is an orthodoxy which not only considers prior censorship antithetical in its very form to free speech, but which views any compromises with the censorship interest at all as ignoble and unnecessary. This orthodoxy sees the free speech problem principally in philosophical, legal, and formal terms, rather than in its political, social, and informal aspects. The enemy is government itself, and the aim is to use the power of the law to deny the censorship interest. In the extreme, the orthodox approach takes an almost ideological turn. The struggle against censorship becomes a kind of crusade on behalf of an eternal verity against the forces of ignorance, fear, and evil. The extent to which freedom is threatened, the justifications offered for limitation, or other such pragmatically dispositioned considerations may be ignored or actually ruled out-of-bounds.

Such an orientation leads to certain misconceptions about the censorship interest itself. Classically, the libertarian orthodoxy battles against government, especially government formally arrayed. Officials themselves are looked upon as the main source of censorship energies. Yet, actually, speech involving sex and manners is the very sort which does *not* threaten the stability or existence of the government. On these issues government is likely to act as it acts on most others in a democratic polity—as an *agent* of marshaled interests perhaps themselves amounting to a majoritarian will.

Since the orthodox view often fails to see the popular character of censorship interest, it is apt to consider the censorship problem capable of legal solution, with a Comstockian censorship interest formally defeated in open battle. This view misconceives not only the nature of the enemy but also that of the war itself. Its formalism overestimates the efficacy of legal power, in the same fashion that another kind of formalism often overestimates the efficacy of military power, as applied to problems essentially social and political in character.

It is unlikely that any mass medium in the American mass democratic society today can be completely, or even nearly, free of control except at a tremendous potential cost to the political system itself. The censorship interest, however misguided it may be thought to be, is nevertheless political force; and though, as a practical matter, there is little chance that it can or will be completely frustrated, the consequences of such a development would be serious. Because the values censorship defends are often of an emotionally elemental character, their repeated denial could lead to a reaction of generalized intolerance or to some other pathological resolution, such as support for extremist politics already built upon tensions produced by group, class, race or individual insecurities, or to even a sense of alienation from the political system itself. In fact, from the standpoint of conflict management, the fact that censorship energy is essentially accommodated informally may itself be a signal of a systemic malfunctioning.

Finally, in the light of the present state of knowledge about the effects of motion pictures, the merits of the censorship interest—which have not been considered in this book—lay claim to a degree of legitimacy. Though much censorship interest is unquestionably irrational, some of the interest is reasonably and intelligently held. The idea that some motion picture content may be harmful to viewers, especially youthful viewers, is not one that can be completely dismissed as the product of wild or morbid imaginings. The absence of conclusive evidence on one side or the other of this question adds a moral complexity to the entire censorship problem.

Two measures would go far toward an accommodation of opposing interests in the controversy over the movies. One is the establishment of some kind of double standard for proscribable erotica, among the media of speech, that would take the movies' unusual communicative power into account. The other is the development of a reliable stratification for the medium that would afford a more finely drawn audience–content balance. The first is a problem for the courts; the second, for the film industry in the first instance, though it is clearly unlikely to come about through the efforts of the industry alone. Developments such as these, though not of libertarian character in themselves, are, in the long run, likely to make freedom of speech in motion pictures more secure and allow its writ to run more widely than it does today.

The great victories already won for freedom of speech in the movies have resulted in much in their content that is beyond the level of acceptability of a large part of the population. These free speech victories have applied to the entire population a standard that, at least in terms of the tolerance it demands, is essentially elitist. To be sure, the popular threshold of acceptability is not static, and the "people," or at least large numbers of persons, can be led or educated to a higher degree of practicing tolerance. Yet where the issues involve fundamental emotional concerns like those of sex and morality, this process is apt to run by a far different clock than the one which has governed changes in the legal doctrine and in motion picture industry economics. The problem for freedom of speech in the movies today is not the winning of legal battles, which is easily enough done, but the winning of battles that are not later lost outside the courtroom. This involves recognition that censorship is in large measure a social and political problem and therefore one that is only partially curable through legal action, however forceful that may be.

NOTES

TABLE OF CASES

INDEX

Notes

Chapter 2. From "Business" to "Speech"

1 For the historical background of the movies I have relied, in part, on two leading histories: Lewis Jacobs, *The Rise of the American Film* (New York, 1939) and Terry Ramsaye, *A Million and One Nights* (New York, 1926), Vols. 1 and 2; as well as on Morris Ernst and Pare Lorentz, *Censored; the Private Life of the Movie* (New York, 1930); Benjamin B. Hampton, *A History of the Movies* (New York, 1931); Ruth Inglis, *Freedom of the Movies* (Chicago, 1947); Arthur Knight, *The Liveliest Art* (The New American Library, Mentor ed., New York, 1957); Raymond Moley, *The Hays Office* (New York, 1945); Leo Rosten, *Hollywood: the Movie Colony and the Movie Makers* (New York, 1941); Richard Schickel, *The Stars* (New York, 1962); Murray Schumach, *The Face on the Cutting Room Floor* (New York, 1964); Margaret Thorp, *America at the Movies* (New York, 1939); Terry Ramsaye, "The Rise and Place of Motion Pictures," in *The American Academy of Political and Social Science Annals*, 254, 1.

2 *People* v. *Doris*, 14 App. Div. 117, 43 N.Y.S. 571 (1st Dep't 1897).

3 *State* v. *Morris*, 24 Del. 330, 76 A. 479 (Ct. Gen. Sess. Del. 1910).

4 *People* v. *Gaynor*, 77 Misc. 576, 137 N.Y.S. 196 (Sup. Ct. N.Y. Co. 1912).

5 *Higgins* v. *Lacroix*, 119 Minn. 145, 137 N.W. 417 (1912).

6 *City of Chicago Charter* art. 5, cl. 45 (1907), as quoted in *Block* v. *Chicago*, 239 Ill. 251, 87 N.E. 1011 (1909).

7 239 Ill. 251, 265, 87 N.E. 1011, 1020 (1909).

8 Act of June 19, 1911 (P.L. 1067), as quoted in *Buffalo Branch, Mutual Film Corp.* v. *Breitlinger*, 250 Pa. 225, 95 A. 433 (1915).

9 H.R. 456, 64th Cong., 1st Sess.

10 38 Stat. 151 (1913).

11 19 U.S.C. §1305 (a).

12 10 U.S.C. §1393 (1958).

13 Act of Sept. 21, 1922, 42 Stat. 968–72, ch. 356, tit. IV, §§510–11. The law was upheld in *Weber* v. *Freed*, 224 F. 355 (3d Cir., 1915), *aff'd per curiam*, 239 U.S. 325 (1915) as a valid exercise of commerce power. The

Supreme Court did not consider any First Amendment contentions. For an analysis of the effect of this statute, see Roger Marchetti, *Law of the Stage, Screen, and Radio* (Los Angeles, 1936), pp. 113–19.

14   Act of June 29, 1940, 54 Stat. 686, ch. 443, §1; 15 U.S.C. 1001 (1940).

15   Knight, *The Liveliest Art*, p. 111.

16   Martin Quigley, Sr., *Decency in Motion Pictures* (New York, 1937), p. 31.

17   Donald R. Young, "Motion Pictures: A Study in Social Legislation," Ph.D. diss., U. of Pa., 1922, quoted in Inglis, *Freedom of the Movies*, p. 63.

18   Louisiana enacted a licensing law in 1935, but no board was ever appointed. *La. Rev. Civ. Code*, §§4:301—4:307 (1950).

19   *Mass. Gen. Laws* ch. 136, §§1–4 (1932). Section 4 relating to motion pictures was invalidated in *Brattle Films* v. *Commissioner of Public Safety*, 333 Mass. 58, 127 N.E.2d 891 (1955), *Op. Att'y Gen.*, Aug. 22, 1955, p. 32.

20   *Conn. Pub. Acts,* ch. 177 (1925). Though upheld in *Fox Film Corp.* v. *Trumbull,* 7 F.2d 715 (D. Conn. 1925), *appeal dismissed by stipulation,* 269 U.S. 597 (1925), the law was repealed in 1927. *Conn. Pub. Acts,* ch. 318 (1927).

21   *R.I. Gen. Laws,* ch. 362, §§1–2 (1938). The law was upheld in *Thayer Amusement Co.* v. *Moulton*, 63 R.I. 682, 7 A.2d 682 (1939).

22   Ernst and Lorentz, *Censored*, p. 170.

23   236 U.S. 230, 246–47 (1915).

24   *Ibid.,* at 244.

25   *Winters* v. *New York*, 333 U.S. 507, 510 (1948).

26   236 U.S., at 246–47.

27   In re *Franklin Film Mfg. Corp.*, 253 Pa. 422, 425, 98 A. 623, 625 (1916).

28   *State* ex. rel. *Midwestern Film Exchange* v. *Clifton*, 118 Ohio St. 91, 160 N.E. 625 (1928).

29   *Schuman* v. *Pickert*, 277 Mich. 225, 229, 269 N.W. 152, 154 (1936).

30   *Pathe Exchange* v. *Cobb*, 202 App. Div. 450, 195 N.Y.S. 661 (3d Dep't 1922), *aff'd*, 236 N.Y. 539, 142 N.E. 274 (1923).

31   In re *Vitagraph*, 295 Pa. 471, 145 A. 518 (1929).

32   334 U.S. 131, 166 (1948).

33   E.g., *RD-DR Corp.* v. *Smith*, 183 F.2d 562 (5th Cir. 1950), *cert. den.*, 340 U.S. 853 (1950); *United Artists* v. *Memphis*, 189 Tenn. 397, 225 S.W.2d 550 (1949), *cert. den.*, 339 U.S. 853 (1950); Leo Kupferman and Thomas O'Brien, "Motion Picture Censorship—The Memphis Blues," 36 *Cornell L.Q.* 273 (1951); Note, "Motion Picture Censorship," 60 *Yale L.J.* 696 (1951).

34   Zechariah Chafee, Jr., *Free Speech in the United States* (Cambridge, Mass., 1941), p. 541.

35   E.g., Chief Justice Warren's dissenting opinion, *Times Film Corp.* v. *Chicago*, 365 U.S. 43, 69–72 (1961); Morris Ernst and Alexander Lindey, *The Censor Marches On* (New York, 1940); Ernst and Lorentz, *Censored;* Robert Haney, *Comstockery in America* (Boston, 1960); Kupferman and O'Brien, 36 *Cornell L.Q.;* Note, 60 *Yale L.J.;* Note, "Censorship of Mo-

tion Pictures," 49 *Yale L.J.* 87 (1939); Lester Velie, "You Can't See That Movie," *Collier's*, May 6, 1950, p. 11.

36 In re *Goldwyn Distributing Corp.*, 265 Pa. 335, 343, 108 A. 816, 819 (1919).

37 *Fox Film Corp.* v. *Collins*, 236 Ill. App. 281 (1925).

38 In re *Appeal of Board of Censors*, Pa. C.P. No. 6, no. 5259 (1937), noted in 86 *U. Pa. L. Rev.* 305 (1938). Although the court actually held the film, *Spain in Flames*, exempt because it was a newsreel, it declared in a dictum that, had it been a feature, the board "would not have acted arbitrarily or capriciously."

39 E.g., a mayor's ban on *Birth of a Nation* was upheld "in the interest of public welfare and the peace and good order of the city." *Bainbridge* v. *Minneapolis*, 131 Minn. 181, 184, 154 N.W. 964, 966 (1915).

40 *United Artists* v. *Memphis*, 189 Tenn. 397, 225 S.W.2d 550 (1949), *cert. den.*, 339 U.S. 853 (1950).

41 *Ibid.*, at 399 and 551–552.

42 Infrequent mention of the words "rape" and "contraceptive" in *Anatomy of a Murder* were held not to make the film obscene. *Columbia Pictures* v. *Chicago*, 184 F. Supp. 817 (N.D. Ill. 1959).

43 H.R. 5990, § 205, 77th Cong., 2d Sess. (1942).

44 E.g., *Kunz* v. *New York*, 340 U.S. 290 (1951); *Niemotko* v. *Maryland*, 340 U.S. 268 (1951); *Saia* v. *New York*, 334 U.S. 558 (1948); *Thomas* v. *Collins*, 323 U.S. 516 (1945); *Murdock* v. *Pennsylvania*, 319 U.S. 105 (1943); *Largent* v. *Texas*, 318 U.S. 418 (1943); *Cantwell* v. *Connecticut*, 310 U.S. 296 (1940); *Schneider* v. *Irvington*, 308 U.S. 147 (1939); *Hague* v. *C.I.O.*, 307 U.S. 496 (1939); *Lovell* v. *Griffin*, 303 U.S. 444 (1938).

45 E.g., *Feiner* v. *New York*, 340 U.S. 315 (1951); *Terminiello* v. *Chicago*, 337 U.S. 1 (1949); *Chaplinsky* v. *New Hampshire*, 315 U.S. 568 (1942); *Bridges* v. *California*, 314 U.S. 252 (1941); *Thornhill* v. *Alabama*, 310 U.S. 88 (1940); *Herndon* v. *Lowry*, 301 U.S. 242 (1937).

46 E.g., *Winters* v. *New York*, 333 U.S. 507 (1948).

47 283 U.S. 697, 720 (1931).

48 *Ibid.*, at 716.

49 For the factual background of the case, I have drawn largely from two excellent accounts: Alan F. Westin, *The Miracle Case: the Supreme Court and the Movies* (Inter-University Case Program Series, No. 64, Tuscaloosa, Ala., 1961); Bosley Crowther, "The Strange Case of 'The Miracle'," *Atlantic Monthly*, April, 1951, p. 35.

50 *Burstyn* v. *McCaffrey*, 198 Misc. 884, 101 N.Y.S.2d 892 (Sup. Ct. 1951).

51 *Burstyn* v. *Wilson*, 303 N.Y. 242, 101 N.E.2d 665 (1951).

52 *Burstyn* v. *Wilson*, 343 U.S. 495, 501–2 (1952).

53 *Ibid.*, at 504–5.

54 *Ibid.*

55 *Ibid.*, at 506.

56 *Ibid.*, at 506–7.

57 Westin, *The Miracle Case*, p. 33.

58 Bosley Crowther in the *The New York Times*, quoted in Westin, *The Miracle Case*, p. 32.

Chapter 3.   Procedures: Pragmatic Assessment

1   *Times Film Corp.* v. *Chicago*, 355 U.S. 35 (1957); *Holmby Productions* v. *Vaughn*, 350 U.S. 870 (1955); *Superior Films* v. *Dep't of Education* and *Commercial Pictures* v. *Board of Regents*, 346 U.S. 587 (1954); *Gelling* v. *Texas*, 343 U.S. 960 (1952).

2   *RKO Radio Pictures* v. *Dep't of Education*, 162 Ohio St. 263, 122 N.E.2d 769 (1954).

3   *Brattle Films* v. *Commissioner of Public Safety*, 333 Mass. 58, 127 N.E.2d 891 (1955).

4   *Kansas* ex. rel. *Fatzer* v. *Shanahan*, 178 Kan. 400, 286 P.2d 742 (1955).

5   See Paul A. Freund, "The Supreme Court and Civil Liberties," 4 *Vand. L. Rev.* 533, 539 (1950–1951).

6   354 U.S. 436, 441 (1957).

7   *Times Film Corp.* v. *Chicago*, 365 U.S. 43, 46 (1961).

8   *Ibid.*, at 50.

9   *Ibid.*, at 49; 343 U.S. 495, 502–3 (1952).

10 365 U.S. 43, 55 (1961).

11 Alexander Bickel, *The Least Dangerous Branch* (New York, 1962), pp. 133–43.

12 *Ibid.*, p. 143.

13 E.g., *Christian Century*, Feb. 8, 1961, p. 163; *Commonweal*, Feb. 10, 1961, pp. 495–96, and March 31, 1961, p. 17; *New Republic*, Feb. 17, 1961, p. 8; *Publishers' Weekly*, Feb. 6, 1961, p. 68; *New York Times*, Jan. 25, 1961, p. 32; *Washington Post*, Jan. 25, 1961, p. 16.

14 *Atlanta* v. *Twentieth Century Fox*, 219 Ga. 271, 133 S.E. 2d 12 (1963); *K. Gordon Murray Productions* v. *Floyd*, 217 Ga. 784, 125 S.E.2d 207 (1962); *Wm. Goldman Theatres* v. *Dana*, 405 Pa. 83, 173 A.2d 59 (1961); *Portland* v. *Welch*, 229 Ore. 427, 367 P.2d 403 (1961).

15 *Zenith International Film Corp.* v. *Chicago*, 291 F.2d 785 (7th Cir. 1961).

16 *Fanfare Films* v. *Motion Picture Censor Board*, 234 Md. 10, 197 A.2d 839 (1964); *The Connection Co.* v. *Board of Regents*, 17 App. Div. 2d 671, 230 N.Y.S.2d 103 (3d Dep't 1962).

17 *Atlanta* v. *Lopert Pictures*, 217 Ga. 432, 122 S.E.2d 916 (1961); *Kingsley International Pictures* v. *Providence*, 166 F. Supp. 456 (D.R.I. 1958).

18 *Janus Films* v. *Fort Worth*, 163 Tex. 616, 354 S.W.2d 597 (1962).

19 *1959 International Motion Picture Almanac* (New York, 1958), pp. 722–24.

20 *1963 International Motion Picture Almanac* (New York, 1962), pp. 733–35.

21 *Wm. Goldman Theatres* v. *Dana*, 405 Pa. 83, 173 A.2d 59 (1961).

22 *Portland* v. *Welch*, 229 Ore. 427, 367 P.2d 403 (1961).

23 *K. Gordon Murray Productions* v. *Floyd*, 217 Ga. 784, 125 S.E.2d 207 (1962).

24 Since the Ohio Constitution, Art. 4, §2, provides that at least six justices of
    the state supreme court must concur in order to render a law unconstitu-
    tional, the licensing statute held invalid, five to two, was merely declared
    "unreasonable and unlawful." *RKO Radio Pictures* v. *Dep't of Education,*
    162 Ohio St. 263, 122 N.E.2d 769 (1954).
25 *Pa. Const.,* art. 1, § 7.
26 *Ga. Const.,* art. 1, par. 15.
27 *Ore. Const.,* art. 1, § 8.
28 405 Pa. 83, 87, 173 A.2d 59, 62 (1961).
29 229 Ore. 427, 431, 367 P.2d 403, 405 (1961).
30 *Ibid.,* at 321 and 406.
31 *Zenith International Film Corp.* v. *Chicago,* 291 F.2d 785, 791 (7th Cir.
    1961).
32 Brief for Appellant at 20, *Freedman* v. *Maryland,* 380 U.S. 51 (1965).
33 380 U.S. 51, 53 (1965). The quotation is from *Bantam Books* v. *Sullivan,*
    372 U.S. 58, 70, n. 10 (1963).
34 380 U.S. 51, 54 (1965).
35 *Ibid.,* at 57–58.
36 *Ibid.,* at 61.
37 Brief for American Civil Liberties Union and Maryland Branch, ACLU,
    Amicus Curiae at 12, *Freedman* v. *Maryland,* 380 U.S. 51 (1965).
38 Brief for Appellant at 29–30, *Freedman* v. *Maryland,* 380 U.S. 51 (1965).
39 *Trans-Lux Distributing Corp.* v. *Board of Regents,* 380 U.S. 259 (1965).
40 *Cambist Films* v. *Board of Regents,* 46 Misc. 2d 513, 260 N.Y.S.2d 804
    (Sup. Ct. 1965).
41 *Ibid.,* at 517–18 and 809.
42 *State* ex. rel. *Londerholm* v. *Columbia Pictures,* 197 Kan. 448, 417 P.2d
    255 (1966).
43 *Victoria Films* v. *Division of Motion Picture Censorship,* Richmond Cir-
    cuit Court (unreported). *Motion Picture Daily,* April 21, 1965, p. 1.
44 *Embassy Pictures* v. *Hudson,* 242 F. Supp. 975 (W.D. Tenn. 1965).
45 *Md. Ann. Code,* art. 66A, § 19(a) (Vol. 6 Replace. 1967).
46 *Trans-Lux Distributing Corp.* v. *Board of Censors,* 240 Md. 98, 213 A.2d
    235 (1965).
47 *Dunn* v. *Board of Censors,* 240 Md. 249, 213 A.2d 751 (1965).
48 *Hewitt* v. *Board of Censors,* 241 Md. 283, 216 A.2d 557 (1966).
49 *Hewitt* v. *Board of Censors,* 243 Md. 574, 221 A.2d 894 (1966).
50 *Chicago Municipal Code,* ch. 155, §§ 7.1 and 7.2. These redrafted provi-
    sions were held unconstitutional in *Teitel Film Corp.* v. *Cusack,* 36 *U.S.L.W.*
    3304 (U.S. Jan. 30, 1968), decided *per curiam* on authority of *Freedman*
    v. *Maryland.*
51 *Interstate Circuit* v. *Dallas,* 247 F. Supp. 906 (N.D. Tex. 1965).
52 Dallas, Tex. Ordinance 11284, Nov. 22, 1965, amending *Dallas Rev. Code
    of Civ. & Crim. Ords.,* ch. 46 (1960).
53 *Interstate Circuit* v. *Dallas,* 366 F.2d 590 (5th Cir. 1966); *aff'g* 249 F.
    Supp. 19 (N.D. Tex. 1965).
54 19 U.S.C., §1305(a).

55 19 C.F.R., ch. 1, § 12.40(e) (Supp. 1967).
56 *Eureka Productions* v. *Lehman,* 17 F. Supp. 259 (S.D.N.Y. 1936); *aff'd per curiam,* 302 U.S. 634 (1936).
57 *United States* v. *One Carton Positive Motion Picture Film Entitled "491,"* 367 F.2d 889 (2d Cir. 1966).
58 *United States* v. *One Book Entitled "The Adventures of Father Silas,"* 249 F. Supp. 911 (S.D.N.Y. 1966).

Chapter 4. Objectives: Obscenity and Classification

1 *Gelling* v. *Texas,* 343 U.S. 960 (1952), *rev'g* 156 Tex. Crim. 516, 247 S.W.2d 95 (1952).
2 *Superior Films* v. *Dep't of Education,* 346 U.S. 587 (1954), *rev'g* 159 Ohio St. 315, 112 N.E.2d 311 (1953).
3 *Commercial Pictures* v. *Board of Regents,* 346 U.S. 587 (1954), *rev'g* 305 N.Y. 336, 113 N.E.2d 502 (1953).
4 *Holmby Productions* v. *Vaughn,* 350 U.S. 870 (1955), *rev'g* 177 Kan. 728, 282 P.2d 412 (1955).
5 *Times Film Corp.* v. *Chicago,* 355 U.S. 35 (1957), *rev'g* 241 F.2d 432 (7th Cir. 1957).
6 See interpretations made in *RKO Radio Pictures* v. *Dep't of Education,* 162 Ohio St. 263, 122 N.E.2d 769 (1954); *Brattle Films* v. *Commissioner of Public Safety,* 333 Mass. 58, 127 N.E.2d 891 (1955).
7 See Melville Nimmer, "The Constitutionality of Official Censorship of Motion Pictures," 25 *U. Chi. L. Rev.* 625 (1958); "Per Curiam Decisions of the Supreme Court: 1957 Term," 26 *U. Chi. L. Rev.* 279 (1959); "Supreme Court Per Curiam Practice: A Critique," 69 *Harv. L. Rev.* 707 (1955).
8 *N.Y. Educ. Law,* §122-a (McKinney 1954).
9 *Kingsley International Pictures* v. *Board of Regents,* 4 N.Y.2d 349, 151 N.E.2d 197, 175 N.Y.S. 39 (1958).
10 360 U.S. 684, 687 (1959).
11 *Ibid.,* at 699.
12 *Ibid.,* at 708.
13 *Chicago Municipal Code,* ch. 155,§4.
14 Fort Worth, Tex., Ordinance No. 2475. See Appendix to Brief for American Civil Liberties Union and Maryland Branch, ACLU, Amicus Curiae at 3a, *Freedman* v. *Maryland,* 380 U.S. 51 (1965).
15 *United Artists* v. *Board of Censors,* 210 Md. 586, 124 A.2d 292 (1956); *Broadway Angels* v. *Wilson,* 282 App. Div. 643, 125 N.Y.S.2d 546 (3d Dep't 1953).
16 *Md. Ann. Code,* art. 66A, §6(d) (Vol. 6 Replace. 1967); "Rules of the Board of Regents," Art. XVI, Motion Picture Division, §220 in *Law, Rules, and Regulations for Review and Licensing of Motion Pictures,* The University of the State of New York, Handbook 38, June, 1963.
17 282 App. Div. 643, 646, 125 N.Y.S.2d 546, 549 (3d Dep't 1953).

18 Zechariah Chafee, Jr., *Government and Mass Communications* (Chicago, 1947), I, 210.

19 For discussion of values that may be seen as jeopardized by obscenity, see Chafee, *Free Speech*, pp. 210–11; James C. N. Paul and Murray L. Schwartz, *Federal Censorship: Obscenity in the Mail* (New York, 1961), pp. 191–202; and Harry Kalven, Jr., "The Metaphysics of the Law of Obscenity," in Philip B. Kurland, ed., *1960 Supreme Court Review* (Chicago, 1960), pp. 3–4.

20 For a review and discussion of studies and other available data on the effects of obscenity, see Terrence J. Murphy, *Censorship: Government and Obscenity* (Baltimore, 1963), pp. 131–51; Robert B. Cairns, James C. N. Paul, and Julius Wishner, "Sex Censorship, the Assumptions of Obscenity Laws, and the Empirical Evidence," 46 *Minn L. Rev.* 1009 (1962).

21 See James J. Kilpatrick, *The Smut Peddlers* (New York, 1960), pp. 207–41.

22 See David Loth, *The Erotic in Literature* (New York, 1961), pp. 230–32; Maurice Girodias, "More Heat than Light," in John Chandos, ed., '*To Deprave and Corrupt . . . ,*' (New York, 1962), p. 125.

23 See Justice Douglas' dissenting opinion in *Roth* v. *United States* and *Alberts* v. *California,* 354 U.S. 476, 508 (1957); American Civil Liberties Union pamphlet, *Obscenity and Censorship,* March, 1963.

24 See, for example, Opinion of the New York Court of Appeals, *Kingsley International Pictures* v. *Board of Regents,* 4 N.Y.2d 349, 151 N.E.2d 197, 175 N.Y.S. 39 (1958).

25 American Civil Liberties Union, *Obscenity and Censorship.*

26 354 U.S. 476, 484 (1957).

27 *A Book Named "John Cleland's Memoirs"* v. *Massachusetts,* 383 U.S. 413, 418 (1966). Brennan, with Warren and Fortas, wrote the opinion announcing the judgment of the Court. In *Manual Enterprises* v. *Day,* 370 U.S. 478 (1962), Harlan, joined by Stewart, said that in addition to prurient appeal, the *Roth-Alberts* test required that an utterance on its face affront community standards of decency, a characteristic he referred to as "patent offensiveness." However, the *Manual* case involved a question of mailability and therefore of federal power. It is not clear whether Harlan would apply the requirement of "patent offensiveness" to state power, which he has consistently maintained is broader than federal power in the control of obscenity. See his dissenting opinions in *Jacobellis* v. *Ohio,* 378 U.S. 184, 203 (1964), and in *Roth* v. *United States,* 354 U.S. 476, 496 (1957).

28 *A Book Named "John Cleland's Memoirs"* v. *Massachusetts,* 383 U.S. 413, 419 (1966). See also Brennan's opinion in *Jacobellis* v. *Ohio,* 378 U.S. 184, 191 (1964).

29 See their respective dissenting opinions in *A Book Named "John Cleland's Memoirs"* v. *Massachusetts,* 383 U.S. 413 at 441 and 460 (1966).

30 383 U.S. 413 at 445.

31 *Jacobellis* v. *Ohio,* 378 U.S. 184, 193 (1964). In *Manual Enterprises* v. *Day,* 370 U.S. 478 (1962), Harlan, joined by Stewart, thought the relevant "community" for deciding a case under the federal mailability statute was national. *Ibid.,* at 488.

32 *Jacobellis* v. *Ohio,* 378 U.S. 184, 200 (1964).

33 *Ibid.,* at 187.

34 *Ibid.,* at 203.

35 See his dissenting opinion in *Jacobellis* v. *Ohio,* 378 U.S. 184, 203 (1964); opinion announcing the judgment of the Court in *Manual Enterprises* v. *Day,* 370 U.S. 478 (1962); dissenting opinion in *Roth* v. *United States,* 354 U.S. 476, 496 (1957).

36 *Jacobellis* v. *Ohio,* 378 U.S. 184, 204 (1964). The point is reiterated in his dissenting opinion in *A Book Named "John Cleland's Memoirs"* v. *Massachusetts,* 383 U.S. 413, 455 (1966).

37 See Douglas' concurring opinion in *A Book Named "John Cleland's Memoirs"* v. *Massachusetts,* 383 U.S. 413, 424 (1966); dissenting opinion in *Roth* v. *United States* and *Alberts* v. *California,* 354 U.S. 476, 508 (1957).

38 See his dissenting opinion in *Mishkin* v. *New York,* 383 U.S. 502, 513 (1966); concurring opinions in *Jacobellis* v. *Ohio,* 378 U.S. 184, 196 (1964); *Kingsley International Pictures* v. *Board of Regents,* 360 U.S. 684, 692 (1959).

39 241 F.2d 772, 777 (9th Cir. 1957).

40 *Sunshine Book Co.* v. *Summerfield,* 355 U.S. 372 (1958), *rev'g* 249 F.2d 114 (D.C. Cir. 1957).

41 128 F. Supp. 565, 571–72 (D.D.C. 1955).

42 *Mounce* v. *United States,* 355 U.S. 180 (1957), *rev'g* 247 F.2d 148 (9th Cir. 1957).

43 *Mounce* v. *United States,* 247 F.2d 148 (9th Cir. 1957).

44 William B. Lockhart and Robert C. McClure, "Censorship of Obscenity: The Developing Constitutional Standards," 45 *Minn. L. Rev.* 5, 58 (1960); "Per Curiam Decisions of the Supreme Court: 1957 Term," 26 *U. Chi. L. Rev.* 279, 309–13 (1959).

45 *Redrup* v. *New York, Austin* v. *Kentucky,* and *Gent* v. *Arkansas,* 386 U.S. 767 (1967).

46 370 U.S. 478, 489–90 (1962).

47 *A Book Named "John Cleland's Memoirs"* v. *Massachusetts,* 383 U.S. 413, 445–46 (1966).

48 Lockhart and McClure, in 45 *Minn. L. Rev.,* p. 60; Kalven, in *1960 Supreme Court Review,* p. 43; "Per Curiam Decisions of the Supreme Court: 1957 Term," 26 *U. Chi. L. Rev.* 279, 313 (1959). For a strong argument that the measure of proscribable erotica *should* be that of hard-core pornography, see C. Peter Magrath, "The Obscenity Cases: Grapes of Roth," in Phillip B. Kurland, ed., *1966 Supreme Court Review* (Chicago, 1960), pp. 69–77.

49 See his dissenting opinion in *Ginzburg* v. *United States,* 383 U.S. 463, 493 (1966); opinion announcing the judgment of the Court in *Manual Enter-*

prises v. *Day,* 370 U.S. 478 (1962); dissenting opinion in *Roth* v. *United States,* 354 U.S. 476, 496 (1957).

50 *Jacobellis* v. *Ohio,* 378 U.S. 184, 197 (1964). Many students of the obscenity problem speak of hard-core pornography as though its essential nature were self-evident. See, for example, Benjamin Bromberg, "Five Tests for Obscenity," 41 *Chi. B. Record* 416, 418–19 (1960); D. H. Lawrence, *Pornography and Obscenity* (New York, 1930), p. 13. Others, like Drs. Phyllis and Eberhard Kronhausen, maintain that upon comparative examination, hard-core pornography is clearly distinguishable from other questionable material because its single purpose is always the stimulation of erotic response in the viewer or reader uncomplicated by any "truthful description of the basic realities of life as the individual experiences it." *Pornography and the Law* (New York, 1959), pp. 18 and 20.

51 Brief for the United States at 37–38, *Roth* v. *United States,* 354 U.S. 476 (1957).

52 *Jacobellis* v. *Ohio,* 378 U.S. 184, 201 (1964).

53 See Paul and Schwartz, *Federal Censorship,* pp. 205–13; M. C. Slough and P. D. McAnany, "Obscenity and Constitutional Freedom—Part II," 8 *St. Lou. L.J.* 449, 461–66 (1964); and Lockhart and McClure, in 45 *Minn. L. Rev.* 77–80. For a critique of the "variable obscenity approach," see Magrath, *1966 Supreme Court Review,* pp. 62–69.

54 *Times Film Corp.* v. *Chicago,* 355 U.S. 35 (1957). Lower court decisions include *United States* v. *One Carton Positive Motion Picture Film Entitled "491,"* 367 F.2d 889 (2d Cir. 1966); *Hewitt* v. *Maryland,* 243 Md. 574, 221 A.2d 894 (1966); *Leighton* v. *Board of Censors,* 242 Md. 705, 218 A.2d 179 (1966); *Hewitt* v. *Maryland,* 241 Md. 283, 216 A.2d 557 (1966); *Dunn* v. *Board of Censors,* 240 Md. 249, 213 A.2d 751 (1965); *Trans-Lux Distributing Corp.* v. *Board of Censors,* 240 Md. 98, 213 A.2d 235 (1965); *Audubon Films* v. *Board of Regents,* 15 N.Y.2d 802, 205 N.E.2d 694 (1965); *Fanfare Films* v. *Motion Picture Censor Board,* 234 Md. 10, 197 A.2d 839 (1964); *The Connection Co.* v. *Board of Regents,* 17 App. Div. 2d 671, 230 N.Y.S.2d 103 (3d Dep't 1962); *Excelsior Pictures* v. *Chicago,* 182 F. Supp. 400 (N.D. Ill. 1960); *Columbia Pictures* v. *Chicago,* 184 F. Supp. 817 (N.D. Ill. 1959); *Capitol Enterprises* v. *Chicago,* 260 F.2d 670 (7th Cir. 1958); *Excelsior Pictures* v. *Board of Regents,* 3 N.Y.2d 237, 144 N.E.2d 31 (1957); *Maryland Board of Censors* v. *Times Film Corp.,* 212 Md. 454, 129 A.2d 833 (1957); *American Civil Liberties Union* v. *Chicago,* 13 Ill. App. 2d 278, 141 N.E.2d 56 (1957); *Capitol Enterprises* v. *Board of Regents,* 1 App. Div. 2d 990, 149 N.Y.S.2d 920 (3d Dep't 1956).

55 *Janus Films* v. *Fort Worth,* 354 S.W.2d 597 (Tex. Civ. App. 1962), *aff'd per curiam,* 163 Tex. 616, 358 S.W.2d 589 (1962).

56 244 F.2d 432 (7th Cir. 1957).

57 Record at 10–11, 360 U.S. 684 (1959).

58 378 U.S. 184, 195–96 (1964).

59 *Ibid.,* at 203.

60   *Ibid.*, Record at 500.

61   *Audubon Films* v. *Board of Regents,* 15 N.Y.2d 802, 205 N.E.2d 694 (1965).

62   *Variety,* April 4, 1962, p. 13.

63   *American Civil Liberties Union* v. *Chicago,* 13 Ill. App. 2d 278, 141 N.E.2d 56 (1957).

64   *Trans-Lux Distributing Corp.* v. *Board of Censors,* 240 Md. 98, 112–14, 213 A.2d 235, 243–44 (1965). The same film had been found obscene by the New York Court of Appeals. *Trans-Lux Distributing Corp.* v. *Board of Regents,* 14 N.Y.2d 88, 198 N.E.2d 242 (1964). However, the decision was reversed *per curiam* by the United States Supreme Court on authority of *Freedman* v. *Maryland,* 380 U.S. 51 (1965), because of procedural deficiencies in the New York licensing law. 380 U.S. 259 (1965).

65   *United States* v. *One Carton Positive Motion Picture Film Entitled "491,"* 367 F.2d 889, 896 (2d Cir. 1966).

66   *Janus Films* v. *Fort Worth,* 354 S.W.2d 597 (Tex. Civ. App. 1962), *aff'd per curiam,* 163 Tex. 616, 358 S.W.2d 589 (1962).

67   *Excelsior Pictures* v. *Board of Regents,* 3 N.Y.2d 237, 239, 144 N.E.2d 31, 32 (1957).

68   *Excelsior Pictures* v. *Chicago,* 182 F. Supp. 400, 403 (N.D. Ill. 1960).

69   *Fanfare Films* v. *Motion Picture Censor Board,* 234 Md. 10, 12, 197 A.2d 839, 840 (1964).

70   *Maryland Board of Censors* v. *Times Film Corp.,* 212 Md. 454, 459, 129 A.2d 833, 836 (1957).

71   *Ibid.,* at 462 and 838.

72   *Columbia Pictures* v. *Chicago,* 184 F. Supp. 817, 818 (N.D. Ill. 1959).

73   *The Connection Co.* v. *Board of Regents,* 17 App. Div. 2d 671, 230 N.Y.S.2d 103 (3d Dep't 1962).

74   *Capitol Enterprises* v. *Chicago,* 260 F.2d 670, 674 (7th Cir. 1958).

75   *Capitol Enterprises* v. *Board of Regents,* 1 App. Div. 2d 990, 991, 149 N.Y.S.2d 920, 922 (3d Dep't 1956).

76   *Grove Press* v. *Christenberry,* 175 F. Supp. 488 (S.D.N.Y. 1959).

77   *Trans-Lux Distributing Corp.* v. *Board of Regents,* 14 N.Y.2d 88, 93, 198 N.E.2d 242, 245 (1964), *rev'd per curiam,* 380 U.S. 259 (1965).

78   For an interesting discussion of a similar concept applied to several media, see George P. Elliott, "Against Pornography," *Harper's,* March, 1965, p. 51.

79   *Variety,* June 20, 1962, p. 4.

80   *Commonwealth* v. *Gordon,* 66 Pa. D. & C. 101, 137–38 (1949).

81   In *Ginzburg* v. *United States,* 383 U.S. 463 (1966), the Supreme Court considered the promotional context of printed matter in upholding the conviction of a publisher for using the mails to distribute obscene materials.

82   According to one survey, 52.6 per cent of those who attend movies once a week or more are between the ages of 10 and 19. *1966 International Motion Picture Almanac* (New York, 1965), p. 62A.

83   *Jacobellis* v. *Ohio,* 378 U.S. 184, 195 (1964). Justice Brennan, joined by Justice Goldberg, wrote the opinion announcing the judgment of the Court.

84   *Butler* v. *Michigan,* 352 U.S. 380 (1957).

85   320 U.S. 158, 167 (1944).

86   *Interstate Circuit* v. *Dallas,* 366 F.2d 590 (5th Cir. 1966), *aff'g* 249 F. Supp. 19 (N.D. Tex. 1965); *Interstate Circuit* v. *Dallas,* 402 S.W.2d 770 (Tex. Civ. App. 1966); *Interstate Circuit* v. *Dallas,* 247 F. Supp. 906 (N.D. Tex. 1965); *Paramount Film Distributing Corp.* v. *Chicago,* 172 F. Supp. 69 (N.D. Ill. 1959).

87   *Interstate Circuit* v. *Dallas,* 249 F. Supp. 19, 24 (N.D. Tex. 1965). See also *Interstate Circuit* v. *Dallas,* 402 S.W.2d 770 (Tex. Civ. App. 1966).

88   *Chicago Municipal Code,* ch. 155, §5.

89   Copy of "An act to amend the education law in relation to classifying motion pictures as acceptable for exhibition to minors under the age of sixteen years." New York State Board of Regents release. The proposal was to amend *N.Y. Educ. Law,* §122-b.

90   Copy of a letter to Marvin E. Aspen, Assistant Corporation Counsel, City of Chicago, Dec. 10, 1964.

91   See Note, " 'For Adults Only', the Constitutionality of Governmental Film Censorship by Age Classification," 69 *Yale L. J.* 141, 150 (1959).

92   *Paramount Film Distributing Corp.* v. *Chicago,* 172 F. Supp. 69 (N.D. Ill. 1959).

93   *Chicago Municipal Code,* ch. 155, §5.

94   *Interstate Circuit* v. *Dallas,* 249 F. Supp. 19, 24 (N.D. Tex. 1965), *aff'd* 366 F.2d 590 (5th Cir. 1966).

95   172 F. Supp. 69, 72 (N.D. Ill. 1959).

96   See Lockhart and McClure, 45 *Minn. L. Rev.,* p. 87.

97   *Chicago Municipal Code,* ch. 155, §5.

98   *Interstate Circuit* v. *Dallas,* 249 F. Supp. 19, 25 (N.D. Tex. 1965).

Chapter 5.   Boards, Procedures, and Decisions

1   Brief for American Civil Liberties Union and Maryland Branch, ACLU, Amicus Curiae, Appendix, *Freedman* v. *Maryland,* 380 U.S. 51 (1965).

2   *1964 Film Daily Yearbook of Motion Pictures* (New York, 1964), pp. 703–6.

3   Charles Aronson, ed., *1965 International Motion Picture Almanac* (New York, 1965), pp. 785–87.

4   Brief for American Civil Liberties Union, Appendix, p. 5a.

5   *Detroit Municipal Code,* ch. 5, art. 2, §7 (1963–1964).

6   Brief for American Civil Liberties Union, Appendix, p. 4a.

7   *Ibid.,* pp. 7a–8a.

8   *Ibid.,* p. 11a.

9   *Ibid.,* p. 13a.

10   *Ibid.,* p. 5a.

11 *Ibid.,* p. 6a.
12 Morris Ernst and Pare Lorentz, *Censored, the Private Life of the Movie* (New York, 1930), pp. 82–83. The authors fail to say, however, how they obtained their information.
13 *Variety,* Feb. 26, 1962, p. 5.
14 *Variety,* Dec. 20, 1961, p. 4.
15 Final Ruling, Motion Picture Appeal Board of the City of Chicago In the Matter of the Motion Picture Entitled *Europe in the Raw,* p. 11.
16 *Trans-Lux Distributing Corp.* v. *Board of Regents,* 380 U.S. 259 (1965). In the decision, *per curiam,* the Supreme Court cited only *Freedman* v. *Maryland,* 380 U.S. 51 (1965). The merits of the *A Stranger Knocks* censorship were apparently not considered.
17 *Variety,* Nov. 7, 1962, p. 4.
18 *Ibid.*
19 *Columbia Pictures* v. *Chicago,* 184 F. Supp. 817 (N.D. Ill. 1959).
20 Maryland State Board of Motion Picture Censors, *Forty-Eighth Annual Report,* 1963–1964, p. 6.
21 *United Artists* v. *Board of Censors,* 210 Md. 586, 124 A.2d 292 (1956).
22 Dallas, Texas, Ordinance 11284, Nov. 22, 1965, § 46A–1(f), amending *Dallas Rev. Code of Civ. & Crim. Ords.,* ch. 46 (1960), as interpreted in *Interstate Circuit* v. *Dallas,* 366 F.2d 590, 599, n. 18 (5th Cir. 1966).
23 The earlier totals are calculated from a table of annual New York censorship figures in Samuel Beckoff, "An Inquiry into the Operative Principles Applicable to Licensing Motion Pictures in New York State," Ph.D. diss., New York University, 1959, p. 78. Unfortunately, except for the period 1943–1949, Beckoff's table, which is one of the few compilations of censorship statistics anywhere, does not include the number of films rejected outright by the Motion Picture Division.
24 Virginia, Division of Motion Picture Censorship, *Report* (1964).

Chapter 6. Limits, Costs, Constituents, Personnel, and Customs Censorship

1 *Variety,* Dec. 4, 1963, p. 15.
2 *Variety,* Aug. 16, 1961, p. 14.
3 *Ibid.*
4 Copy of an address, "Report on Censorship," by T. Manning Clagett, Motion Picture Association of America, delivered at the annual meeting of the Congress of Motion Picture Organizations, Nov. 6, 1964, New York.
5 "Interview with Ephraim London," *Film Comment,* Vol. 1, no. 4 (1963), p. 6.
6 *Chicago Municipal Code,* ch. 155, §7.3 as amended Dec. 27, 1961.
7 *Variety:* Feb. 26, 1964, p. 28; May 13, 1964, p. 17.
8 *Variety,* March 18, 1964, p. 19.
9 *Areopagitica* (New York, Appleton-Century Crofts, 1951), p. 28.
10 A severe indictment of film censors in the 1920's is Morris Ernst's and

Pare Lorentz' *Censored, The Private Life of the Movie* (New York, 1930). More recently film censors have been criticized by Zechariah Chafee, Jr., *Free Speech in the United States* (Cambridge, Mass., 1941); Robert Haney, *Comstockery in America* (Boston, 1960); Murray Schumach, *The Face on the Cutting Room Floor* (New York, 1964); Ira H. Carmen, *Movies, Censorship, and the Law* (Ann Arbor, 1966); Thomas I. Emerson, "The Doctrine of Prior Restraint," 20 *Law & Contemp. Probs.* 648 (1955); Lester Velie, "You Can't See That Movie," *Collier's*, May 6, 1950, p. 11.

11 Emerson, 20 *Law & Contemp. Probs.*, p. 658.

12 *Md. Ann. Code,* art 66A, §3 (1965).

13 *Chicago Municipal Code,* ch. 155, §7.1 as amended Dec. 27, 1961.

14 See, for example, *Chicago's American*, Oct. 15, 1959, p. 1.

15 Chicago *Daily News*, April 9, 1959, p. 22.

16 *Motion Picture Daily*, Jan. 4, 1967, p. 1.

17 *Criticism and Censorship* (Milwaukee, 1956), p. 40.

18 *United States* v. *One Book Entitled "Ulysses" by James Joyce*, 72 F.2d 705 (2d Cir. 1934).

19 *United States* v. *One Carton Positive Motion Picture Film Entitled "491,"* 247 F. Supp. 450 (S.D.N.Y. 1965).

20 *United States* v. *Two Tin Boxes*, 79 F.2d 1017 (2d Cir. 1935).

Chapter 7. Informal Censorship and Control by the Criminal Process

1 See Chief Justice Warren's dissenting opinion in *Times Film Corp.* v. *Chicago*, 365 U.S. 43, 50 (1961) and Justice Douglas' dissenting opinion in the same case, *Ibid.*, at 84; Thomas I. Emerson, "The Doctrine of Prior Restraint," 20 *Law & Contemp. Prob.* 648 (1955); James M. Landis, "A Lawyer Looks at Censorship," 5 *Social Meaning of Legal Concepts* 1, 15 (1953); and Brief for American Civil Liberties Union and Maryland Branch, ACLU, Amicus Curiae, *Freedman* v. *Maryland*, 380 U.S. 51 (1965).

2 The publications and periods covered were *Variety*, Dec. 1, 1961 to Jan. 1, 1967; *Boxoffice*, July 1, 1964 to Jan. 1, 1967; *Motion Picture Daily*, Sept. 1, 1964 to Jan. 1, 1967; *Motion Picture Exhibitor*, July 1, 1964 to Jan. 1, 1967; and *Motion Picture Herald*, Sept. 1, 1964 to Oct. 1, 1966.

3 *Motion Picture Daily*, Nov. 25, 1964, p. 3.

4 *Variety*, Aug. 21, 1963, p. 4.

5 *Boxoffice*, Jan. 5, 1965, p. SE–1.

6 *Motion Picture Exhibitor*, Dec. 23, 1964, p. 17.

7 *Boxoffice*, Oct. 17, 1966, p. NE–1.

8 *Motion Picture Exhibitor*, Feb. 3, 1965, p. 16.

9 *Boxoffice*, May 31, 1965, p. ME–1.

10 *Variety*, Aug. 10, 1966, p. 25.

11 *Variety*, Feb. 6, 1963, p. 15.

12 *Boxoffice,* Sept. 21, 1964, p. C–1.
13 *Motion Picture Herald,* Jan. 20, 1965, p. 18.
14 *New York Laws* ch. 327 (McKinney 1965).
15 "Motion Picture Censorship in Light of 1965 Supreme Court Decisions," prepared by Barbara Scott, ACLU, Memorandum to the Censorship Committee, Oct. 21, 1965, p. 3.
16 *Chemline, Inc.* v. *Grand Prairie,* 364 F.2d 721 (5th Cir. 1966).
17 *Boxoffice,* June 8, 1966, p. SE–1.
18 *Variety,* June 27, 1962, p. 14.
19 *Variety,* Jan. 2, 1963, p. 16.
20 *Variety,* April 28, 1962, p. 15.
21 *Motion Picture Daily,* Jan. 12, 1965, p. 1.
22 *Variety,* Jan. 29, 1964, p. 17.
23 *Variety,* April 7, 1965, p. 16.
24 *Variety,* Aug. 31, 1966, p. 18.
25 *Boxoffice,* Feb. 1, 1965, p. NC–1.
26 *Motion Picture Daily,* Oct. 14, 1966, p. 2.
27 Note, "Entertainment: Public Pressures and the Law," 71 *Harv. L. Rev.* 326, 346 (1957).
28 *Motion Picture Exhibitor,* Feb. 17, 1965, p. 4.
29 *Variety,* April 1, 1965, p. 5.
30 San Francisco *Chronicle,* Oct. 9, 1964, p. 2.
31 *Motion Picture Exhibitor,* Sept. 23, 1964, p. 5.
32 *Variety,* Feb. 21, 1962, p. 13.
33 *Wisconsin State Journal,* Oct. 28, 1962, §2, p. 3.
34 *Variety,* Jan. 3, 1962, p. 7.
35 *Variety,* Aug. 5, 1964, p. 5.
36 *Variety,* Nov. 25, 1964, p. 22.
37 Quoted in *Variety,* Sept. 5, 1962, p. 4.
38 *Variety,* Feb. 5, 1962, p. 5.
39 *Boxoffice,* Jan. 4, 1965, p. E–1.
40 *The New York Times,* Feb. 15, 1958, p. 19.
41 *Variety,* Nov. 28, 1962, p. 5.
42 *Boxoffice,* March 22, 1965, p. W–6.
43 *Variety,* Oct. 23, 1963, p. 20.
44 *Variety,* Dec. 18, 1963, p. 18.
45 *The New York Times,* Dec. 30, 1956, p. 24.
46 *Variety,* March 20, 1963, p. 14.
47 *Motion Picture Daily,* Dec. 29, 1964, p. 2.
48 *Boxoffice,* Jan. 24, 1966, p. W–6.
49 *Boxoffice,* Feb. 15, 1965, p. SE–3.
50 *The New York Times,* Aug. 2, 1958, p. 19.
51 *Jacobellis* v. *Ohio,* 378 U.S. 184 (1964).
52 *State* v. *Warth,* 173 Ohio St. 15, 179 N.E.2d 772 (1962).
53 Cleveland *Plain Dealer,* Dec. 6, 1959.
54 Cleveland *Plain Dealer,* Nov. 14, 1959, p. 1.

55 *The Cleveland Press,* Nov. 15, 1959.
56 *Catholic Universe Bulletin,* Nov. 20, 1959.
57 Cleveland Heights *Sun Press,* Dec. 10, 1959.
58 *Variety,* Dec. 18, 1963, p. 18.
59 71 *Harv. L. Rev.,* p. 362, n. 258.
60 *Boxoffice:* Feb. 15, 1965, p. NC–1; Feb. 22, 1965, p. NC–1.
61 *Variety,* June 3, 1964, p. 11.
62 Madison *Capital Times,* Jan. 7, 1963, p. 9.
63 See Note, "Extra-Legal Censorship of Literature," 33 *N. Y. U. L. Rev.* 989 (1958); Note, "Liabilities of Extra-Legal Censors," 5 *Buff. L. Rev.* 328 (1955); Note, "Censorship of Obscene Literature by Informal Government Action," 22 *U. Chi. L. Rev.* 216 (1954).
64 *Variety,* April 27, 1966, p. 5.
65 *New York Penal Law* §1141–1 (McKinney 1965).
66 *Variety,* Oct. 14, 1964, p. 20.
67 *Boxoffice,* Jan. 18, 1965, p. E–1.
68 *Variety,* Dec. 23, 1964, p. 13.

Chapter 8. Nongovernmental Censorship: Advisory Ratings and Self-Regulation

1   *Variety,* March 4, 1964, p. 20.
2   *Variety,* April 1, 1964, p. 21.
3   *Variety,* March 4, 1964, p. 20.
4   *Boxoffice,* April 26, 1965, p. ME–1.
5   *Boxoffice,* April 5, 1965, p. SW–1.
6   *Variety,* Feb. 13, 1963, p. 1.
7   Quoted in Murray Schumach, *The Face on the Cutting Room Floor* (New York, 1964), p. 85.
8   The Rev. Joseph A. Daly, first director of the Legion of Decency, quoted in Harold C. Gardiner, S.J., *Catholic Viewpoint on Censorship* (Garden City, N.Y., 1958), p. 89.
9   Quoted in Gardiner, *Catholic Viewpoint,* p. 99.
10 Frank Getlein and Harold C. Gardiner, S.J., *Movies, Morals, and Art* (New York, 1961), p. 132.
11 Quoted in Gardiner, *Catholic Viewpoint,* pp. 101–2.
12 Schumach, *The Face on the Cutting Room Floor,* p. 91.
13 *Motion Picture Daily,* Sept. 1, 1965, p. 1.
14 This statement is part of a decree of the Vatican Council, quoted in a statement issued by the Roman Catholic Episcopal Committee for Motion Pictures, Radio, and Television, April 5, 1964, p. 9 (Mimeographed)
15 Press Release, National Legion of Decency, June 9, 1965, p. 1.
16 Letter to the author, May 1, 1967.
17 National Catholic Office for Motion Pictures, *Films, 1965: Reviews, Commentary and Ratings* (New York), pp. 49–55.

18 National Catholic Office for Motion Pictures, *Films, 1966: Reviews, Commentary and Ratings* (New York), p. 52.
19 Judy Stone, "The Legion of Decency, What's Nude?" *Ramparts,* Sept., 1965, p. 49.
20 Quoted in Stone, *Ramparts,* p. 55.
21 Quoted in Stone, *Ramparts,* p. 54.
22 Quoted in Stone, *Ramparts,* p. 55.
23 Quoted in Schumach, *The Face on the Cutting Room Floor,* p. 76–77.
24 *Ibid.,* p. 78. The change in paragraph order is mine.
25 *The New York Times,* April 7, 1965, p. 37.
26 *Variety,* May 19, 1965, p. 23.
27 Michael Conant, *Antitrust in the Motion Picture Industry* (Berkeley and Los Angeles, 1960), p. 41.
28 *The Motion Picture Code of Self-Regulation,* The Motion Picture Association of America, pp. 5–6.
29 Peter Bunzel, "Yes, They Did It: 'Lolita' *Is* a Movie," *Life,* May 25, 1962, p. 93.
30 *Variety,* Dec. 20, 1961, p. 17.
31 *Variety,* Feb. 14, 1962, p. 2.
32 Beth Day, *This Was Hollywood* (Garden City, N.Y., 1960), p. 241.
33 *Variety,* Sept. 28, 1966, p. 5.
34 "Passing the Buck," *The Journal of the Screen Producers Guild,* March, 1965, p. 27.
35 Interview, New York, Nov. 30, 1964.
36 *Variety,* Feb. 21, 1962, p. 5.
37 John Alan Sargent, "Self-Regulation: The Motion Picture Production Code, 1930–1961," Ph.D. diss., U. of Mich., 1963, pp. 226 and 227–28.
38 Ruth Inglis, *Freedom of the Movies* (Chicago, 1947), p. 186.
39 *The New York Times,* April 4, 1965.
40 Conant, *Antitrust in the Motion Picture Industry,* p. 41.
41 *Motion Picture Daily,* Jan. 6, 1967, p. 1.
42 *Variety,* Sept. 28, 1966, p. 5.
43 *The New York Times,* July 31, 1961, p. 14.
44 *Ibid.*
45 *Boxoffice,* Sept. 21, 1964, p. C–1.
46 Bunzel in *Life,* p. 86.
47 Interview, New York, Nov. 30, 1964.
48 Note, "Entertainment: Public Pressures and the Law," 71 *Harv. L. Rev.* 326, 346 (1957).
49 See A. H. Howe, "A Banker Looks at the Picture Business," *The Journal of the Screen Producers Guild,* Dec., 1965, p. 9.
50 *Variety,* Feb. 10, 1965, p. 1.
51 *Variety,* June 19, 1963, p. 5.
52 *Variety,* Feb. 10, 1965, p. 1.
53 *Variety,* July 11, 1962, p. 15.
54 *Variety,* Oct. 12, 1966, p. 7.

55 *Variety*, April 1, 1964, p. 2.
56 *Variety*, July 18, 1962, p. 18.
57 Katherine Hamill, "The Supercolossal—Well, Pretty Good—World of Joe Levine," *Fortune*, March, 1964, p. 130.
58 *Motion Picture Exhibitor*, Aug. 12, 1964, p. 10.
59 *Newsweek*, June 6, 1966, p. 102.
60 "Cinema Underground," *The New Yorker*, July 13, 1963, p. 16.
61 Arthur Knight, "New American Cinema?" *Saturday Review*, Nov. 2, 1963, p. 41.
62 Quoted in Michael Milner, *Sex on Celluloid* (New York, 1964), pp. 33–34.

Table of Cases

Page references to this book are listed in italics.

Index